Situating the Self

For Wolf,
who frequently disagreed

Situating the Self

Gender, Community and Postmodernism in
Contemporary Ethics

Seyla Benhabib

Routledge
New York

First published in 1992 by Routledge, an imprint of
Routledge, Chapman & Hall, Inc.
29 West 35th Street
New York, NY 10001

Published in Great Britain by Polity Press

Library of Congress Cataloging-in-Publication Data

Benhabib, Seyla.
    Situating the self : gender, community, and postmodernism in contemporary ethics / Seyla Benhabib.
        p.   cm.
    Includes bibliographical references and index.
    ISBN 0-415-90546-X.—ISBN 0-415-90547-8 (pbk.)
    1. Ethics.   2. Liberalism—Philosophy.   3. Communication—Moral and ethical aspects.   4. Postmodernism.   5. Feminist theory.
I. Title.
BJ1012.B45   1992
170—dc20   91-45826
                                                                                                         CIP

Printed in Great Britain
This book is printed on acid-free paper.

Contents

Acknowledgments

Many of these essays were inspired by my close encounter with liberal political theory and its communitarian critics during my stay in the Harvard University Department of Government from 1987 to 1989. This exchange led me to articulate more precisely the premises which contemporary critical theory, and in particular the discourse ethic, shared with liberal moral and political theory, while having in common with communitarianism deep roots in Hegel's critique of Kantian moral philosophy. Discourse ethic is situated somewhere between liberalism and communitarianism, Kantian universalism and Hegelian Sittlichkeit. My thanks go to Judith Shklar, Michael Sandel, Stephen Macedo, Shannon Stimson and Nancy Rosenblum for many inspiring, fortuitous conversations on liberalism and its critics. I would also like to thank my feminist friends Nancy Fraser, Iris Young, and in particular Drucilla Cornell for leading me to see the moral and political significance of postmodernism for women. I owe a different sort of gratitude to another group of friends and colleages: Kenneth Baynes and Maurizio Passerin d'Entrèves, as my former students, have through their own work on contemporary liberalism and communitarianism, both influenced and inspired my own thoughts. It is a pleasure not only to have taught them but also to have learned from them. Finally, conversations over the years with T. A. McCarthy, Richard J. Bernstein, Jean Cohen, Andrew Arato and Alessandro Ferrara have not only been inspirational but have strengthened my sense that the tradition of critical theory is very much alive. Special thanks are due to Fred Dallmayr, who in a careful and judicious review of this collection at an early stage, provided me with incisive recommendations about the whole. The earliest of these essays ("Epistemologies of Postmodernism," partially included in chapter 7) was written in 1984; the rest were completed and published between 1987 and 1990. My thanks go to the publishers of the books and journals where they have previously appeared, acknowledged after the essays themselves. They have all been revised for inclusion in this volume. I would also like to thank the Department of Philosophy at the State University of New York at Stony Brook, and particularly former Dean of the Humanities Don Ihde, for providing me with a one-semester research assignment which enabled me to put the finishing touches on this book. As always, it has been a pleasure to work with the staff and editors of Polity Press, particularly with Ann Bone, and with Maureen MacGrogan from Routledge.

Introduction

Communicative Ethics and the Claims of Gender, Community and Postmodernism

As the twentieth century draws to a close, there is little question *late 1990s* that we are living through more than the chronological end of an epoch. To invoke a distinction familiar to the Greeks, it is not only *kronos* which is holding sway over our lives; but our *kairos* as well, our lived time, time as imbued with symbolic meaning, is caught in the throes of forces of which we only have a dim understanding at the present. The many "postisms," like posthumanism, post-structuralism, postmodernism, post-Fordism, post-Keynesianism, and post-histoire circulating in our intellectual and cultural lives, are at one level only expressions of a deeply shared sense that certain aspects of our social, symbolic and political universe have been profoundly and most likely irretrievably transformed.

During periods of profound transformations such as these, as contemporaries of an epoch, we are more often than not in the position of staring through the glass darkly. We do not have the privilege of hindsight; we are not like the "owl of Minerva" which spreads its wings only at dusk. As engaged intellectuals we cannot write from the vantage point of "the grey which paints itself on green" and we do not even want to. Contrary to this Hegelian prognosis of "standing at the end of history," which has been recently revived by Francis Fukuyama – this late student of Hegel as read through the eyes of Alexandre Kojève[1] – the present harbors many ironies, contradictions and perplexities. Ernst Bloch's phrase of "non-contemporaneous contemporaneities" or *ungleichzeitige Gleichzeitigkeiten* is more appropriate to capture the fractured spirit of our times.[2]

Among the many ironies nourished by this fractured spirit is certainly the fact that while the cultural and political ideals of modernity, and among them what Richard Rorty has called "the meta-narratives of liberal democracies,"[3] have become suspect to the

humanistic and artistic avant-garde of western late-capitalist societies, political developments in Eastern Europe and the Soviet Union
have given these ideals a new purchase on life. While the peoples of
Eastern Europe and the Soviet Union have taken to the streets and
defied state police as well as the potential threat of foreign troops in
the name of parliamentary democracy, the rule of law and a market
economy, the academic discourse of the last decades, particularly
under the label of "postmodernism," has produced an intellectual
climate profoundly skeptical toward the moral and political ideals of
modernity, the Enlightenment and liberal democracy.

This current mood of skepticism among intellectual, academic and
artistic circles toward continuing the "project of modernity" is based
upon an understandable disillusionment with a form of life that
still perpetrates war, armament, environmental destruction and
economic exploitation at the cost of satisfying basic human needs
with human dignity, a form of life that still relegates many women,
non-Christian and non-white peoples to second-class moral and
political status, a form of life that saps the bases of solidaristic
coexistence in the name of profit and competition. Whether the form
of life of advanced capitalist mass democracies can reform itself from
within is a pressing one. It is my conviction, however, that the
project of modernity can only be reformed from within the intellectual, moral and political resources made possible and available to
us by the development of modernity on a global scale since the
sixteenth century. Among the legacies of modernity which today
need reconstructing but not wholesale dismantling are moral and
political universalism, committed to the now seemingly "old-
fashioned" and suspect ideals of universal respect for each person in
virtue of their humanity; the moral autonomy of the individual;
economic and social justice and equality; democratic participation;
the most extensive civil and political liberties compatible with principles of justice; and the formation of solidaristic human associations.

This book attempts a reconstruction of this legacy by address-
ing the following question: what is living and what is dead in
universalist moral and political theories of the present, after their
criticism in the hands of communitarians, feminists and postmodernists? More specifically, this book is an attempt to defend the
tradition of universalism in the face of this triple-pronged critique by
engaging with the claims of feminism, communitarianism and
postmodernism and by learning from them.

Communitarian critics of liberalism like Alasdair MacIntyre,
Michael Sandel, Charles Taylor and Michael Walzer have questioned
the epistemological assumptions as well as the normative vision of
liberal political theories. Feminist thinkers like Carol Gilligan, Carole
Pateman, Susan Moller Okin, Virginia Held, Iris Young, Nancy

Fraser, and Drucilla Cornell have continued the communitarian critique of liberal visions of the "unencumbered self." They have also pointed out that neither liberals nor communitarians have overcome their gender blindness such as to include women and their activities in their theories of justice and community. Postmodernists, a somewhat vague label by which we have come to designate the works of Michel Foucault, Jacques Derrida and Jean-François Lyotard among others, while sharing the communitarian and feminist skepticism toward the meta-narratives of liberal Enlightenment and modernity have radicalized this critique to the point of questioning the ideal of an autonomous subject of ethics and politics and the normative foundations of democratic politics altogether. Each of these lines of thought has contributed to a forceful rethinking of the Enlightenment tradition in ethics and politics extending from Immanuel Kant to John Rawls and Jürgen Habermas.

I wish to isolate three general themes around which the rethinking of Enlightenment universalism initiated by feminism, communitarianism and postmodernism ought to be continued. Communitarians, feminists and postmodernists have ① voiced skepticism toward the claims of a "legislating" reason to be able to articulate the necessary conditions of a "moral point of view," an "original position," or an "ideal speech situation;" ② they have questioned the abstract and disembedded, distorting and nostalgic ideal of the autonomous male ego which the universalist tradition privileges; ③ they have unmasked the inability of such universalist, legislative reason to deal with the indeterminacy and multiplicity of contexts and life-situations with which practical reason is always confronted. I shall argue in this book that there is a powerful kernel of truth in these criticisms, and that contemporary universalist theories must take seriously the claims of community, gender and postmodernism. Nevertheless, neither the pretenses of a legislative reason, nor the fiction of a disembedded autonomous male ego, nor for that matter indifference and insensitivity to contextual reasoning are the *sine qua non* of the universalist tradition in practical philosophy. A post-Enlightenment defense of universalism, without metaphysical props and historical conceits, is still viable. Such universalism would be interactive not legislative, cognizant of gender difference not gender blind, contextually sensitive and not situation indifferent. The goal of the essays collected in this volume is to argue for such a post-Enlightenment project of interactive universalism.

By bringing competing intellectual discourses of the present into dialogue, and by measuring their claims against each other, I intend to soften the boundaries which have often been drawn around universalist theories and feminist positions, communitarian aspirations and postmodernist skepticism. These oppositions and juxta-positions are too simple to grasp the complex criss-crossing of theoretical and political commitments in the present. Not only is a feminist universalism, for example, a discursive possibility rather than a sheer contradiction in terms; no matter how contradictory their political messages may be, in their critique of progress and modernity communitarianism and postmodernism are allies rather than opponents. By focussing on the fragile and shifting nature of such conceptual alliances and confrontations, I hope to illuminate the contradictory potentials of the present moment in our intel-lectual lives. It is my hope to create cracks and fissures in the edifice of discursive traditions large enough so that a new ray of reason which still reflects the dignity of justice along with the promise of happiness may shine through them.

A central premise of this book is that the crucial insights of the universalist tradition in practical philosophy can be reformulated today without committing oneself to the metaphysical illusions of the Enlightenment. These are the illusions of a self-transparent and self-grounding reason, the illusion of a disembedded and dis-embodied subject, and the illusion of having found an Archimedean standpoint, situated beyond historical and cultural contingency. They have long ceased to convince. But since how long one lingers on in their company and basks in their comforting warmth more often than not depends upon the intensity of the original farewell, let me state here my own adieu to these ideals. Enlightenment thinkers from Hobbes and Descartes to Rousseau, Locke and Kant believed that reason is a natural disposition of the human mind, which when governed by proper education can discover certain truths. It was furthermore assumed that the clarity and distinctness of these truths or the vivacity of their impact upon our senses would be sufficient to ensure intersubjective agreement among like-thinking rational minds. Even Kant whose Copernican revolution uncovered the active contribution of the knower to the process of knowing, nevertheless conflated the discovery of those conditions under which the objectivity of experience was possible with those conditions under which the truth or falsehood of propositions con-cerning experience could be ascertained. By contrast, I proceed from the premise that we must distinguish between the conditions for ascertaining the validity of statements and those characteristics pertaining to the cognitive apparatus of the human subject and which lead it to organize perceptual and experiential reality in a certain fashion.[4] Such a universal-pragmatic reformulation of transcendental philosophy, as undertaken by Karl-Otto Apel and Jürgen Habermas,[5] is postmetaphysical in the sense that truth is no

longer regarded as the psychological attribute of human consciousness, or to be the property of a reality distinct from the mind, or
even to consist in the process by which "givens" in consciousness
are correlated with "givens" in experience. In the discursive justification and validation of truth claims no moment is privileged as a
given, evidential structure which cannot be further questioned. It is
the discourse of the community of inquirers (Charles Sanders Peirce)
which first assigns an evidential or other type of value to aspects
of our consciousness or experience, and brings them into play as
factors which support our claims to the veracity of our beliefs. In the
continuing and potentially unending discourse of the community
of inquiry there are no "givens," there are only those aspects of
consciousness and reality which at any point in time may enter into
our deliberations as evidence and which we find cogent in backing
our statements. The first step then in the formulation of a postmetaphysical universalist position is to shift from a substantialistic to
a discursive, communicative concept of rationality.

The second step comes with the recognition that the subjects of
reason are finite, embodied and fragile creatures, and not disembodied cogitos or abstract unities of transcendental apperception
to which may belong one or more bodies. The empiricist tradition,
which in contradistinction from Descartes and Kant, let us say,
would describe the self as an "I know not what," or as a "bundle of
impressions," does not so much ignore the body as it tries to
formulate the unity of the self along the model of the continuity of a
substance in time. As opposed to the dismissal of the body in the
one case, and the reduction of self-identity to the continuity of a
substance in the other, I assume that the subject of reason is a
human infant whose body can only be kept alive, whose needs can
only be satisfied, and whose self can only develop within the human
community into which it is born. The human infant becomes a "self," *Mead*
a being capable of speech and action, only by learning to interact
in a human community. The self becomes an individual in that it
becomes a "social" being capable of language, interaction and cognition. The identity of the self is constituted by a narrative unity,
which integrates what "I" can do, have done and will accomplish
with what you expect of "me," interpret my acts and intentions to
mean, wish for me in the future, etc. The Enlightenment conception
of the disembedded cogito no less than the empiricist illusion of a
substance-like self cannot do justice to those contingent processes of
socialization through which an infant becomes a person, acquires
language and reason, develops a sense of justice and autonomy, and
becomes capable of projecting a narrative into the world of which
she is not only the author but the actor as well. The "narrative
structure of actions and personal identity" is the second premise

which allows one to move beyond the metaphysical assumptions of Enlightenment universalism.

If reason is the contingent achievement of linguistically socialized, finite and embodied creatures, then the legislative claims of practical reason must also be understood in interactionist terms. We may mark a shift here from *legislative to interactive rationality*.[6] This shift radically alters the conceptualization of "the moral point of view." The moral point of view is not an Archimedean center from which the moral philosopher pretends to be able to move the world. The moral point of view articulates rather a certain stage in the development of linguistically socialized human beings when they start to reason about general rules governing their mutual existence from the standpoint of a hypothetical questioning: under what conditions can we say that these general rules of action are valid not simply because it is what you and I have been brought up to believe or because my parents, the synagogue, my neighbors, my tribe say so, but because they are fair, just, impartial, in the mutual interest of all? The moral point of view corresponds to the stage of reasoning reached by individuals for whom a disjunction emerges between the social validity of norms and of normative institutional arrangements on the one hand, and their hypothetical validity from the standpoint of some standard of justice, fairness, impartiality. "Tell me Euthyphro," is the Socratic question, "is something pious because the gods love it, or do the gods love it because it is pious?" In the first case, the morally valid is dictated by the gods of my city, in the second, even the gods of my city recognize the presence of standards of piety and justice which would be valid for all. The moral point of view corresponds to the developmental stage of individuals and collectivities who have moved beyond identifying the "ought" with the "socially valid," and thus beyond a "conventional" understanding of ethical life, to a stance of questioning and hypothetical reasoning. Most high cultures in human history which differentiate between the natural and the social worlds are capable of producing such questioning, and such a disjunction between "the moral ought" (*das moralische Sollen*) and "social validity or acceptability" (*soziale Geltung*).[7]

The elements of a postmetaphysical, interactive universalism are: the universal pragmatic reformulation of the basis of the validity of truth claims in terms of a discourse theory of justification; the vision of an embodied and embedded human self whose identity is constituted narratively, and the reformulation of the moral point of view as the contingent achievement of an interactive form of rationality rather than as the timeless standpoint of a legislative reason. Taken together, these premises form a broad conception of reason, self and society. What is their status in the project of a postmetaphysical and interactive universalism?

Perhaps this question can be best approached by contrasting John Rawls's claims for a "political conception of justice" with the broad vision of reason, self and society outlined above. In the wake of objections raised by communitarians like Michael Sandel in particular to the concept of the self and the vision of the good presupposed or at least implied by his theory of justice, John Rawls distinguished between "metaphysical" and "political" conceptions of justice. While the former view would entail fundamental philosophical premises about the nature of the self, one's vision of society and even one's concept of human rationality, the political conception of justice proceeded from assumptions about self, society and reason which were "formulated not in terms of any comprehensive doctrine but in terms of certain fundamental intuitive ideas viewed as latent in the public political culture of a democratic society."[8] Rawls believes in the legislative task of reason and he limits the scope of philosophical inquiry in accordance with conceptions of what is appropriate for the public culture of liberal democracies. He formulates his philosophical presuppositions in such a fashion as would elicit an "overlapping consensus" and thus be acceptable to the implicit self-understanding of the public actors of a democratic polity. The essays collected in this volume do not restrict the scope of normative inquiry to the actually existing limitations on the public discourses of actually existing democracies. In the final analysis, conceptions of self, reason and society and visions of ethics and politics are inseparable. One should regard such conceptions of self, reason and society not as elements of a "comprehensive" Weltanschaung which cannot be further challenged, but as presuppositions which are themselves always also subject to challenge and inquiry. As I will argue below, such assumptions about self, reason and society are the "substantive" presuppositions without which no "proceduralism," including Rawls's own program of an "overlapping consensus," can be cogently formulated. There is a kind of normative philosophical analysis of fundamental presuppositions which serves to place ethical inquiry in the larger context of epistemic and cultural debates in a society. Such analysis of presuppositions should be viewed not as the attempt to put forth a comprehensive moral doctrine acceptable to all, but as the dialectical uncovering of premises and arguments which are implicit not only in contemporary cultural and intellectual debates but in the institutions and social practices of our lives as well. In Hegelian language this would be the study of ethics as a doctrine of "objective spirit." In my language this is a study of ethics in the context of a critical theory of society and culture.[9]

While continuing the broad philosophical shift from legislative to interactive reason initiated by the work of Jürgen Habermas in par-

ticular, in this book I depart from his version of a discourse or communicative ethic in crucial ways. I attempt to highlight, emphasize
and even radicalize those aspects of a discourse ethic which are
universalist without being rationalistic, which seek understanding among humans while considering the consensus of all to be a
counterfactual illusion, and which are sensitive to differences of
identity, needs and modes of reasoning without obliterating these
behind some conception of uniform rational moral autonomy. There
are (three) decisive foci around which I propose to save discourse
ethics from the excesses of its own rationalistic Enlightenment
legacy. These are the conceptualization of the moral point of view
in light of the reversibility of perspectives and the cultivation in
Hannah Arendt's terms of "representative thinking;" to "engender"
the subject of moral reasoning, not in order to relativize moral
claims to fit gender differences but to make them gender sensitive
and cognizant of gender difference; to develop a rudimentary
phenomenology of moral judgment in order to show how a principled, universalist morality and context-sensitive moral judgment
can fit together. My goal is to situate reason and the moral self more
decisively in contexts of gender and community, while insisting
upon the discursive power of individuals to challenge such situatedness in the name of universalistic principles, future identities and as
yet undiscovered communities.

Chapter 1 entitled "In the Shadow of Aristotle and Hegel: Communicative Ethics and Current Controversies in Practical Philosophy"
presents the general outlines of my attempt to defend communicative ethics while heeding the criticism of neo-Aristotelians like Hans-
Georg Gadamer and Alasdair MacIntyre on the one hand and of
neo-Hegelians like Charles Taylor on the other. I begin by seeking
an answer to the standard Hegelian objection to formalist ethical
universalism that procedures of universalizability are at best inconsistent and at worst empty. Applying this objection to the case of
discourse ethics, I maintain that neither inconsistency nor emptiness
are unavoidable defects of a conversationally conceived model of
moral reasoning. What I propose is a procedural reformulation of
the universalizability principle along the model of a moral conversation in which the capacity to reverse perspectives, that is, the willingness to reason from the others' point of view, and the sensitivity to
hear their voice is paramount. Following Kant, Hannah Arendt has
given this core intuition of universalistic ethical and political theories
a brilliant formulation:

> The power of judgment rests on a potential agreement with others,
> and the thinking process which is active in judging something is not,
> like the thought process of pure reasoning, a dialogue between me

and myself, but finds itself always and primarily, even if I am quite alone in making up my mind, in an anticipated communication with others with whom I know I must finally come to some agreement. And this enlarged way of thinking, which as judgment knows how to transcend its individual limitations, cannot function in strict isolation or solitude; it needs the presence of others "in whose place" it must think, whose perspective it must take into consideration, and without whom it never has the opportunity to operate at all.[10]

The nerve of my reformulation of the universalist tradition in ethics is this construction of the "moral point of view" along the model of a moral conversation, exercising the art of "enlarged thinking." The goal of such conversation is not consensus or unanimity (*Einstimmigkeit* or *Konsens*) but the "anticipated communication with others with whom I know I must finally come to some agreement" (*Verständigung*). This distinction between "consensus" and "reaching an agreement" has not always been heeded in objections to communicative ethics. At times Habermas himself has overstated the case by insisting that the purpose of universalizability procedures in ethics must be the uncovering or discovering of some "general interest" to which all could consent.[11] I propose to view the concept of "general interest" in ethics and politics more as a regulative ideal and less as the subject matter of a substantive consensus. In ethics, the universalizability procedure, if it is understood as a reversing of perspectives and the willingness to reason from the other's (others') point of view, does not guarantee consent; it demonstrates the will and the readiness to seek understanding with the other and to reach some reasonable agreement in an open-ended moral conversation. Likewise, in politics, it is less significant that "we" discover "the" general interest, but more significant that collective decisions be reached through procedures which are radically open and fair to all. Above all these decisions should not exclude the voice of those whose "interests" may not be formulable in the accepted language of public discourse, but whose very presence in public life may force the boundaries between private needs and public claims, individual misfortunes and collectively representable grievances.

One consequence of reformulating universalizability in terms of the model of reversibility of perspectives and the cultivation of "enlarged thinking" is that the *identity of the moral self* must be reconceptualized as well. More precisely, this reformulation allows us to challenge those presuppositions of "legalistic universalism" from Kant to Rawls which have privileged a certain vision of the moral self. In order to think of universalizability as reversing of perspectives and a seeking to understand the standpoint of the other(s), they must be viewed not only as generalized but also as concrete others. According to the standpoint of the "generalized other", each individual is a moral person endowed with the same moral rights as ourselves; this moral person is also a reasoning and acting being, capable of a sense of justice, of formulating a vision of the good, and of engaging in activity to pursue the latter. The standpoint of the concrete other, by contrast, enjoins us to view every moral person as a unique individual, with a certain life history, disposition and endowment, as well as needs and limitations. One consequence of limiting procedures of universalizability to the standpoint of the generalized other has been that the other as distinct from the self has disappeared in universalizing moral discourse. As I argue in the essay, "The Generalized and the Concrete Other," there can be no coherent reversibility of perspectives and positions unless the identity of the other as distinct from the self, not merely in the sense of bodily otherness but as a concrete other, is retained.

I envision the relationship of the generalized to the concrete other as along the model of a continuum. In the first place there is the universalistic commitment to the consideration of every human individual as a being worthy of universal moral respect. This norm which I share with the liberal tradition is institutionalized in a democratic polity through the recognition of civil, legal and political rights – all of which reflect the morality of the law or, if you wish, the principles of justice in a well-ordered polity. The standpoint of the concrete other, by contrast, is implicit in those ethical relationships in which we are always already immersed in the lifeworld. To be a family member, a parent, a spouse, a sister or a brother means to know how to reason from the standpoint of the concrete other. One cannot act within these ethical relationships in the way in which standing in this kind of a relationship to someone else demands of us without being able to think from the standpoint of our child, our spouse, our sister or brother, mother or father. To stand in such an ethical relationship means that we as concrete individuals know what is expected of us in virtue of the kind of social bonds which tie us to the other.

If the standpoint of the generalized and the concrete other(s) are thought of as existing along a continuum, extending from universal respect for all as moral persons at one end to the care, solidarity and solicitation demanded of us and shown to us by those to whom we stand in the closest relationship at the other,[12] then the privileging in traditional universalistic theories of the legal domain and the exclusive focus upon relationships of justice must be altered. I argue against Kohlberg and Habermas that relations of justice do not exhaust the moral domain, even if they occupy a privileged position within it (see pp. 184ff.). Again to introduce a Hegelian locution, ethical life encompasses much more than the relationship of right-bearing generalized others to each other. Even if the Kantian tradition distinguishes between legality and morality, a tendency in Kantian ethics which has persisted till our own days is to model ethical bonds along juridical (*rechtsfroemmig*) ones. Viewed from the standpoint of the interactive universalism which I seek to develop in this book, the problem appears differently: my question is how ethical life must be thought of – life in the family no less than life in the modern constitutional state – from the standpoint of a post-conventional and universalist morality. Sometimes Hegel argued as if "the moral point of view" and Sittlichkeit were incompatible, but the really challenging task suggested by his *Philosophy of Right* is to envisage a universalistic moral point of view as situated within an ethical community. Call this the vision of a *postconventional Sittlichkeit*.

It is this search for a "postconventional Sittlichkeit" which distinguishes my vision from that of communitarian thinkers like Michael Sandel and Alasdair MacIntyre in particular. In the chapter on "Autonomy, Modernity and Community: Communitarianism and Critical Social Theory in Dialogue," I argue that there are two strands of communitarian thinking on the question of reconstituting a community under conditions of modernity. The first I describe as the "integrationist" and the second as the "participationist." While the first group of thinkers seek to reconstitute community via recouping and reclaiming an integrative vision of fundamental values and principles, the participationists envisage such a community as emerging from common action, engagement and debate in the civic and public realms of democratic societies. I reject the integrationist vision of community as being incompatible with the values of autonomy, pluralism, reflexivity and tolerance in modern societies.

In the constitution of such a postconventional Sittlichkeit via participatory politics in a democratic polity, the faculty of "enlarged thinking" plays a crucial role. This was one of Hannah Arendt's cardinal insights, and ultimately why she considered judgment a political rather than a moral faculty. In "thinking with Arendt against Arendt" in several of the chapters below, I will attempt to make her conception of enlarged thinking useful both for morality and for politics. In the democratic polity, the gap between the demands of justice, as these articulate principles of moral right, and the demands of virtue, as this defines the quality of our relations to others in the lifeworld, can be bridged by cultivating qualities of civic friendship and solidarity. These qualities of civic friendship and solidarity mediate between the standpoints of the "generalized" and the "concrete others," by teaching us to reason, to understand and to appreciate the standpoint of "collective concrete others." Such understanding, however, is a product of political activity. It cannot be performed either by the political theorist or by the moral agent in vacuo. For, as Arendt well knew, the multiplicity of perspectives which constitute the political can only be revealed to those who are willing to engage in the foray of public contestation. The perspectival quality of the public world can only manifest itself to those who "join together in action in concert." Public space is formed through such action in concert. In a postconventional Sittlichkeit, the public sphere is the crucial domain of interaction which mediates between the macropolitical institutions of a democratic polity and the private sphere.

The public sphere is a common theme in several chapters of this book. I set up a contrast between the liberal, the Arendtian and the Habermasian models of the public sphere. As representative of the liberal position, Bruce Ackerman's model of a public conversation under the constraints of neutrality is chosen. My argument is that the constraint of neutrality illicitly limits the agenda of public conversation and excludes particularly those groups like women and blacks who have not been traditional partners in the liberal dialogue. I maintain that democratic politics redefines and reconstitutes the line between the right and the good, justice and the good life. Although this agonal and contestatory dimension of politics is at the heart of Hannah Arendt's work, what makes her concept of public space so deficient from the standpoint of complex, modern societies is a constraint similar to that introduced by Ackerman with his concept of "liberal neutrality." Arendt also seeks to limit the scope and the agenda of the public sphere via essentialist assumptions about the "natural place" of human activities and the "political" or "non-political" nature of certain topoi of debate. By contrast, I plead for a radically proceduralist model of the public sphere, neither the scope nor the agenda of which can be limited a priori, and whose lines can be redrawn by the participants in the conversation. Habermas's concept of a public sphere embodying the principles of a discourse ethics is my model here.

One of the chief contributions of feminist thought to political theory in the western tradition is to have questioned the line dividing the public and the private. Feminists have argued that the "privacy" of the private sphere, which has always included the relations of the male head of household to his spouse and children, has been an opaque glass rendering women and their traditional spheres of activity invisible and inaudible. Women, and the activities to which they have been historically confined, like childrearing, housekeeping, satisfying the emotional and sexual needs of the male, tending to the sick and the elderly, have been placed until very recently beyond the pale of justice. The norms of free-dom, equality and reciprocity have stopped at the household door. Two centuries after the American and the French revolutions, the entry of women into the public sphere is far from complete, the gender division of labor in the family is still not the object of moral and political reflection, and women and their concerns are still invisible in contemporary theories of justice and community. It is not my purpose to lament the invisibility of gender in contemporary thought, but rather to ask the question: what consequences does this invisibility have for the theories under consideration? A theory of universalist morality or of the public sphere cannot simply "ignore" women and be subsequently "corrected" by their reinsertion into the picture from which they were missing. Women's absence points to some categorial distortions within these theories; that is to say, because they exclude women these theories are systematically skewed. The exclusion of women and their point of view is not just a political omission and a moral blind spot but constitutes an epistemological deficit as well.

I call attention to the epistemological deficits of contemporary universalism in the following areas. First, I argue that the neglect by universalist theories of the moral emotions and of everyday moral interactions with concrete others has everything to do with the gender division of labor in western societies subsequent to modernity. Justice becomes the core of collective moral life when the extended households of antiquity and the Middle Ages lose their productive functions with the rise of the capitalist exchange economy, and become mere reproductive units whose function is to satisfy the daily bodily and psychosexual needs of their members. Second, every concept of public space presupposes a corresponding delimitation of the private. In the chapter entitled "Models of Public Space: Hannah Arendt, the Liberal Tradition and Jürgen Habermas," I show that these theories of the public sphere are gender blind to the extent that they either draw a rigid and dogmatic boundary between the public and the private (Arendt), or as is the case with Habermas, because they develop binary oppositions which exclude the thematization of issues most important for women from public discussion. The oppositions between "justice" and "the good life," "generalizable interests" versus "private need interpretations," between "public norms" and "private values", have the consequence of leaving the line between the public and the private pretty much where it has always been, namely between the public spheres of the polity and the economy on the one hand and the familial-domestic realm on the other. Engaging in a dialectical battle with Habermas, I try to reconstruct his model of the public sphere in a way which would both accommodate feminist criticisms and also help feminists in our own thinking about alternative public spheres.

Finally, there is a relationship between the neglect of the problem of moral judgment in universalist moral theories and the neglect of women and their activities. Because women's sphere of activity has traditionally been and still today is so concentrated in the private sphere in which children are raised, human relationships maintained and traditions handed down and continued, the female experience has been more attuned to the "narrative structure of action" and the "standpoint of the concrete other." Since they have had to deal with concrete individuals, with their needs, endowments, wants and abilities, dreams as well as failures, women in their capacities as primary caregivers have had to exercise insight into the claims of the particular. In a sense the art of the particular has been their domain, as has the "web of stories", which in Hannah Arendt's words constitutes the who and the what of our shared world. It is in the context of discussing Hannah Arendt's theory of judgment that I provide the outlines of a phenomenology of moral judgment, which would nonetheless be compatible with a universalist and principled morality.

The claim that the gender blindness of universalist theories is not merely a matter of moral indifference or political inclination but that it points to a deeper epistemic failure has been one of the cornerstones of the postmodernist critique of the grand narratives of the logocentric western tradition. If there is one commitment which unites postmodernists from Foucault to Derrida to Lyotard it is this critique of western rationality as seen from the perspective of the margins, from the standpoint of what and whom it excludes, suppresses, delegitimizes, renders mad, imbecilic or childish. In his impressive genealogies of reason Foucault uncovers the discursive practices which have drawn the line between madness and civilization, mental health and sickness, criminality and normality, sexual deviance and sexual conformism.[13] Foucault shows that the other of reason comes to haunt this very reason. The persistence of the other within the text of western metaphysics, the continuing attempts of this metaphysics to erase the presence of the other in the endless game of binary oppositions has been a guiding vision of Jacques Derrida's thought from his early essay on "the ends of man" to his most recent comments on the "force of law."[14] Of course, it would be a mistake to think that the other in Jacques Derrida's thought is merely a nomer for an excluded gender, race, people or geopolitical region of the world. For Derrida, as for Hegel, no identity can be constituted without difference; the other is never merely an other but always also an in- and for-itself. But for Hegel there is a moment of identity which overcomes difference by "appropriating" it, by pretending that the "other" is something merely posited (*etwas gesetzt*) which the one self-identical subject presupposes (*vorausgesetzt*); for Derrida difference is irreducible and never evaporates into the imperialist game of positing one's presuppositions which Hegel's subjects always play. Difference which is ineliminable is différance, the continuing act and process of differing. Although there is no identity, nonetheless there is more than merely a contingent relationship between the logocentrism of the West and the imperialist gesture with which the West "appropriates" its other(s), pretending much like the Hegelian concept that they were its own presuppositions on the way to self-fulfillment. The Orient is there to enable the Occident, Africa is there to enable western civilization to fulfill its mission, the woman is there to help man actualize himself in her womb, etc. . . . The logic of binary oppositions is also a logic of subordination and domination.

In Jean-François Lyotard's work the epistemic exclusion of the other also has moral and political implications although it can by no means be reduced to these. In *The Postmodern Condition* Lyotard contrasted the "grand narratives" of the Enlightenment to the "petit recits" of women, children, fools and primitives. The exclusion of small narrativity, argued Lyotard, was an aspect of the grandiose vision of the modernizing western tradition. *The Postmodern Condition* left ambigious, however, whether by "narrativity" Lyotard meant a kind of ordinary language philosophy à la Wittgenstein, a hermeneutic tradition of judgment à la Gadamer, or a kind of poetic imagination like the one Richard Rorty defends. Perhaps all three were envisioned. In subsequent works like *Le Différend*, *Just Gaming* and *Heidegger and the Jews*[15] there is a linking of the limits of rationalism to the ethics and politics of the other.

As the chapter on "Feminism and the Question of Postmodernism" clarifies, in their critique of the illusions of logocentrism and in their championing of the standpoint of the "other(s)," postmodernist thinkers have been crucial allies for contemporary feminism. By focussing on the problem of the subject, the question of grand narratives, and the standards of rationality and critique, I construct a dialogue here between weak and strong postmodernist claims and feminist positions/oppositions. Postmodernism is an ally with whom feminism cannot claim identity but only partial and strategic solidarity. Postmodernism, in its infinitely skeptical and subversive attitude toward normative claims, institutional justice and political struggles, is certainly refreshing. Yet, it is also debilitating. The so-called critique of "identity politics," which is now dominating feminist thought, is not only an acknowledgment of the necessity of "rainbow politics," as Iris Young has claimed.[16] The critique of "identity politics" attempts to replace the vision of an autonomous and engendered subject with that of a fractured, opaque self; the "deed without the doer" becomes the paradigm of subversive activity for selves who joyfully deny their own coherence and relish their opacity and multiplicity. This problematic vision of the self is a radicalization of the Nietzschean critique of modernity in the name of an aesthetics of the everyday. It is Zarathustra who can be lamb and lion, sage and rebel at once. For women the aesthetic transcendence of the everyday is of course a temptation. But precisely because women's stories have so often been written for them by others, precisely because their own sense of self has been so fragile, and their ability to assert control over the conditions of their existence so rare, this vision of the self appears to me to be making a virtue out of necessity. No less important is that social criticism of the kind required for women's struggles is not even possible without positing the legal, moral and political norms of autonomy, choice and self-determination. Aesthetic modernism has always parasitically depended upon the achievements of modernity in the spheres of law and morality – insofar as the right of the moral person to pursue her sense of the good, be it ever so fractured, incoherent and opaque, has first to be anchored in law and morality before it can become an everyday option for playful selves. In this respect, as in many others, postmodernism presupposes a super-liberalism, more pluralistic, more tolerant, more open to the right of difference and otherness than the rather staid and sober versions presented by John Rawls, Ronald Dworkin and Thomas Nagel. As far as I am concerned this is not troublesome. What is baffling though is the lightheartedness with which postmodernists simply assume or even posit those hyper-universalist and superliberal values of diversity, heterogeneity, eccentricity and otherness. In doing so they rely on the very norms of the autonomy of subjects and the rationality of democratic procedures which otherwise they seem to so blithely dismiss. What concept of reason, which vision of autonomy allows us to retain these values and the institutions within which these values flourish and become ways of life? To this question postmodernists have no answer; perhaps because, more often than not, as sons of the French revolution, they have enjoyed the privileges of the modern to the point of growing blasé vis à vis them.

This book ends as it began in a tug with Hegel. "On Hegel, Women and Irony" brings together many strands of argumentation. By examining Hegel's relationship to the movement of the early romantics in the Jena circle, and in particular by looking at the life of one of these early "modernist" women, Caroline Michaelis von Schlegel Schelling, I show that the women's question in Hegel's philosophy is not only a conceptual result necessitated by a series of binary oppositions which define the logic of gender relations in his philosophy. Nor is the confinement of women to a traditionalist vision of Sittlichkeit in the *Philosophy of Right* merely a consequence of the historical limitations of Hegel's times. Hegel could have argued otherwise, just as some of his contemporaries and most notably the early Friedrich von Schlegel did. Yet he chose not to; he was not necessitated to do so. He chose not to follow the consequences of modernity in ethical life all the way into the sphere of personal, intimate, sexual relations between men and women. He refused to accept the ideals of hetoresexual equality and egalitarian reciprocity which his romantic friends for a short while at least advocated. Yet as the person of Caroline von Schlegel Schelling shows, women cannot but have an ambivalent relationship to modernity, which on the one hand promises them so much and which yet on the other constantly subverts its own *promesse du bonheur*. In joining the French revolutionary armies and the shortlived republic of Mainz, Caroline appears to me to have appreciated the dialectic of bourgeois republicanism which initially allowed women as participants into the public sphere, only at a second stage to send them scurrying home. The recovery of a sense of irony in the face of the modernist project and bemusement at its dialectical twists and turns is truer not only to the dilemmas of contemporary feminism but in the face of an epoch approaching its end as well.

Notes

1   F. Fukuyama has argued that transformations in the Soviet Union and Eastern Europe show that we have in effect reached "the end of history". F. Fukuyama, "The End of History?" *The National Interest* (Summer 1989), pp. 3–18. Of course, this is not meant in the trivial chronological sense that time will now stand still, but rather in the sense that the economic and political *kairos* of the future (how long is the future?) will not add anything new to the principles of western capitalism and liberal democracy. Just as Hegel saw the post-French revolutionary modern state, based on the principles of the right of persons and property, to represent the conceptual end of the history of freedom, Fukuyama also believes that the second half of the twentieth century has vindicated capitalism and liberal democracy over their enemies, namely fascism and communism. See ibid., pp. 9ff.

2   See Ernst Bloch, *Erbschaft dieser Zeit*, first published 1935 (Suhrkamp, Frankfurt, 1973), pp. 110ff.

3   See Richard Rorty, "Habermas and Lyotard on Postmodernity," *Praxis International*, 4.1 (April 1984), pp. 34ff. Also see "The Contingency of a Liberal Community," in *Contingency, Irony and Solidarity* (Cambridge University Press, Cambridge, 1989), pp. 44ff.

4   Wilfried Sellars's discussion of this point, which is after all a

restatement of Hegel's critique of "Sense Certainty" in the first chapter of *The Phenomenology of Spirit*, has been very influential on my thinking. See Wilfried Sellars, "Empiricism and the Philosophy of Mind," in *Science, Perception and Reality* (Humanities, New York, 1963), pp. 127ff., and Michael Williams, *Groundless Belief: An Essay on the Possibility of Epistemology* (Yale University Press, New Haven, 1977), esp. pp. 25ff. for a more recent statement.

5 See Karl-Otto Apel, "From Kant to Peirce: The Semiotic Transformation of Transcendental Logic," in *Towards a Transformation of Philosophy*, trans. Glyn Adey and David Frisby (Routledge and Kegan Paul, London, 1980), pp. 77–93; see also J. Habermas, "What is Universal Pragmatics?," in *Communication and the Evolution of Society*, trans. Thomas McCarthy (Beacon, Boston, 1979), pp. 1–69, and "Wahrheitstheorien," in *Wirklichkeit und Reflexion*, ed. H. Fahrenbach (Neske, Pfüllingen, 1973), and most recently Jürgen Habermas, *Postmetaphysisches Denken* (Suhrkamp, Frankfurt, 1989).

6 In chapter 5 below, "The Generalized and the Concrete Other: The Kohlberg–Gilligan Controversy and Moral Theory," I use the terms "substitutionalist" and "interactive" universalisms to mark this contrast.

7 The kind of developmental universalism defended by Kohlberg and Habermas has at times been subject to the misleading reading that Socrates and Jesus, Buddha or Francis of Assisi as members of cultures and societies which were prior in world history to western Enlightenment and modernity should be considered for that reason to be on a "lower level of moral development" than Voltaire or Nietzsche, Kant or Karl Marx! Obviously, an absurd view which reeks of the self-satisfied evolutionism of the eighteenth and nineteenth centuries. I have argued elsewhere that this is a gross misunderstanding of Habermas's work in particular, see S. Benhabib, *Critique, Norm and Utopia: A Study of the Foundations of Critical Theory* (Columbia University Press, New York, 1986), pp. 253ff. Although the relationship of cognitive universalist moral positions to modernity is a complex one, which I shall address in various chapters below, the developmental interpretation of the moral point of view in no way sanctions the construal of world history and human cultures as if they were stages in the growth of a super-ego writ large. I reject attempts to apply a cognitive developmental scheme with a teleological endpoint to world history and cultures. One can utilize a much weaker scheme of distinctions between preconventional, conventional, and postconventional modalities of cultural traditions, without also having to maintain that these are "natural" sequences of evolution which will invariably take place in a normal course of "development." For in the case of individual development it is the interaction of a finite bodily individual with the social and the physical world which initiates learning in this individual, activates memory and reflection and brings about progressions to "higher," more integrated stages of situation comprehension and problem solving. The "subject" of world history by contrast is an abstraction at best and a fiction at worst. One cannot attribute to this fiction a dynamic source of interaction and learning such as propels individuals. Although I find the categories of "pre, post

and conventional moralities" descriptively useful in thinking about patterns of normative reasoning in cultures, I attribute no teleological necessity to the progression from one stage to another.

8 John Rawls, "The Priority of Right and Ideas of the Good," *Philosophy and Public Affairs*, 17.4 (Fall 1988), pp. 251–76, here p. 252.

9 I have dealt with the logic and presuppositions of critical social theory in my book, *Critique, Norm and Utopia*. The current volume continues the exploration of the project of communicative ethics, outlined in chapter 8 of that book.

10 Hannah Arendt, "The Crisis in Culture," in *Between Past and Future: Six Exercises in Political Thought* (Meridian, New York, 1961), pp. 220–1.

11 See in particular Habermas's continuing reliance on the concept of "general interest," formulated first in the context of his theory of legitimation crisis, and subsequently in the context of his moral theory. J. Habermas, *Legitimation Crisis*, trans. Thomas McCarthy (Beacon, Boston, 1975), pp. 111ff, and "Discourse Ethics: Notes on a Program of Philosophical Justification," in *Moral Consciousness and Communicative Action*, trans. Christian Lehnhardt and Shierry Weber Nicholsen (MIT Press, Boston, 1990), pp. 43ff; and my critique in chapter 1 below.

12 This, of course, does not mean that only family or kinship groups can define such a space for us. In modern societies most individuals recreate family and kinlike structures for themselves on the basis of ties other than blood lineage; the relationship of friendship, which is a special bonding of two individuals, beyond and sometimes against the demands of kinship, nationality, ethnicity and politics, is one of the most cherished dimensions of ordinary lives under conditions of modernity.

13 For an early but extremely illuminating statement of the purpose of "genealogical inquiry," see Michel Foucault, "Nietzsche, Genealogy, History," in *Language, Counter-Memory, Practice: Selected Essays and Interviews*, ed. and introd. Donald F. Bouchard (Cornell University Press, New York, 1977), pp. 139–65.

14 Jacques Derrida, "The Ends of Man," reprinted in *After Philosophy*, ed. Kenneth Baynes, James Bohman and Thomas McCarthy (MIT Press, Boston, 1987), pp. 125–61, and "The Force of Law: The 'Mythical Foundation of Authority'," in special issue on Deconstruction and the Possibility of Justice, *Benjamin N. Cardozo Law Review*, 11.5–6 (July–Aug. 1990), pp. 919–1047.

15 See Jean-François Lyotard, *The Differend: Phrases in Dispute*, trans. G. van den Abbeele (University of Minnesota Press, Minneapolis, 1988); Jean-François Lyotard and Jean-Loup Thebaud, *Just Gaming*, trans. Wald Godzich (University of Minnesota Press, Minneapolis, 1979); and Lyotard, *Heidegger and the Jews*, trans. Andreas Michel and Mark Roberts (University of Minnesota Press, Minneapolis, 1990).

16 See Iris Young, "The Ideal of Community and the Politics of Difference," reprinted in *Feminism and Postmodernism*, ed. Linda Nicholson (Routledge, New York, 1990), pp. 300–1.

PART I

Modernity, Morality and Ethical Life

1 In the Shadow of Aristotle and Hegel

Communicative Ethics and Current Controversies in Practical Philosophy

In their Introduction to *Revisions: Changing Perspectives in Moral Philosophy*, Stanley Hauerwas and Alasdair MacIntyre write:

> This is not the first time that ethics has been fashionable. And history suggests that in those periods when a social order becomes uneasy and even alarmed about the weakening of its moral bonds and the poverty of its moral inheritance and turns for aid to the moral philosopher and theologian, it may not find these disciplines flourishing in such a way as to be able to make available the kind of moral reflection and theory which the culture actually needs. Indeed on occasion it may be that the very causes which have led to the impoverishment of moral experience and the weakening of moral bonds will also themselves have contributed to the formation of a kind of moral theology and philosophy which are unable to provide the needed resources.[1]

If this statement can be viewed as a fairly accurate indication of the Zeitgeist concerning ethical theory today, then this certainly does not bode well for yet another program of ethical universalism and formalism in the Kantian tradition. Such ethical formalism is considered a part of the Enlightenment project of rationalism and of the political project of liberalism, and it is argued that precisely these intellectual and political legacies are an aspect, if not the main cause, of the contemporary crisis. If communicative or discourse ethics is to be at all credible, it must be able to meet the kind of challenges posed by MacIntyre and Hauerwas.

Communicative or discourse ethics, as formulated by Karl-Otto Apel and Jürgen Habermas over the last two decades, is informed both by the Anglo-American and Continental traditions of thought and is witness to a provocative interaction between them. This project has been influenced by the work of such moral philosophers as Kurt Baier, Alan Gewirth, H. M. Hare, Marcus Singer and Stephen Toulmin on moral reasoning and universalizability in ethics.[2] Above all, it is in John Rawls's neo-Kantian constructivism and Lawrence Kohlberg's cognitive-developmental moral theory that Apel and Habermas have found the most kindred projects of moral philosophy in the Anglo-American world.[3]

The central insight of communicative or discourse ethics derives from modern theories of autonomy and of the social contract, as articulated by John Locke, Jean-Jacques Rousseau, and in particular by Immanuel Kant. Only those norms and normative institutional arrangements are valid, it is claimed, which individuals can or would freely consent to as a result of engaging in certain argumentative practices. Apel maintains that such argumentative practices can be described as "an ideal community of communication" (*die ideale Kommunikationsgemeinschaft*), while Habermas calls them "practical discourses." Both agree that such practices are the only plausible procedure in the light of which we can think of the Kantian principle of "universalizability" in ethics today. Instead of asking what an individual moral agent could or would will, without self-contradiction, to be a universal maxim for all, one asks: what norms or institutions would the members of an ideal or real communication community agree to as representing their common interests after engaging in a special kind of argumentation or conversation? The procedural model of an argumentative praxis replaces the silent thought-experiment enjoined by the Kantian universalizability test.

In this chapter I would like to acknowledge the challenge posed to communicative ethics from a standpoint which I will roughly describe as "neo-Aristotelian" and "neo-Hegelian." Since Aristotle's criticism of Plato's theory of the good and of the ideal state in his *Nicomachean Ethics* and *Politics*,[4] and since Hegel's critique of Kantian ethics in his various writings,[5] formalist and universalist ethical theories have been continuously challenged in the name of some concrete historical-ethical community or, in Hegelian language, of some *Sittlichkeit*. In fact, Apel and Habermas admit that one cannot ignore the lessons of Hegel's critique of Kantian morality.[6] Whether they have successfully integrated these lessons into communicative ethics is worth examining more closely.

A word of terminological clarification at the outset. In recent discussions "neo-Aristotelianism" has been used to refer to three, not always clearly distinguished, strands of social analysis and philosophical argumentation. Particularly in the German context, this term has been identified with a neoconservative social diagnosis of the problems of late-capitalist societies.[7] Such societies are viewed as suffering from a loss of moral and almost civilizational orientation, caused by excessive individualism, libertarianism, and the general temerity of liberalism when faced with the task of establishing fundamental values. Neither capitalist economic and societal modernization, nor technological changes are seen as basic causes of the current crisis; instead political liberalism and moral pluralism are regarded as the chief causes of this situation. From Robert Spaemann to Allan Bloom, this position has found vigorous exponents today.

The term "neo-Aristotelian" is also frequently used to designate the position of thinkers like Alasdair MacIntyre, Michael Sandel, Charles Taylor and Michael Walzer, who lament the decline of moral and political communities in contemporary societies.[8] But unlike the neoconservatives, the "communitarian" neo-Aristotelians are critical of contemporary capitalism and technology. The recovery of "community" need not only or even necessarily mean the recovery of some fundamentalist value scheme; rather communities can be reconstituted by the reassertion of democratic control over the runaway megastructures of modern capital and technology. The communitarians share with neoconservatives the belief that the formalist, ahistorical and individualistic legacies of Enlightenment thinking have been historically implicated in developments which have led to the decline of community as a way of life. Particularly today, they argue, this Enlightenment legacy so constricts our imagination and impoverishes our moral vocabulary that we cannot even conceptualize solutions to the current crises of welfare-state type democracies which would transcend the "rights-entitlement-distributive justice" trinity of political liberalism.

Finally, "neo-Aristotelianism" refers to a hermeneutical philosophical ethics, taking as its starting point the Aristotelian understanding of *phronesis*. Hans-Georg Gadamer was the first to turn to Aristotle's model of phronesis as a form of contextually embedded and situationally sensitive judgment of particulars.[9] Gadamer so powerfully synthesized Aristotle's ethical theory and Hegel's critique of Kant that after his work the two strands of argumentation became almost indistinguishable. From Aristotle's critique of Plato, Gadamer extricated the model of a situationally sensitive practical reason, always functioning against the background of the shared ethical understanding of a community.[10] From Hegel's critique of Kant, Gadamer borrowed the insight that all formalism presupposes a context that it abstracts from and that there is no formal ethics which does not have some material presuppositions concerning the self and social institutions.[11] Just as there can be no understanding which is not situated in some historical context, so there can be no "moral standpoint" which would not be dependent upon a shared ethos, be it that of the modern state. The Kantian moral point of view is only intelligible in light of the revolutions of modernity and the establishment of freedom as a principle of the modern world.

These three strands of a neoconservative social diagnosis, a politics of community and a philosophical ethics of a historically informed practical reason form the core elements of the contemporary neo-Aristotelian position. This chapter will deal with neo-Aristotelianism not as a social diagnosis or as a political philosophy but primarily as philosophical ethics. The political and social implications of neo-Aristotelian and communitarian positions will be discussed in the following chapter.

Let me now formulate a series of objections to communicative ethics. Some version of these has been voiced by thinkers inspired by Aristotle and Hegel against Kantian-type ethical theories at some point or another. My goal is to show that these objections have not succeeded in delivering a *coup de grâce* (a blow of mercy) to a dialogically reformulated universalist ethical theory. A serious exchange between such a universalist ethical theory, which presupposes neither the methodological individualism nor the ahistoricism of traditional Kantian ethics, and a hermeneutically inspired neo-Aristotelianism can lead us to see that some traditional oppositions and exclusions in moral philosophy are no longer convincing. Such oppositions as between universalism and historicity, between an ethics of principle and one of contextual judgment, or as between ethical cognition and moral motivation, within the confines of which much recent discussion has run, are no longer compelling. Just as it is not the case that there can be no historically informed ethical universalism, it is equally not the case that all neo-Aristotelianism must defend a conservative theory of communal ethics. In this chapter I will be concerned to indicate how such false oppositions can be transformed into a more fruitful set of contentions between two types of ethical theorizing which have marked the western philosophical tradition since its beginnings in Socrates' challenge to the Sophists and his condemnation to death by the city of Athens.

1 Skepticism toward the Principle of Universalizability. Is it at best Inconsistent and at worst Empty?

Hegel had criticized the Kantian formula, "Act only on that maxim through which you can at the same time will that it should become a universal law," on numerous occasions as being inconsistent at best and empty at worst.[12] Hegel argued that the test alone whether or not a maxim could be universalized could not determine its moral rightness. As he pointed out in his early essay on *Natural Law*, whether or not I should return deposits entrusted to me is answered in the affirmative by Kant with the argument that it would be self-contradictory to will that deposists should not exist. The young Hegel answers that there is no contradiction in willing a situation in which deposits and property do not exist, unless of course we make some other assumptions about human needs, scarce resources, distributive justice and the like. Out of the pure form of the moral law alone, no concrete maxims of action can follow and if they do, it is because other unidentified premises have been smuggled into the argument.[13]

In view of this Hegelian critique, which influences discussions of Kantian ethics even today,[14] the response of Kantian moral theorists has been twofold: first, some have accepted Hegel's critique that the formal procedure of universalizability can yield no determinate test of the rightness of maxims; they admit that one must presuppose some minimally shared conception of human goods and desires as goals of action, and must test principles of action against this background. This line of response has weakened the Kantian distinction between autonomy and heteronomy by accepting that the goals of action may be dictated by contingent features of human nature rather than by the dictates of pure practical reason alone. John Rawls's list of "basic goods," which rational agents are supposed to want whatever else they also want, is the best example of the introduction of material assumptions about human desires into the universalizability argument. The test of universalizability is not about whether we want these goods but rather about the moral principles guiding their eventual distribution.[15] Other Kantian moral philosophers, and most notably among them Onora O'Neill and Alan Gewirth, have refused to jettison the pure Kantian program, and have attempted to expand the principle of the non-contradiction of maxims by looking more closely at the *formal features of rational action*. O'Neill, for example, distinguishes between "conceptual inconsistency" and "volitional inconsistency" in order to differentiate among types of incoherence in action.[16] "The non-universalized maxim," she writes, "embodies a conceptual contradiction only if it *aims* at achieving mutually incompatible objectives and so cannot under any circumstances be acted on with success."[17] Volitional inconsistency, by contrast, occurs when a rational agent violates what O'Neill names "principles of rational intending."[18] Applying universalizability to maxims of action both to test their conceptual consistency and their volitional consistency avoids, so argues O'Neill, "the dismal choice between triviality and implausible rigorism."[19] In a similar vein, Alan Gewirth expands on the idea of the "rational conditions of action" in order to derive from them non-trivial and intersubjectively binding maxims of moral action.[20]

Both strategies have problems. In the first case, by allowing material presuppositions about human nature and desires into the picture, one runs the risk of weakening the distinction between Kantian and other types of utilitarian or Aristotelian moral theories. The result is a certain eclecticism in the structure of the theory. The second position runs a different danger: by focussing exclusively on the conditions of rational intending or acting, as O'Neill and Gewirth do, one can lose sight of the question of intersubjective moral validity. After all, the Kantian principle of universalizability was formulated in order to generate morally binding maxims of action which all can recognize. As Alasdair MacIntyre shows in his sharp critique of Gewirth, from the premise that I as a rational agent require certain conditions of action to be fulfilled, it can never follow that you have an *obligation* not to hinder me from enjoying these conditions.[21] The grounds for this obligation are left unclear; but it is precisely such grounds that the universalizability requirement was intended to produce. Put in terms which are those of Apel and Habermas, the analysis of the rational structure of action for a single agent produces an *egological* moral theory which cannot justify intersubjective moral validity. Instead of asking what I as a single rational moral agent can intend or will to be a universal maxim for all without contradiction, the communicative ethicist asks: what principles of action can we all recognize or agree to as being valid if we engage in practical discourse or a mutual search for justification?

With this reformulation, universalizability is defined as an intersubjective procedure of argumentation, geared to attain communicative agreement. This reformulation brings with it several significant shifts: instead of thinking of universalizability as a test of *non-contradiction*, we think of universalizability as a test of *communicative agreement*. We do not search for what would be non-self-contradictory but rather for what would be mutually acceptable for all. Furthermore, there is also a shift from the model of the goal-oriented or strategic action of a single agent intending a specific outcome to the model of *communicative action* which is speech and action to be shared with others.

What has been gained through this reformulation such as to counter the Hegelian objection? Have we not simply pushed the problem from one procedure on to another? Instead of deriving moral principles from some procedure of conceptual or volitional coherence, do we not simply derive them now from our definition of the conversational situation? Theorists can construct or design conversations to yield certain outcomes: the preconditions of conversation may guarantee that certain outcomes will result.[22] In an earlier article I formulated this problem as follows: either models of practical discourse or the ideal communication community are defined so minimally as to be trivial in their implications or there are more controversial substantive premises guiding their design, and which do not belong among the minimal conditions defining the argumentation situation, in which case they are inconsistent.[23] We are back to the "dismal choice" between triviality or inconsistency (to modify slightly Onora O'Neill's felicitous phrase).

The way out of this dilemma, I suggest, is to opt for a strong and possibly controversial construction of the conversational model which would nonetheless be able to avoid the charges of dogmatism and/or circularity.[24] My thinking is as follows. What Habermas has previously named the conditions of an "ideal speech situation," and which in the essay "Discourse Ethics: Notes on a Program of Philosophical Justification" are called the "universal and necessary communicative presuppositions of argumentative speech,"[25] entail strong ethical assumptions. They require of us: (1) that we recognize the right of all beings capable of speech and action to be participants in the moral conversation – I will call this *the principle of universal moral respect*; (2) these conditions further stipulate that within such conversations each has the same symmetrical rights to various speech acts, to initiate new topics, to ask for reflection about the presuppositions of the conversation, etc. Let me call this *the principle of egalitarian reciprocity*.[26] The very presuppositions of the argumentation situation then have a normative content that precedes the moral argument itself. But can one then really avoid the charges of circularity and dogmatism?

One of the central disagreements between Apel and Habermas concerns precisely this issue of the justification of the constraints of the moral conversation. Apel maintains that:

> If, on the one hand, a presupposition cannot be challenged in argumentation without actual performative self-contradiction, and if, on the other hand, it cannot be deductively grounded without formal-logical petitio principii, then it belongs to those transcendental-pragmatic presuppositions of argumentation that one must always (already) have accepted, if the language game of argumentation is to be meaningful.[27]

For Apel, the principle that all beings capable of speech and action are potential members of the same communication community with me, and that they deserve equal and symmetrical treatment are two such conditions.

In view of this Apelian strategy of fundamental grounding or *Letztbegründung*, Habermas argues that such a strong justification of communicative ethics cannot succeed and may not even be necessary. Rather than viewing the normative constraints of the ideal communication community as being "disclosable" via an act of transcendental self-reflection, Habermas argues that we view them as "universal pragmatic presuppositions" of speech acts corresponding to the know-how of competent "moral" agents at the postconventional stage. But as Thomas McCarthy has pointed out, there is no univocal description of the "know-how" of moral actors who have reached the postconventional stage of moral reasoning.[28] Habermas's description of this know-how is one among many others like those of John Rawls and Lawrence Kohlberg. At the stage of postconventional moral reasoning, reversibility, universalizability and impartiality, under some description, are all aspects of the moral point of view, but the real point of philosophical contention is the acceptable or adequate description of these formal constraints. The appeal to moral psychology and development brings no exemption from the justificatory process. Lawrence Kohlberg was wrong in thinking that the "ought" can be deduced from the "is." The formal structure of postconventional moral reasoning allows a number of substantive moral interpretations, and these interpretations always take place by presupposing a hermeneutic horizon of norms and values which have become aspects of a modern lifeworld.

As opposed to Apel's strategy of *Letztbegründung* and Habermas's strategy of a "weak transcendental argument," based on the rational reconstruction of competencies, I would like to plead for a "historically self-conscious universalism." The principles of universal respect and egalitarian reciprocity are our philosophical clarification of the constituents of the moral point of view from *within* the normative hermeneutic horizon of modernity. These principles are neither the *only allowable* interpretation of the formal constituents of the competency of postconventional moral actors nor are they unequivocal transcendental presuppositions which every rational agent, upon deep reflection, must concede to. These principles are arrived at by a process of "reflective equilibrium," in Rawlsian terms, whereby one, as a philosopher, analyzes, refines and judges culturally defined moral intuitions in light of articulated philosophical principles. What one arrives at at the end of such a process of reflective equilibrium is a "thick description" of the moral presuppositions of the cultural horizon of modernity.

The steps leading to the establishment of the norms of universal moral respect and egalitarian reciprocity can be formalized as follows:

1 A philosophical theory of morality must show wherein the justifiability of moral judgments and/or normative assertions reside.

2 To justify means to show that if you and I argued about a particular moral judgment ('It was wrong not to help the

refugees and to let them die on the wide sea') and a set of normative assertions ('Education should be free for all for the first eighteen years of their lives') that we could in principle come to a reasonable agreement (*rationales Einverständnis*).

3 A "reasonable agreement" must be arrived at under conditions which correspond to our idea of a fair debate.

4 These rules of fair debate can be formulated as the "universal-pragmatic" presuppositions of argumentative speech and these can be stated as a set of procedural rules.

5 These rules reflect the moral ideal that we ought to *respect* each other as beings whose standpoint is worthy of equal consideration (the principle of universal moral respect) and that furthermore.

6 We ought to treat each other as concrete human beings whose capacity to express this standpoint we ought to enhance by creating, whenever possible, social practices embodying the discursive ideal (the principle of egalitarian reciprocity).

As I have reformulated this historically self-conscious weak justification program, steps 5 and 6 are substantive moral norms. Step 5 is the norm of universal respect. What is the force of the "ought" which attaches to it? This "ought" is not arrived at by a philosophical deduction from steps 1 to 4. A weak justification strategy consists in showing that there is not a single *deductive chain* of reasoning establishing this principle, but that there is a family of arguments and considerations each supporting the centrality of this principle as a basic moral norm. One of the arguments leading to the plausibility of the norm of universal respect is indeed a "universal pragmatic" one. This goes as follows: All argumentation entails respect for one's conversation partners; such respect belongs to the idea of fair argumentation; to be a competent partner in such a conversation then entails recognizing the principle of equal respect. Step 5 in this sense is an explication of the material normative content of the idea of argument, fair debate, etc. But note that this argument begs the question as to who, which groups of humans, are worthy of being considered as "conversation partners" and who are not. The step which leads from the specification of the rules of fair debate and argument to the material moral norm of universal moral respect for all is still missing.

Now a second argument lending support to the ideals of universal respect and egalitarian reciprocity comes from social action theory. The norm of "reciprocity" is embedded in the very structures of communicative action into which we are all socialized, for reciprocity entails that we are treated by others equally insofar as we are a member of a particular human group.[29] All communicative action entails symmetry and reciprocity of normative expectations among group members. In fact to become a member of a human group involves our being treated in accordance with such reciprocity. "Respect" is an attitude and a moral feeling first acquired through such processes of communicative socialization. The bases for respect can be disturbed if the conditions for developing a sense of self-worth and appreciation from others are lacking; respect may cease to be an aspect of our life experience under conditions of war and hostility leading to the breakdown of mutuality, and finally, respect may shrivel in a culture which is given to extreme indifference and forms of atomized individualism.

Thus at one level the intuitive idea behind the norms of universal respect is ancient and corresponds to the "golden rule" of the tradition – "Do unto others as you would have others do unto you." Universalizability enjoins us to reverse perspectives among members of a "moral community" and judge from the point of view of the other(s). Such reversibility is essential to the ties of reciprocity that bind human communities together. All human communities define some "significant others" in relation to whom reversibility and reciprocity must be exercised – be they members of my kin group, my tribe, my city-state, my nation, my co-religionists. What distinguishes "modern" from "premodern" ethical theories is the assumption of the former that the moral community is coextensive with all beings capable of speech and action, and potentially with all of humanity.[30] In this sense, communicative ethics sets up a model of moral conversation among members of a modern ethical community for whom the theological and ontological bases of inequality among humans has been radically placed into question.

This is not an admission of dogmatism in favor of modernity, for even this "dogma" of modernity, if you wish, can be challenged within the moral conversation itself. The racist, the sexist or the bigot can challenge the principle of universal moral respect and egalitarian reciprocity within the moral conversation, but if they want to establish that their position is right not simply because it is mighty, they must convince with argument that this is so. The presuppositions of the moral conversation can be challenged within the conversation itself, but if they are altogether suspended or violated then might, violence, coercion and suppression follow. One thus avoids the charge of circularity: by allowing that the presuppositions of the moral conversation can be questioned from within the conversation itself, they are placed within the purview of argumentation. But insofar as they are pragmatic rules necessary to keep the moral conversation going, we can only bracket them in order to challenge them but we cannot suspend them altogether. The shoe is really on the other foot. It is up to the critic of such egalitarian universalism to show, with good grounds, why some individuals on account of certain characteristics should be effectively excluded from the moral conversation.

Now defenders of inegalitarianism – men and women are "by nature" different and hence must be assigned differential rights and privileges; the white race is "by nature" superior to others and hence must be granted "higher" rights than other races; practitioners of the "one true" religion are closer to the truths of God and hence must have more authority than practitioners of other false religions in determining collective moral matters – combine with such claims also the belief that they can be demonstrated to be "valid" even to members of those groups whom one singles out for unequal treatment. Only the very extreme cases of sexism, racism and religious bigotry consider any kind of argument futile or unnecessary. Women should not only be treated differently but they should "want" to be treated differently by assenting to the fact that this is "natural"; non-white peoples should willingly accept the superiority of the white man and be grateful for it; infidels should be converted to see the true path to God. Inegalitarian arguments usually also require that others "see" the validity of these principles. And herein lies the paradox of such inegalitarianism: if such inegalitarianism is to be "rational" it must woo the assent of those who will be treated unequally, but to woo such assent means admitting the "others" into the conversation. But if these "others" can see the rationality of the inegalitarian position, they can also dispute its justice. To assent entails just as much the capacity to dissent, to say no. Therefore, either inegalitarianism is irrational, i.e. it cannot win the assent of those it addresses, or it is unjust because it precludes the possibility that its addressees will reject it.

Of course, our moral and political world is more characterized by struggles unto death among moral opponents than by a conversation among them. This admission reveals the fragility of the moral point of view in a world of power and violence, but this is not an admission of irrelevance. Political ideologies as well as more subtle forms of cultural hegemony have always sought to make plausible the continuation of violence and power to those who most suffered from their consequences. When such ideology and hegemony no longer serve to justify such relations, then struggles unto death for moral recognition can follow. As a critical social theorist, the philosopher is concerned with the unmasking of such mechanisms of continuing political ideology and cultural hegemony; as a moral theorist, the philosopher has one central task: to clarify and justify those normative standards in the light of which such social criticism is exercised.[31]

Let us return once more to the Hegelian objection: can a universalist ethical theory, which views universalizability in ethics as a moral conversation governed by certain procedural constraints, avoid the "dismal choice" (O'Neill) between triviality or inconsistency? Hegel's critique assumes but does not clarify a distinction between universalizability as a procedure for testing and universalizability as a procedure for generating maxims. As a procedure for *testing* the intersubjective validity of moral principles and norms of action, communicative ethics is neither trivial nor inconsistent; as a procedure for *generating* valid principles of action, the model of moral conversation is a necessary but insufficient test case that requires, in any given instance, adequate contextualization. In other words, we can say of a course of action, the principle of which has passed the test of conversational universalizability, that it is morally permissible, but also assert that it was the wrong thing to do under the circumstances. The universalizability test should produce standards of what are morally permissible and impermissible in general; however, such tests are by no means sufficient to establish the "morally good," in the sense not simply of what is allowed, but of what is morally meritorious in any given context.

Habermas formulates the test of universalizability thus: "Unless all affected can *freely* accept the consequences and the side effects that the *general* observance of a controversial norm can be expected to have for the satisfaction of the interests of *each individual* . . ." (emphasis in the text).[32] What we are asking them is not whether on the basis of this procedure the moral theorist can deduce concrete moral principles guiding action. The adoption of "all contents," writes Habermas, "no matter how fundamental the action norm involved may be, must be made to depend on real discourses (or advocatory discourses conducted as substitutes for them)."[33]

Even if this principle of universalizability ("U") is not intended to generate concrete principles or norms of action, can it serve as a test procedure for determining what is morally permissible and impermissible? As a test procedure "U" enjoins us to engage in a counterfactual thought-experiment in which we enter into conversation with all who would be potentially affected by our actions. Let us consider some standard moral maxims to assess what has been gained by this reformulation. Take the example used by Kant, "deposits once made must be returned for otherwise there would be no property." The relevant question is: does the principle "there ought to be property" satisfy the test that "all affected can freely accept the consequences and the side effects that the general observance of a controversial norm can be expected to have for the satisfaction of the interests of *each individual*?" The answer is that both the existence of property relations and its opposite can be adopted as a collective maxim of their actions by moral actors, if the consequences of such arrangements for the satisfaction of the interests of each can be freely accepted by all. In other words, the existence or non-existence of property relations cannot be determined via a moral deduction. Contrary to what Kant assumed, as long as they serve the satisfaction of the interests of each individual and this can be freely accepted by all, numerous forms of property arrangements are morally permissible. Kant was wrong in attempting to generate a categorical imperative to uphold property relations; what is at stake is not property as such but other moral values like general welfare and the correct mode of dispensing scarce resources. To this extent, the universalizability procedure in communicative ethics upholds Hegel's critique of Kant.

Yet, as formulated by Habermas, "U" also leads to morally disturbing and counter-intuitive consequences. Take the maxim, "Do not inflict unnecessary suffering." Whether or not we are to inflict unnecessary suffering is to be determined by whether all affected can freely accept the consequences and side effects that the general observance of a controversial norm can be expected to have for the satisfaction of the interests of each individual. Can we imagine a situation in which it would be in the interests of each individual and freely accepted by them that they would be not only perpetrators but receivers of unnecessary suffering? The answer to this question appears to depend on an equivocation concerning "interests." Suppose there are masochists and sadists among us who interpret their interests as consisting precisely in the opportunity to inflict and receive such suffering.[34] Are we ready to say that under these conditions *Neminem laede* (Cause suffering to none) ceases to be a morally valid principle? In other words, what appears to be the virtue of "U" in the property example, that is its indeterminacy, is its weakness in the second case. But the least that a universalist ethical theory ought to do is to cover the same ground as what Kant had described as "negative duties," i.e. duties not to violate the rights of humanity in oneself and in others. Yet "U" does not appear to do this.

I believe the difficulty is that Habermas has given "U" such a *consequentialist* formulation that his theory is now subject to the kinds of arguments that deontological rights theorists have always successfully brought against utilitarians. Without some stronger constraints about how we are to interpret "U", we run the risk of regressing behind the achievements of Kant's moral philosophy, and behind his distinction between negative and positive duties. The categorical imperative proves as morally impermissible what Kant names "negative duties," not to lie, not to harm, not to cheat, or otherwise violate the dignity of the moral person. Positive moral duties cannot be deduced from the universalizability test alone but

require contextual moral judgment in their concretization.[35] I have
suggested above that the communicative ethics version of "U" must
deliver criteria for distinguishing among the morally permissible and
the morally impermissible, without, however, being able to yield
adequate criteria of the morally good, virtuous or appropriate action
in any given circumstance.

Albrecht Wellmer, Agnes Heller and Otfried Höffe have all
recently expressed stronger criticisms of communicative ethics:
even as a test procedure for what is intersubjectively permissible,
"U", they argue, is either too indeterminate or too complex or too
counterfactual. In Heller's sharp formulation:

> Put bluntly, if we look to moral philosophy for guidance in our actions
> here and now, we cannot obtain any positive guidance from the
> Habermasian version of the categorical imperative. Rather, what we
> could get is a *substantive limitation* placed on our intellectual intuitions:
> we, as individuals, should only claim universal validity for those moral
> norms which we can assume would be accepted by everyone as valid
> in an ideal situation of symmetric reciprocity.[36]

Albrecht Wellmer writes:

> If we interpret U as an explication of our preunderstanding of moral
> validity, then this means that in our moral convictions and in our
> moral judgments, only such judgments must be involved that the
> consequences and side-effects which the general observance of a
> specific norm would have for each individual could be *freely* (*zwangslos*)
> accepted by all. This, however, so it appears to me, would make
> justified moral judgment a total chimera (*Ein Ding der Unmöglichkeit*).[37]

Heller argues that the Habermasian theory cannot be saved for it
is in effect a theory of "legitimation rather than one of validation."[38]
Wellmer recommends that we interpret the ideals of "rational consent" or "agreement" as regulative principles, but that in the solution of *real* moral problems under real moral *conditions*, we can "only
think of what the reasonable person or those competent judges or
those affected by our actions *would* say if they were sufficiently
reasonable, good willing and competent in judgment."[39] I think
Wellmer's response weakens the distinction between justification
and contextualization. While I agree that such contextualization is
absolutely crucial for *moral* judgment in real situations, I think his
response makes the test of the validity of moral judgment a matter
of phronesis alone. I am interested in seeing whether there is anything at all, any guidelines, in the procedure of discourse ethics that
could place a "substantive limitation on our intellectual intuition,"
in the way of necessary but insufficient criteria. Heller considers the
placing of such limitations alone too minimal an achievement for

moral theory. In my opinion, however, it would be quite sufficient for a universalist moral theory which is self-conscious about the historical horizon of modernity within which it is situated, if it could succeed in placing such a substantive limitation on our intuitions.

I want to suggest that "U" is actually redundant in Habermas's theory and that it adds little but consequentialist confusion to "D" – the basic premise of discourse ethics. "D" states that only those norms can claim to be valid that meet (or could meet) with the approval of all concerned in their capacity as participants in a practical discourse. "D", together with those rules of argument governing discourses, the normative content of which I summarized as the principles of universal moral respect and egalitarian reciprocity, are in my view quite adequate to serve as the only universalizability test.

The chief difference between my proposal and Habermas's is that for him "U" has the effect of guaranteeing consensus. As long as their interests are not violated, all could freely consent to some moral content. But the difficulty with consent theories is as old as Rousseau's dictum – "On les forcera d'être libre." Consent alone can never be a criterion of anything, neither of truth nor of moral validity; rather, it is always the rationality of the procedure for attaining agreement which is of philosophical interest. We must interpret consent not as an end-goal but as a process for the co-operative generation of truth or validity. The core intuition behind modern universalizability procedures is not that everybody could or would agree to the same set of principles, but that these principles have been adopted as a result of a procedure, whether of moral reasoning or of public debate, which we are ready to deem "reasonable and fair." It is not the *result* of the process of moral judgment alone that counts but the *process* for the attainment of such judgment which plays a role in its validity, and I would say, moral worth. Consent is a misleading term for capturing the core idea behind communicative ethics: namely the processual generation of reasonable agreement about moral principles via an open-ended moral conversation. It is my claim that this core intuition, together with an interpretation of the normative constraints of argument in light of the principle of universal respect and egalitarian reciprocity, are sufficient to accomplish what U was intended to accomplish, but only at the price of consequentialist confusion.

Let us return once more to the principle, "Do not inflict unnecessary suffering" to test this claim.[40] According to my formula, we are to imagine whether if I and all those whose actions would affect me, and by whose actions I would be affected, were to engage in a moral conversation, governed by the procedural constraints of universal respect and egalitarian reciprocity, we could adopt this as a principle of action. By adopting the infliction of unnecessary suffering as a norm of action, however, we would in effect be undermining the very idea of a moral dialogue in the first place. But it would be absurd to want to adopt as valid or correct a principle of action – the infliction of arbitrary suffering – such as would impair or jeopardize the very possibility of an ongoing conversation among us. Since such ongoing moral conversation involves sustaining relations of universal respect and egalitarian reciprocity, if we all were to engage in the infliction of unnecessary suffering, we would undermine the very basis of our ongoing moral relationship. In this sense, universalizability is not only a *formal procedure* but involves the utopian projection of a way of life in which respect and reciprocity reign.

There is an interesting consequence here: when we shift the burden of the moral test in communicative ethics from consensus to the idea of an ongoing moral conversation, we begin to ask not what all would or could agree to as a result of practical discourses to be morally permissible or impermissible, but what would be allowed and perhaps even necessary from the standpoint of continuing and sustaining the practice of the moral conversation among us. The emphasis now is less on *rational agreement*, but more on sustaining those normative practices and moral relationships within which reasoned agreement *as a way of life* can flourish and continue.

2   The Right and the Good

Sympathetic critics of communicative ethics have persistently pointed out that this project formulates a model of *political legitimacy* rather than one of *moral validity*. To ask whether certain normative institutional arrangements would or could be freely adopted by all as being in their common interests, is precisely to continue the central idea of the modern natural right and social contract traditions from Locke and Rousseau to Kant.[41] While many agree that such a principle of rational consent is fundamental to the modern ideas of democratic legitimacy and justice, equally many contest that it can serve as a moral procedure that would be relevant in guiding individual action and judgment.

In my interpretation, the basic principle of discourse ethics together with the normative constraints of argumentation can serve as "substantive tests" of our moral intuitions. Furthermore if we do not want to jettison the distinction between *contextualization* and *justification* in ethics altogether, we can still preserve the model of a moral conversation taking place under the constraints of discourses as a limiting test for our intuitions and judgments of the morally permissible and impermissible. Clearly then, whether discourse ethics is a model of legitimacy or one of moral validity will depend on what implications and usefulness this model may have for guiding individual moral action and judgment. Precisely because I think that it can have such implications when interpreted properly, I want to suggest that the restriction of communicative ethics to a model of political legitimacy alone is not convincing. Communicative ethics promotes a universalist and postconventionalist perspective on all ethical relations: it has implications for familial life no less than for the democratic legislatures.

Whereas some critics of discourse ethics want to regard it as a program of political legitimacy, others of a more neo-Aristotelian persuasion argue that no principles of legitimacy can be formulated without presupposing some substantive theory of the good life. Quite in line with Hegel's critique of Kant, these contemporary Aristotelians and especially communitarian critics of liberalism, maintain that the very idea of a *minimal-universalist* ethic, which would be supposedly "neutral" vis à vis the multiplicity of ethical life-forms, is untenable. Charles Taylor's objections to communicative ethics have followed this line of argument.[42] This issue has been frequently referred to as that of the "right" versus the "good."

From the outset, we must distinguish among the liberal-communitarian version of this controversy and the controversy as it applies to communicative ethics. The first controversy concerns whether liberal principles of justice, as formulated by John Rawls and Ronald Dworkin in particular, are "neutral," in the sense of allowing the coexistence of many forms of belief, value systems and lifestyles in the polity, or whether these principles both presuppose and privilege a specific way of life – let us say an individualist one, centered around the virtues of the rule of law at the expense of solidarity, of privacy at the expense of community, and of justice at the expense of friendship. While liberals continue to aspire to such neutrality, communitarians insist on the illusory quality of their search.[43]

This debate among liberals and communitarians cannot be simply extended to communicative ethics, for the obvious reason that neither Apel nor Habermas has developed a normative theory of justice out of communicative ethics, although communicative ethics has definite institutional implications (cf. section 3 below). When applied to communicative ethics, the issue of the "right" versus the "good" has several dimensions which have hitherto not been distinguished from each other. First is the question of how the distinction between matters of "justice" and those of the "good life" is to be drawn within communicative ethics. Habermas has formulated this distinction in light of certain assumptions concerning the proper *object domain* of moral theory under conditions of modernity. Briefly put, his argument is that modern ethical theory must restrict itself to articulating a minimal universalist conception of justice. All other moral matters as pertain to the virtues, to moral emotions, to life conduct are questions which belong to the domain of "ethical life." They are non-universalizable and non-formalizable. I will argue in the next chapter that this argument, restricting the domain of modern moral theory to matters of justice alone, is untenable.

Second is the issue of how a metatheory of moral justification might limit our conceptions of the moral good. In language that has been made familiar to us by Rawls's *Theory of Justice*, we can say that a deontological ethics like communicative ethics that privileges the "right" places certain restrictions on what can be defended as conceptions of the "good." But how can such restrictions themselves be justified? Don't they jeopardize the moral neutrality of the purported framework?[44]

In answering this extremely important objection, let me distinguish between "philosophical neutrality," "moral neutrality," and "political-legislative neutrality." Philosophically, communicative ethics is based on certain epistemological, pscyhological and historical assumptions as articulated in the previous sections of this chapter. There can be no "philosophically neutral" justification of a procedural meta-ethic of dialogue. Here one must enter the philosophical foray and offer the best, the most cogent and the most informed reasons one can think of for holding the position that one does.[45]

"Moral neutrality" is a different matter. Here the issue is whether the communicative ethics conception of the right can accommodate varieties of goodness or whether it privileges certain forms of the good life over others. Alasdair MacIntyre has plausibly argued that often the distinction between meta-ethics and substantive ethics is spurious to the degree that a philosophical meta-ethics, including a theory of moral justification, has substantive moral implications.[46] "If your metatheory of procedural justification," such an objection might read, "conceived as a dialogue taking place under the contraints of practical discourse, defines the 'moral point of view' in light of a minimal commitment to discursive justification, are you not thereby precluding all conceptions of the good in which discursive justification plays no role from even being considered as forms of the good?"

Certainly, the standpoint of communicative ethics has been made possible by the culture of modernity in which the justification of norms and values and their reflective questioning have become a way of life. The sociological presupposition of communicative ethics is that the spheres of law and morality on the one hand, individual morality and other forms of collective ethical life on the other have been separated or differentiated from each other. To give a simple example of such differentiation: in a country which enjoys a secular and modern civil code of law, the decision of two individuals to get married, as long as there are no legal hindrances to their union like falsification of one's previous marital status, is a personal "moral" choice in which other "ethical considerations" like the religion of one's partner, his/her profession, social background, cultural life-style, etc., may and often do play a role – but as individual considerations which cannot and should not be enforced by the legal system. Even though members of the same faith do tend to inter-marry, it would be "morally" and "politically" non-neutral for the state to want to prohibit interfaith marriages. In Hegelian language, in the modern state abstract right (legality), morality and ethical life have become distinct spheres and practices. The individual as a member of all these spheres must integrate the claims of each upon her through her own resources. The reflexive questioning of ways of life and of concepts of the good is institutionalized with the full separation from each other of these three spheres under conditions of modernity. Such differentiation constitutes the first social-historical presupposition of communicative ethics.

There is yet another condition for the possibility of communicative ethics to emerge as defining the "moral point of view." In Max Weber's language, the "disenchantment" of the world, the separation from each other of the good, the true and the beautiful, or of science, ethics, aesthetics and theology have to have been initiated even if not completed as cultural and cognitive processes. In the modern world, the overarching value systems of the past which integrated cosmological theories and a certain understanding of nature with the belief that these dictated a specific normative regulation of the social order because this was grounded in such a natural system have been subject to radical dismemberment. The separation of fact from value, although a contingent achievement of modern science, once in place, places additional burdens of justification upon the claims of those that would proceed from their given unity.[47] Communicative ethics presupposes processes of such "value differentiation," which decenter our world-view by cognitively distinguishing the knowledge of nature from the justification of norms. Processes of value differentiation also initiate traditions of discursive justification in independent value spheres. Modern science, for example, no less than theology and art criticism since the sixteenth century has developed methods and procedures for the assessment of validity claims in its domain. The cumulative logic of these "sphere specific" processes of discursive justification cannot be simply subverted. Such processes of value differentiation and societal differentiation are the historical and cultural conditions for the possibility of a communicative ethic.[48]

Now the issue of moral neutrality returns with a new vengeance. Christos Mantziaris writes:

> Benhabib's communicative ethics, "sets up a model of moral conversation among members of a modern ethical community, for whom the theological and ontological bases of inequality among humans has been radically placed into question." The circularity in the argument for political neutrality[49] becomes apparent if communicative ethics can be confronted with the justification of norms proposed by holders of differing conceptions of the good which are not *necessarily* developed within the framework of post-conventional morality assumed in the "modern ethical community."[50]

I would like to suggest that although communicative ethics is not "morally neutral," in that it does privilege a secular, universalist, reflexive culture in which debate, articulation and contention about value questions as well as conceptions of justice and the good have become a way of life, it has a singular cognitive virtue when compared to systems of conventional morality, namely comprehensive reflexivity. By a "conventional moral system," I understand one in which a distinction between social acceptance and hypothetical validity has become articulable, even though one possible justification of norms may be that "they are good and fair because they reflect our way of life, which is superior to those of others."[51] As a system of postconventional morality, by contrast, communicative ethics distinguishes among modes of argument leading to hypothetical validity. Thus no way of life is prima facie superior to another and the prima facie validity it confers upon certain normative practices cannot be taken for granted if one cannot demonstrate with reasons to others who are not members of this way of life and even to skeptics among one's way of life as to why these practices are more just and fair than another. Note that the advocate of conventional morality is not *excluded* from the conversation; but the kinds of grounds such a person will bring into the moral conversation will not be sufficiently universalizable from the standpoint of all involved.

Suppose that you are a member of the Mormon sect or of an Arab dynasty and consider polygamy the morally correct way to live. That polygamy is just is assured for you by the dictates of the teaching of Joseph Smith or of Muhammad the Prophet. Can you, however, imagine a situation in which you can justify to others who are neither Mormons nor traditionalist Muhammadans (non-traditionalists do not accept polygamy either) that polygamy is the most just marital order among the sexes? Such a conversation will most likely end by appealing either to the ultimate veracity of the one true teaching, the correct interpretation of the word of the Koran, or maybe even to the fact that women are naturally inferior to men and thus must be protected by them and must submit to their authority. Now, as a defender of communicative ethics I know that those who adhere to a conventional morality have a cognitive barrier beyond which they will not argue; that they will invoke certain kinds of reasons which will divide the participants of the moral conversation into insiders and outsiders, into those who share their presuppositions and those who do not. Because the adherents of such moralities are willing to stop the conversation and because they have to withdraw from the process of reflexive justification in order not to let their world-view crumble, their position is not comprehensive and reflexive enough. They cannot distance themselves from their own position and accept that it may be right not to practice polygamy on moral grounds. And here is the paradox of the "conventional moral point of view" in a universe of discourse which has experienced value reflexivity and differentiation. If the adherent of a conventional morality is willing to admit that practices which contradict her position can also be moral, then she is no longer a conventional moralist.[52] For then what decides whether a practice is moral or not is not whether it corresponds to the system of belief which is given to her by the holy book or by revelation but that there are other criteria by which to establish this. One may have to concede that even members of a different religion who do not practice polygamy may be "morally right." But if she can concede this then she can also concede that there is a step beyond conventional morality, maybe some common ideal of humanity, from which these moral precepts draw their binding force.

Moral reflexivity and moral conventionalism then are not compatible; but in a disenchanted universe, to limit reflexivity is an indication of a rationality deficit. That is to say, only a moral point of view which can radically question all procedures of justification, including its own, can create the conditions for a moral conversation which is open and rational enough to include other points of view, including those which will withdraw from the conversation at some point. In this sense, communicative ethics "trumps" other less reflexive "moral points of view." It can coexist with them and recognize their cognitive limits; communicative ethics is aware not only of other moral systems as representing a "moral point of view" (albeit one which may no longer be defensible on rational grounds), but it is also aware of the historical conditions which made its own point of view possible. Such reflexivity, however, is decidedly not a defense of moral monism or bigotry. There is no reason not to respect a way of life which considers that the game of moral justification has its limits, and that the point is not to argue about the good incessantly but to do the good. Yet we have to realize that only a mode of collective existence based upon norms which accept the institution of moral justification as a way of life can be tolerant and pluralistic enough to support the right of those who opt out of it. Communicative ethics therefore is not "morally neutral," in that it maintains that only certain moral positions are comprehensive and reflexive enough such as to be able to generate norms of coexistence and conduct which would be acceptable to *all* in a modern society.

With these considerations, I reach the third sense of "neutrality" usually invoked in debates about the right and the good, namely "political and legal neutrality." In my discussion of Bruce Ackerman's theory of liberal neutrality in chapter 3, I shall distinguish more explicitly between the meanings of legal and political neutrality. Suffice it to say in this context though that "neutrality" is a rather bloodless and shapeless term in defending those values of tolerance, plurality and difference that a deontological theory like communicative ethics which constrains our conception of the moral good in light of a procedure of moral justification would like to promote. What is meant by the term "neutrality" cannot be that universalist ethical theories are indifferent when faced with a way of life based on violence versus one based on parliamentary democracy, or unable to choose between a way of life which defines a woman's place on the basis of scripture versus a way of life which considers women as equal moral beings endowed with the right and the capacity to choose and pursue their conceptions of the good. What should be meant by the term "neutrality" is that the norms embodied in the legal and public institutions of our societies should be so abstract and general as to permit the flourishing of many different ways of life and many different conceptions of the good. It is plurality, tolerance and diversity in culture, religion, lifestyles, aesthetic taste and personal expression which are to be encouraged; but to encourage the flourishing of these values and practices one must be the partisan advocate of a moral vision of postconventional universalism. Precisely because such a framework can challenge all its presuppositions, and precisely because it is ready to submit its fundamental principles to debate, it can provide the bases for the public philosophy of a pluralist, tolerant, democratic-liberal polity. Although communicative ethics is not only a public philosophy of justice, it shares with other neo-Kantian theories like Rawls's the virtue that it is a theory of coexistence in accordance with principles of the morally right. "The pluralism of life choices, styles and moral pursuits" may be thus a more appropriate phraseology to capture the sense of "political" and "legislative" neutrality I am advocating here.

There is, of course, a dilemma which any liberal theorist as well as the communicative ethicist must face in this context. For the defender of communicative ethics, even more than for the liberal theorist, her ethical position involves a strong commitment to the norms of universal moral respect and egalitarian reciprocity. Is such a commitment also compatible with the consequences of pluralism, tolerance and experimentation advocated above? Not always, and in instances when there is a clash between the meta-norms of communicative ethics and the specific norms of a moral way of life, the latter must be subordinated to the former. In situations of coexistence of different ethical communities in one polity, universal human and citizen's rights take precedence over the specific norms of a specific ethical community. To illustrate: both the liberal theorist and the communicative ethicist would agree that the modern democratic state ought to tolerate the Mormon sect just as it ought to allow the orthodox Muslim way of life to continue. However, the practice of polygamy which also is part of the belief system of these sects should not be condoned by the state.[53] Members of this sect should not be able to gain *legal recognition* for their practice of polygamy, although the state should not persecute those who practice polygamy as long as the equal consent of the adult males and females in their various practices is secured. But, for example, when the wife of a Mormon protests that she is being held against her will and has been forced into this union against her consent then the state should defend the life, liberty and security of this women against her alleged husband. The metanorms of communicative ethics like universal respect and egalitarian reciprocity are often embodied in the constitutions of liberal democracies as basic principles of human and civil and political rights. These rights are the ultimate moral principles to which appeal must be made in a situation of prima facie ethical conflict between different ways of life. The modern legal system mediates among the conflicting claims of various life-forms, lifestyles and visions of the good. In cases of a conflict between the principles of right which make coexistence possible among adherents of divergent conceptions of the good and principles of other more partial conceptions of the good, of which we know that they cannot be generalized beyond their specific adherents, the right trumps over that particular conception of the good.

Communicative ethics is a deontological theory to the extent that it constrains conceptions of the moral good in accordance with certain restrictions upon procedures of moral justification. It is not "neutral," either in the sense of having weak philosophical presuppositions or in the sense of being indifferent vis à vis competing ways of life. Yet it is reflexive, it allows the non-dogmatic questioning of its own presuppositions; it is pluralist and tolerant, in that it promotes the coexistence of all ways of life compatible with the acceptance of a framework of universal rights and justice. In this sense in communicative ethics as well, the right is prior to the good but the right itself promotes a vision of the good life which cherishes the norms of universal respect and egalitarian reciprocity.

3 On the Distinction between Justice, Morality and Politics

The neo-Aristotelian and neo-Hegelian insistence on the centrality of a shared ethos or of a concrete Sittlichkeit in the conceptualization and resolution of moral questions, has unavoidable implications in the domain of political action as well. If this shared ethos and this Sittlichkeit are not viewed as forming the unavoidable hermeneutical horizon over and against which moral questions and problems are always formulated, but if they are considered the normative standard in light of which to assess individual actions, then morality becomes subordinated to the collective ethos of a community.

As the young Hegel wistfully wrote of the polis:

> As freemen the Greeks and Romans obeyed laws laid down by them-selves, obeyed men whom they had themselves appointed to office, waged wars on which they had themselves decided, gave their property, exhausted their passions, and sacrificed their lives by thousands for an end which was their own ... In public as in private and domestic life, every individual was a free man, one who lived by his own laws. The idea (*Idee*) of his country or of his state was the invisible and higher reality for which he strove, which impelled him to effort; it was the final end of *his* world or in his eyes the final end of *the* world, an end which he found manifested in the realities of his daily life or which he himself cooperated in manifesting and maintaining.[54]

Undoubtedly, this idealization of the Greek polis has to be ex-plained today more in light of German romantic attitudes toward Greek antiquity than judged as a historically accurate depiction of Greek society. As the mature Hegel himself recognized, the rights of subjective welfare and conscience are among the constituents of the moral freedom of the individual, and the individuals' pursuits can never be wholly integrated within a concrete ethical totality. The split of ethical life into the family, civil society and the state under conditions of modernity also means that potentially the dictates of individual conscience and welfare on the one hand and the claims of institutions – family, market and the state – can always clash. In a famous passage of the *Philosophy of Right*, Hegel defended the rights of Anabaptists and Quakers to refuse military service in the modern state on the grounds that the state is strong enough to allow for dissent without crumbling in the face of it.[55] Both in his theory of representative institutions and even more so in his reflections on war and world history, Hegel made the "self-preservation" of the universal the *normative* goal to which morality had to be subordinated. Politics, understood as the sphere governed by the dictates of the self-preservation and the welfare of collectivities, is juxtaposed by the mature Hegel to the "abstract cosmopolitanism" and "universalism" of Kantian ethics.

In contemporary debates one can recognize this Hegelian antecedent in two charges which are frequently leveled against communicative ethics. First, communicative ethics is said to lead to anti-institutionalist and fundamentally anarchistic consequences in political life;[56] second, communicative ethics is said to be "moralistic" to the point of complete utopianism in the domain of politics. Imagine conducting a practical discourse on matters of international relations, state security, maybe even banking and fiscal policy under the constraint of an ideal speech situation! The strategic and instrumental relation of the parties to each other is so fundamentally constitutive of these macro-institutions of political life that the kind of moralistic utopianism advocated by partisans of discourse ethics, so argues the political realist, would only result in confusion and insecurity. In the domain of politics, realism enlightened by an ethics of responsibility, in the Weberian sense, is the best approach.[57]

In the face of the charge of anti-institutionalism it must be said that discourse ethics is not a theory of institutions, although it has institutional implications. Whether we interpret them as principles of legitimacy or as principles of moral validity neither "D" nor "U" can yield a concrete theory of institutions, but they have institutional implications.[58] Institutionalist thinkers like Lübbe and Niklas Luhmann maintain that upholding any concrete institution to the demands of such rational consensus would make life impossible. Within the constraints of institutions, decision procedures, limited by space and time and scarce resources, must be respected. To hope for the rational consensus of all under these circumstances would paralyze institutional life to the point of a breakdown.

This objection is justified, but it confuses levels. The discourse theory does not develop a positive model of functioning institutions, which after all will always be subject to time-space constraints as well as to those of scarce resources and personnel. The discourse theory develops a normative and critical criterion by which to judge existing institutional arrangements, insofar as these current arrangements suppress a "generalizable interest." This appeal to the "suppressed generalizable interest" need not be read along Rousseauian lines.[59] In complex societies, it is doubtful that there could be a definition and specification of the suppressed generalizable interest which would meet with the consent of all. But one can use this criterion as a critical yardstick by which to uncover the under-representation, the exclusion and silencing of *certain kinds* of interests. In other words, it is not so much the identification of the "general interest" which is at stake, as the uncovering of those partial interests which represent themselves as if they were general. The assumption is that institutions can function as channels of illegitimate exclusion and silencing, and as I will develop more extensively in the next two chapters the task of a critical discourse theory is to develop a moral presumption in favor of the radical democratization of such processes.

What institutionalists neglect is that power is not only a social resource to be distributed, say like bread or automobiles. It is also a sociocultural grid of interpretation and communication. Public dialogue is not external to but constitutive of power relations. There are always certain implicit constraints on modes of public discourse in a society which together can be said to constitute "the meta-politics of institutional dialogue."[60] As a critical theorist, one is interested in identifying those social relations, power structures and sociocultural grids of communication and interpretation at the present which limit the identity of the parties to the dialogue, which set the agenda for what are considered appropriate or inappropriate matters of institutional debate, and which sanctify the speech of some over those of others as being the language of the public. Certainly this is not the only point of view from which to understand and evaluate institutions; efficiency, stability and predictability are also relevant criteria. To assume though that all discourses of legitimacy are counterproductive or anarchistic is to disguise political authoritarianism as a post-Enlightenment critique of the Enlightenment.

In his essay, "Is the Ideal Communication Community a Utopia?" Karl-Otto Apel deals extensively with the question of the utopian content and implications of communicative ethics.[61] In his view, it would be utopian in the negative sense of extreme irrelevance, to demand that all instances of strategic action, whether individual or collective, be governed by the norms of communicative action, aimed at achieving mutual understanding and reciprocity. Nonetheless, it is both a moral and a political question to ask what the limits of individual and collective strategic action are, and to reflect on how to mediate between the requirements of self-interest and the moral principles of mutuality and cooperative understanding. Once we restate the problem in this fashion, a whole range of interesting considerations begin to emerge. The stark opposition between political utopianism and political realism is to be rejected. Communicative ethics anticipates non-violent strategies of conflict resolution as well as encouraging cooperative and associative methods of problem solving. It is a matter of political imagination as well as collective fantasy to project institutions, practices and ways of life which promote non-violent conflict resolution strategies and associative problem solving methods. Far from being utopian in the sense of being irrelevant, in a world of complete interdependence among peoples and nations, in which the alternatives are between non-violent collaboration and nuclear annihilation, communicative ethics may supply our minds with just the right dose of fantasy such as to think beyond the old oppositions of utopia or realism, containment or conflict. Then, as today, we still can say, "L'imagination au pouvoir"!

4   On the Problem of Moral Motivation and Character

A major weakness of cognitive and proceduralist ethical theories since Kant has been their reductionist treatment of the emotional and affective bases of moral judgment and conduct. Twentieth-century neo-Kantian ethical theories have by and large rejected Kant's dualistic moral psychology, and his repressive treatment of sensuality and the emotions, all the while retaining the distinction between "action done from the motive of duty" and "self-regarding actions." Nevertheless this rejection of the Kantian treatment of the emotional and affective bases of ethics has not brought renewed attention to these issues. Only in recent years, Amelie Rorty, Martha Nussbaum, Annette Baier and Lawrence Blum on the US side of the ocean and Ursula Wolff in Germany, as well as feminist moral theorists like Virginia Held and Sara Ruddick, have developed a rich and significant body of work that has analyzed moral emotions and moral character.[62] Does not the neglect of these issue by advocates of communicative ethics so far point not only to a weak spot in the theory but maybe to a blind spot altogether?

I would like to suggest that very often ethical cognitivism has been confused with ethical rationalism, and the neglect of the affective and emotive bases of ethics is a result of the narrow "rationalism" of most neo-Kantian theories. By "ethical cognitivism" I understand the view that ethical judgments and principles have a cognitively articulable kernel and that they are neither mere statements of preference nor mere statements of taste. They imply validity claims of the sort, "X is right" (where X refers to a principle of action or a moral judgment) means that "I can justify to you with good grounds why one ought to respect, uphold, agree with X." In this sense, ethical cognitivism is opposed to ethical decisionism that reduces such principles and judgments to an "I will" which cannot be further questioned. Ethical cognitivism is also opposed to ethical emotivism that conflates statements like "Child molesting is wrong" with claims like "I like Haägen-Dasz ice-cream."

By "ethical rationalism," by contrast, I mean a theoretical position which views *moral judgments* as the core of moral theory, and which neglects that the moral self is not a moral geometrician but an embodied, finite, suffering and emotive being. We are not born rational but we acquire rationality through contingent processes of socialization and identity formation. Neo-Aristotelians as well as feminist theorists have argued that we are children before we are adults, that as human children we can only survive and develop within networks of dependence with others, and that these networks of dependence constitute the "moral bonds" that continue to bind us even as moral adults. In Virginia Held's words, by ignoring the genealogy of the moral self and the development of the moral person out of a network of dependencies, universalist theorists often view the moral agent as the autonomous, adult male head of household, transacting in the market-place or in the polity with like others.[63] Since Rousseau the demand has been to make "l'homme" whole again, either by making him wholly a "Burgher" or by making him a "citoyen."

This "rationalist" bias of universalist theories in the Kantian tradition has at least two consequences. By ignoring or rather by abstracting away from the embedded, contingent and finite aspects of human beings, these theories are blind to the variety and richness as well as significance of emotional and character development. These are viewed as processes preceding the "genealogy" of the adult moral self; they appear to constitute the murky and shadowy and often female and maternal background out of which the light of reason emerges.

This neglect of the contingent beginnings of moral personality and character also leads to a distorted vision of certain human relationships and of their *moral texture*. Universalist and proceduralist ethical theorists often confuse the moral ideal of autonomy with the vision of the self "as a mushroom" (Hobbes).[64] Far from being a description of the "moral point of view," state-of-nature abstractions as well as visions of the "original position" are often projections of the ideal of moral autonomy which only reflect the experience of the male head of household. But let us proceed cautiously here: I am *not* arguing that a truly universalist articulation of the moral point of view, one that includes the experiences of women and children, mothers and sisters, as well as brothers and fathers is

not possible. The gender blindness of much modern and contemporary universalist theory, in my opinion, does not compromise
moral universalism as such, it only shows the need to judge universalism against its own ideals and to force it make clear its own
unjustified assumptions.

Current constructions of the "moral point of view" so lopsidedly
privilege either the *homo economicus* or the *homo politicus* that they
exclude all familial and other personal relations of dependence from
their purview. While to become an autonomous adult means asserting one's independence vis à vis these relations, the process of
moral maturation need not be viewed along the fictive model of the
nineteenth-century boy who leaves home to become "a self-made
man" out "yonder" in the wide, wild world. Moral autonomy can
also be understood as growth and change, sustained by a network
of relationships. Modern and contemporary constructions of the
moral point of view are like the distorting lens of a camera: if you
focus too badly, the scene in front of you not only becomes murky
but can lose contours altogether and become unrecognizable. Likewise, the construction of those moral procedures which are to act as
"substantive limits on our intuitions" must not be so out of focus
that by looking through them, we lose the moral contours and moral
textures of such personal relationships. Moral vision is a moral
virtue, and moral blindness is the inability to see the moral texture
of the situation confronting the person.[65] Since the eighteenth
century ethical rationalism has promoted a form of moral blindness
with respect to the moral experience and claims of women, children
and other "non-autonomous others," as well as rough handling the
moral texture of the personal and the familial. The standpoints of
the "generalized" and "the concrete other"(s) which will be developed below are necessary in order to expand moral cognitive universalism beyond its rationalistic limitations.

Communicative ethics, in my view, is a form of ethical cognitivism which has so far been presented as a form of ethical rationalism. Particularly the claim that judgments of justice constitute the
hard core of all moral theory is an instance of such rationalism (see
below pp. 72ff., 183ff.). As I shall argue in the next chapter, this hard
distinction between judgments of justice and those of the good life
cannot be sustained even from the standpoint of the constraints of a
discourse theory. Neither can the privileging of moral judgments to
the neglect of moral emotions and character. There is a curious
inconsistency here. The theory of communicative competence
develops a post-Enlightenment conception of reason and views
reason as the contingent acquisition of beings capable of language
and action to articulate and sustain intersubjective validity claims.[66]
The theory of communicative ethics more often than not seems to

perpetrate the Enlightenment illusions of the rational moral self as a moral geometrician.

If this is so, how can one maintain that the model of a universalist moral dialogue, envisaged in accordance with the formal constraints of discourses, can serve as a defensible version of the "moral point of view"? My answer is that if we do not view such discourses in legalistic terms as articulating the standpoint of right-bearing "generalized others," and if we understand them as the continuation of *ordinary moral conversations* in which we seek to come to terms with and appreciate the concrete others' point of view, we do not have to submit to the distorting lens of procedural universalism.[67] To argue that the counterfactual ideals of reciprocity, equality and the "gentle force of reason" are implicit in the very structures of communicative action is to argue that the "moral point of view" articulates more precisely those implicit structures of speech and action within which human life unfolds. Each time we say to a child, "But what if other kids pushed you into the sand, how would you feel then?", and each time we say to a mate, to a relative, "But let me see if I understand your point correctly," we are engaging in moral conversations of justification. And if I am correct that our goal is the process of such dialogue, conversation and mutual understanding and not consensus, then discourse theory can represent the moral point of view without having to invoke the fiction of the *homo economicus* or *homo politicus*. To know how to sustain an ongoing human relationship means to know what it means to be an "I" and a "me", to know that I am an "other" to you and that, likewise, you are an "I' to yourself but an "other" to me. Hegel had named this structure that of "reciprocal recognition." Communicative actions are actions through which we sustain such human relationships and through which we practice the reversibility of perspectives implicit in adult human relationships. The development of this capacity for reversing perspectives and the development of the capacity to assume the moral point of view are intimately linked. In the final analysis, universalizability requires us to practice the reversibility of standpoints by extending this to the viewpoint of humanity. Such a capacity is essential to being a good partner in a moral conversation, and is itself furthered by the practice of moral conversation. In conversation, I must know how to listen, I must know how to understand your point of view, I must learn to represent to myself the world and the other as you see them. If I cannot listen, if I cannot understand, and if I cannot represent, the conversation stops, develops into an argument, or maybe never gets started. Discourse ethics projects such moral conversations, in which reciprocal recognition is exercised, unto a utopian community of humankind. But the ability and the willingness of individuals to do so begins with the admonition of the parent to the child: "What if others threw sand in your face or pushed you into the pool, how would you feel then?"

5 Judging in Context versus Principled Rigorism

Aristotle saw *phronesis* or practical wisdom concerning particulars as the crowning achievement of moral *paideia* and character. A common criticism of Kantian-type ethical theories is that they substitute an ethical rigorism of principles for the art of moral judgment.[68] Justifiable as this critique is, the discussion concerning moral judgment by either group of contenders in this debate has not advanced far. The metaphor of the "archer hitting the mark", the language of moral insight and blindness, still dominate many recent treatments of the issue. If we can register a certain impatience with neo-Aristotelians in this respect, we must also admit that distinguishing between "justification" and "contextualization," as Apel and Habermas do, cannot exempt the discourse theorists from analyzing what it is that we do when we supposedly contextualize moral principles and how this activity is related to the work of judging.[69] Obviously, there is a difference between the contextual application of a cookbook recipe in our kitchens in view of the ingredients and the utensils we have, and the so-called "contextualization" of moral principles. If the discourse model is to succeed in acting as "a substantive limit on our intuitions" of the morally permissible and impermissible, we must be able to suggest how the procedural model of the moral conversation developed so far is involved in the process of moral judgment.

I would like to suggest that if there are certain moral and cognitive skills involved in reaching perspicacious, appropriate, sensitive and illuminating judgments that they bear a "family resemblance" to the conversational skills and virtues involved in the ongoing practice of moral dialogue and discourse. There is a cardinal requirement of contextual judgment, which most theorists from Immanuel Kant to Hannah Arendt who have developed the problem of judgment have suggested, and this is the ability, in Hannah Arendt's words, for "representative thinking."[70] In Kant's discovery of the "enlarged mentality" in his theory of reflective judgment, Arendt saw a model for the kind of intersubjective validity which judgments had to be submitted to in the public realm. Judgment involves the capacity to represent to oneself the multiplicity of viewpoints, the variety of perspectives, the layers of meaning which constitute a situation. This representational capacity is crucial for the kind of sensitivity to particulars which most agree is central for good and perspicacious judgment. The more we can identify the different viewpoints from which a situation can be intepreted and construed, the more we will have sensitivity to the particularities of the perspectives involved. Put differently, judgment involves certain "interpretive" and "narrative" skills which, in turn, entail the capacity for exercising an "enlarged mentality." This "enlarged mentality" can be described precisely as exercising the reversibility of perspectives which discourse ethics enjoins. The link between a universalist model of moral conversation and the exercise of moral judgment is the capacity for the reversing of moral perspectives, or what Kant and Arendt name the "enlarged mentality." In "Judgment and the Moral Foundations of Politics in Hannah Arendt's Thought" I will discuss in more detail why the narrative and interpretive skills involved in judging entail the reversibility of moral perspectives.

What I am suggesting so far then is that if we view discourses as moral conversations in which we exercise reversibility of perspectives either by actually listening to all involved or by representing to ourselves imaginatively the many perspectives of those involved, then this procedure is also an aspect of the skills of moral imagination and moral narrative which good judgment involves whatever else it might involve. There is no incompatability between the exercise of moral intuition guided by an egalitarian and universalist model of moral conversation and the exercise of contextual judgment. Quite to the contrary, the kinds of interpretive and narrative skills that are essential to good judgment, if not guided by moral principles, can also be easily used for "amoral" purposes. The exercise of good judgment can also mean manipulating people – presumably good administrators, politicians, therapists, strategists, social workers and even teachers of young children all exercise "good judgment", not always for the sake of moral reciprocity or with respect to enhancing the moral integrity of the one about whom such judgment is exercised. Moral judgment alone is not the totality of moral virtue. Here as well we need a "substantive limit" on our intuitions: only judgment guided by the principles of universal moral respect and reciprocity is "good" moral judgment, in the sense of being ethically right. Judgments which are not limited by such principles may be "brilliant," "right on the mark," "perspicacious," but also immoral or amoral. Saying this is not to say that in a fragmented universe of value we are never in the situation of juggling moral principles against other political, artistic and administrative ends. Kantian theories have paid little attention to this "fragmentation of value," and to the consequences which the fine tuning and balancing of our moral commitments with other value commitments have for the conduct of our lives.

Here, we reach a frontier where moral theory flows into a larger theory of value, and I would say, into culture at large. Morality is a central domain in the universe of values which define cultures, and it is cultures which supply the motivational patterns and symbolic interpretations in light of which individuals think of narrative histories, project their visions of the good life, interpret their needs and the like. Moral theory finds this material, so to speak, "given." Thus, moral theory is limited on the one hand by the macro-institutions of a polity, politics, administration and the market within the limits of which choices concerning justice are made. On the other hand, moral theory is limited by culture, its repertoire of interpretations of the good life, its projections of visions of happiness and fulfillment, and its personality and socialization patterns. These two domains form the larger ethical context of which morality is always but an aspect. Yet the relation between morality and this larger ethical context is not what neo-Aristotelians and the young Hegel would like us to think it is. Under conditions of modernity, as the old Hegel knew, the moral point of view always judges the institutions of which it is a part; and the modern individual exercises autonomy in distancing him or herself from the given cultural interpretation of social roles, needs and conceptions of the good life. In this sense the dispute between discourse theorists and neo-Aristotelians and neo-Hegelians is at its heart a dispute about modernity, and about whether modern moral theory since Kant has been an accomplice in the process of disintegration of personality and the fragmentation of value which is said to be our general condition today. The next chapter on "Autonomy, Modernity and Community: Communitarianism and Critical Social Theory in Dialogue" will deal with this larger issue about modernity and its discontents.

Notes

This chapter was originally written as the Afterword to *The Communicative Ethics Controversy*, ed. Seyla Benhabib and Fred Dallmayr (MIT Press, Cambridge, Mass., 1990, pp. 330–69) under the title "Communicative Ethics and Contemporary Controversies in Practical Philosophy." It was reprinted with minor revisions in *Philosophical Forum*, special issue on Hermeneutics in Ethics and Social Theory, guest edited by Michael Kelly, vol. 21, nos 1–2 (1989), pp. 1–32. The current version has been rewritten in the context of the present volume. I would like to thank my colleagues Kenneth Baynes and Dick Howard for their comments and criticisms on an early version of this article.

1 Stanley Hauerwas and Alasdair MacIntyre, *Revisions* (University of Notre Dame Press, Notre Dame, Ind., 1983), p. vii.

2   See Kurt Baier, *The Moral Point of View*, abridged edn (Random House, New York, 1965); Alan Gewirth, *Reason and Morality* (University of Chicago Press, Chicago, 1978); H. M. Hare, *Freedom and Reason* (Oxford University Press, Oxford, 1963); Marcus Singer, *Generalizability in Ethics: An Essay in the Logic of Ethics with the Rudiments of a System of Moral Philosophy* (Alfred Knopf, New York, 1961); Stephen Toulmin, *The Place of Reason in Ethics* (Cambridge University Press, Cambridge, 1953).

3   See John Rawls, *A Theory of Justice* (Harvard University Press, Cambridge, Mass., 1972); John Rawls, "Kantian Constructivism in Moral Philosophy: The Dewey Memorial Lectures 1980." *Journal of Philosophy*, 77 (Sept. 1980), pp. 515–72; Lawrence Kohlberg, *Essays on Moral Development*, vol. 1, *The Philosophy of Moral Development*, and vol. 2, *The Psychology of Moral Development* (Harper and Row, San Francisco, 1984).

4   In *The Basic Works of Aristotle*, ed. and trans. Richard McKeon (Random House, New York, 1966).

5   For Hegel's early critique of Kant, see "The Spirit of Christianity and its Fate," in G. W. F. Hegel, *Early Theological Writings*, trans. T. M. Knox (University of Pennsylvania Press, Philadelphia, 1971), pp. 182–302; G. W. F. Hegel, *Hegel's Phenomenology of Spirit*, trans. A. V. Miller (Clarendon, Oxford, 1977), ch. 6, section C; *Hegel's Philosophy of Right*, trans. T. M. Knox (Oxford University Press, Oxford, 1973), para. 40, Addition, pp. 39ff; Hegel, *Science of Logic*, trans. A. V. Miller (Humanities, New York, 1969), pp. 133ff.

6   Karl-Otto Apel, "Kant, Hegel und das aktuelle Problem der normativen Grundlagen der Moral und Recht," in *Diskurs und Verantwortung* (Suhrkamp, Frankfurt, 1988), pp. 69–103; Apel, "Kann der post-kantische Standpunkt der Moralität noch einmal in substantielle Sittlichkeit 'aufgehoben' werden?" in ibid., pp. 103–54; Jürgen Habermas, "Moralität und Sittlichkeit: Treffen Hegels Einwände gegen Kant auch auf die Diskursethik zu?" in *Moralität und Sittlichkeit: Das Problem Hegels und die Diskursethik*, ed. W. Kuhlmann (Suhrkamp, Frankfurt, 1986), pp. 16–38.

7   Herbert Schnädelbach, "Was ist Neoaristotelismus?" in *Moralität und Sittlichkeit*, ed. Kuhlmann, pp. 38–64; trans. as "What is Neo-Aristotelianism?" in *Praxis International*, 7.3–4 (Oct. 1987–Jan. 1988), pp. 225–38.

8   For an excellent survey of the various strands of neo-Aristotelianism in contemporary discussions, and in particular for the serious differences between German and Anglophone neo-Aristotelian trends, see Maurizio Passerin d'Entrèves, "Aristotle or Burke? Some Comments on H. Schnädelbach's 'What is neo-Aristotelianism?'," in *Praxis International*, 7.3–4 (Oct. 1987–Jan. 1988), pp. 238–46. Strictly speaking, neither Michael Walzer's position nor that of Charles Taylor are easily assimilable to neo-Aristotelianism. Although Walzer accepts a hermeneutically inspired philosophical ethics, he does not revive the Aristotelian tradition of the virtues as do MacIntyre and to a lesser extent Sandel. The recent publication of Charles Taylor's *Sources of the Self: The Making of Modern Identity* (Harvard University Press,

Cambridge, Mass., 1989) indicates the degree to which his position is deeply indebted to modernity and its culture. Like Hegel, Taylor remains a critic of universalism from within the modernist horizon. See the next chapter.

9 Hans-Georg Gadamer, *Truth and Method* (Seabury, New York, 1975).

10 Hans-Georg Gadamer, "Hermeneutics as Practical Philosophy," in *Reason in the Age of Science*, trans. Frederick G. Lawrence (MIT Press, Cambridge, Mass., 1981), pp. 88–113. I have not included Hannah Arendt's work under this categorization, because in matters of moral as opposed to political philosophy, Arendt remained a Kantian thinker. I deal with some aspects of this admittedly not generally shared interpretation of Hannah Arendt's work in chapter 4 below, "Judgment and the Moral Foundations of Politics in Hannah Arendt's Thought."

11 Cf. Hans-Georg Gadamer, "Hegel's Philosophy and its Aftereffects until Today" and "The Heritage of Hegel," in *Reason in the Age of Science*, pp. 21–38 and 38–69, and Gadamer, *Hegel's Dialectic*, trans. P. Christopher Smith (Yale University Press, New Haven, 1976).

12 I. Kant, *Grundlegung der Metaphysik der Sitten*, trans. by H. J. Paton as *The Moral Law* (Hutchinson, London, 1953), p. 421.

13 G. W. F. Hegel, *Natural Law*, trans. T. M. Knox, introd. H. B. Acton (University of Pennsylvania Press, Philadelphia, 1975), pp. 77–8.

14 For some recent considerations on Hegel's critique of Kantian ethics, see Jonathan Lear, "Moral Objectivity," in *Objectivity and Cultural Divergence*, ed. S. C. Brown (Cambridge University Press, Cambridge, 1984), pp. 153–71.

15 The Kantian principle of universalizability does not, of course, dictate any specific content to the principles of justice; rather, it is operative in the construction of the "original position," as the privileged moral vantage point from which to enter into deliberations about matters of justice. Cf, Rawls, *A Theory of Justice*.

16 Onora O'Neill, "Consistency in Action," in *Morality and Universality*, ed. Nelson T. Potter and Mark Timmons (Reidel, Dordrecht, 1985), pp. 159–86.

17 Ibid., p. 168.

18 Ibid., p. 169.

19 Ibid., p. 169.

20 See Alan Gewirth, *Reason and Morality* (University of Chicago Press, Chicago, 1978), pp. 48–129.

21 Alasdair MacIntyre, *After Virtue* (University of Notre Dame Press, Notre Dame, 1984), p. 67.

22 Cf. Michael Walzer, "A Critique of Philosophical Conversation," in *Philosophical Forum*, 21.1–2 (Fall–Winter 1989–90), pp. 182–97 (here pp. 185ff); reprinted in *Hermeneutics and Critical Theory in Ethics and Politics*, ed. Michael Kelly (MIT Press, Cambridge, Mass., 1990).

23 S. Benhabib, "The Methodological Illusions of Modern Political Theory: The Case of Rawls and Habermas," in *Neue Hefte für Philosophie*, no. 21 (Spring 1982), pp. 47–74.

24 I have developed this argument more extensively in, "Liberal Dialogue vs. A Discourse Theory of Legitimacy," in *Liberalism and the Moral Life*,

ed. Nancy Rosenblum (Harvard University Press, Cambridge, Mass., 1989), pp. 143–57.

25 J. Habermas, "Diskursethik: Notizen zu einem Begründungsprogramm," in *Moralbewusstsein und kommunikatives Handeln* (Suhrkamp, Frankfurt, 1983), pp. 96–7; trans. by Christian Lenhardt and Shierry Weber Nicholsen as "Discourse Ethics: Notes on a Program of Philosophical Justification," in *Moral Consciousness and Communicative Action* (MIT Press, Cambridge, Mass., 1990), pp. 43–116, here p. 86.

26 In chapter 5 below, I will distinguish further among "formal" and "complementary" norms of reciprocity.

27 Karl-Otto Apel, "The Problem of Philosophical Fundamental Grounding in Light of a Transcendental Pragmatics of Language," in *After Philosophy*, ed. K. Baynes, J. Bohman and T. A. McCarthy (MIT Press, Cambridge, Mass., 1987), p. 277.

28 T. McCarthy, "Rationality and Relativism: Habermas's Overcoming of Hermeneutics," in *Habermas: Critical Debates*, ed. John Thompson and David Held (MIT Press, Cambridge, Mass., 1982), p. 74.

29 Jürgen Habermas, "Moralbewusstsein und kommunikatives Handeln," in *Moralbewusstsein und kommunikatives Handeln*, pp. 169–82; trans. as "Moral Consciousness and Communicative Action," in *Moral Consciousness and Communicative Action*, pp. 116ff.

30 The question at this point is: how can we conceptualize our moral obligations toward those kinds of beings who are either not fully or not at all capable of speech and action? I am thinking of infants and young children, of the handicapped, mute and deaf, of the mentally disabled. No less significant is the possibility of an ethical relation to nature and to living beings in general. Some believe that the fact that communicative ethics has had little to say about these phenomena indicates an essential blindness and aporia in this theory, see Micha Brumlik, "Über die Ansprüche Ungeborener und Unmündiger: Wie advokatorisch ist die diskursive Ethik?" in *Moralität und Sittlichkeit*, ed. Kuhlmann, pp. 265ff. I can only suggest here that if the principle of embodiedness is emphasized, and if an adequate distinction is made between ethical cognitivism and ethical rationalism as suggested below, then the way is opened for a communicative but non-rationalistic formulation of the relation to the body, the emotions and nature. If communication is not understood narrowly and exclusively as language but if body gestures, behavior, facial expressions, mimics and sounds are also viewed as non-linguistic but linguistically articulable modes of communication, then the "ideal communication community" extends well beyond the adult person capable of full speech and accountable action. Every parent of a young infant knows that the act of communication with a being not yet capable of speech and action is the art of being able to understand and anticipate those body signals, cries and gestures as expressing the needs and desires of another human and to act such as to satisfy them. Every communication with an infant counterfactually presupposes that that infant is a being who must be treated as if she had fully developed wants and intentions. I would say that the same is true of our relation to the disabled and the mentally ill. In mothering,

nursing, caring and in education we are always counterfactually presupposing the equality and autonomy of the being whose needs we are satisfying or whose body and mind we are caring for, curing or training. When this counterfactual presupposition of equality, certainly not an equality of ability but one of claims, fails then we have poor pedagogics just as we have stifling, overprotective or punitive care, mothering or nursing. In this sense, there is more of a continuity between the practices of argumentative speech among adults and the practices of non-linguistic communication than the critics of communicative ethics would admit. In each case for a successful communication to be established one must counterfactually presuppose the equal claims of the being one is communicating with, one must reciprocate when confronted with these needs, claims and demands. Whether this insight concerning the non-linguistic yet linguistically articulable aspects of communication is also a sufficient basis upon which to build the ethical aspects of the relation to the emotions, the body and nature is an open question to be explored. For a very interesting attempt to base an ecological ethics on the principle of nature's expressions and our ability to understand these (e.g. the death of a forest can be understood analogously to the loss of one of our limbs; oil spills can be thought of as skin ulcers and lacerations), see Konrad Ott's paper, "Zum Verhältnis von Ökologie und Moral," presented to the Graduate Colloquium at the Faculty of Philosophy, University of Frankfurt.

31 The metastatus of such criticism – whether such criticism needs to be philosophically grounded in some generally acceptable system of norms or whether it can be exercised immanently, by internally appealing to, critiquing or debunking the norms of a given culture, community and group – is what sharply divides social theorists like Habermas and Michael Walzer. Given also the large area of substantive agreement among them upon the need for the radical-democratic reconstruction of late-capitalist societies, it is worth pursuing what status these meta-philosophical disagreements – immanent or transcendental; relativist or universalist – have. For Walzer, see *Interpretation and Social Criticism* (Harvard University Press, Cambridge, Mass., 1987). See also chapter 7 below for a further discussion of the weaknesses of the standpoint of "internal" or "situated" cultural criticism.

32 Habermas, "Discourse Ethics," p. 93.

33 Ibid., p. 94.

34 I realize that in using this example I am inviting the retort that this is a moralistic way of looking at the phenomena of sado-masochism which hardly comes to terms with the complexities of this practice in psychosexual and cultural terms. The psychosexual complexity of this practice is not sufficient argument against the immorality of sado-masochism, insofar as it violates the principles of moral respect and egalitarian reciprocity among humans. Nevertheless, I would agree with the libertarian position and also maintain that as long as these practices are engaged in with the explicit consent of two adults and do not result in "cruel and unusual injury" to the parties, they must be tolerated in the

liberal-democratic polity. It is not the business of the modern state to promote virtue in private life; however, the standpoint of the discourse ethicist has to go beyond the perspective of the "legislator" to a utopian promotion of modes of social interaction and solidarity that realize the norm of egalitarian reciprocity. In arguing that the sado-masochists may be wrong in the perception of their own interests as lying in inflicting and receiving bodily and psychic punishment, I am not arguing as a Kantian legislator but as a moral theorist who realizes that morality is part of a larger universe of culture and values. Communicative ethics projects a utopian way of life in which mutuality, respect and reciprocity become the norm among humans as concrete selves and not just as juridical agents.

35 See Barbara Herman's excellent discussion, "The Practice of Moral Judgment," *Journal of Philosophy* (August 1985), pp. 414–36.

36 Agnes Heller, "The Discourse Ethics of Habermas: Critique and Appraisal," *Thesis Eleven*, no. 10–11 (1984–5), pp. 5–17, here p. 7. See also Albrecht Wellmer, "Ethics and Dialogue: Elements of Moral Judgment in Kant and Discourse Ethics," in *The Persistence of Modernity*, trans. David Midgley (Polity, Cambridge, 1991); Otfried Höffe, "Kantian Skepticism Toward the Transcendental Ethics of Communication," in *The Communicative Ethics Controversy*, ed. Benhabib and Dallmayr, pp. 193–220.

37 Wellmer, "Ethics and Dialogue," pp. 154–5 (extracts my own translation from the German).

38 Heller, "The Discourse Ethics of Habermas," p. 8.

39 Wellmer, "Ethics and Dialogue," p. 156.

40 Wellmer also discusses this principle in ibid., pp. 156ff. Wellmer's argument is that since the universal adherence to this norm would eliminate precisely those cases like the legitimate right to self-defense and justified punishment, the discourse ethics is obliging us to think of what is morally right only in relation to counterfactual ideal conditions and not real ones. Wellmer concludes that the conditions of action suggested by U can properly be thought of as those appropriate for a "kingdom of ends." But the fact that in actual life we must always make justified exceptions to such general moral rules has little to do with the question whether our moral theory is able to justify what we intuitively know to be a right moral principle, i.e. in this case not to inflict unnecessary suffering.

41 Cf. Wellmer, ibid., pp. 194–5; Heller, "The Discourse Ethics of Habermas," p. 9.

42 Charles Taylor, "Die Motive einer Verfahrensethik," in *Moralität und Sittlichkeit*, ed. Kuhlmann, pp. 101ff.

43 See Michael Sandel, "Introduction," in *Liberalism and its Critics*, ed. Michael J. Sandel (New York University Press, New York, 1984), pp. 4ff.

44 For an early version of this objection see Thomas Nagel's critique of Rawls's "original position," in "Rawls on Justice," in *Reading Rawls*, ed. Norman Daniels (Oxford University Press, Oxford, 1975), pp. 97ff.

45 In *Patterns of Moral Complexity* (Cambridge University Press, Cambridge, 1987) Charles Larmore attempted to outline a "neutral justification of

political neutrality," as this latter principle characterized the attitude of the liberal state toward controversial conceptions of the good, see pp. 51–6. In a later article, Larmore reconsiders this position and suggests that "political neutrality is a moral principle, stipulating the conditions on which political principles can be justified" and that in the final analysis such justification of political neutrality is provided by a "moral" conception which relies on the two norms of "rational dialogue" and "equal respect." See Larmore, "Political Liberalism," *Political Theory*, 18.3 (Aug. 1990), pp. 342 and 347 respectively. Although I have reservations about the restrictive conception of politics viewed as the action of the state and its agencies alone which Larmore shares with a long liberal tradition, I have found his discussion in this latter article to be very helpful in illuminating the problem of "neutrality" from the standpoint of communicative ethics as well. For the communicative ethicist as well, "neutrality" concerns the kind of justification offered by the democratic state and other public institutions to justify certain norms, laws and institutions.

46 See some of MacIntyre's earlier essays, "Ought," "Some More about 'Ought'," in *Against the Self-Images of the Age* (University of Notre Dame Press, Notre Dame, 1978), pp. 136–57 and 157–73 respectively.

47 Creationism and sociobiology are two recent thought currents which attempt to subvert such value differentiation. Creationists relativize the truth claims of modern science by juxtaposing to them religious conviction and the word of the scripture as an equally credible source of valid knowledge. Sociobiology, when used to draw normative consequences regarding social roles and the social division of labor, commits the mistake of attributing to scientific assertions authority in the sphere of moral and political norms. In each case, the proponents of such views try to circumvent specific processes of validation and argumentation, the use of rules of evidence and inference which have been developed within these spheres. Creationism violates rules of scientific evidence and inference, while sociobiology conflates the logic of moral argumentation, which always considers general rules of action with respect to the future action of a collectivity, with the logic of scientific facts. Even if all known animal and other primate communities in nature were based upon a sexual division of labor which confined the care of the young to the female, it would not follow that this gender division of labor would have to be the one which we would have to adopt as a norm of our collective action. For the latter conclusion to be established we must first consider the question whether it is just, fair, morally good or in everyone's interest that the gender division of labor be so organized in our societies. This, of course, does not mean that claims from sociobiology or from scripture cannot be introduced as grounds in a process of argumentation. But they alone cannot be the basis of validity for general moral and political norms of action without first standing the test of discursive justification.

48 My recognition of the historical and sociological "contingency" of communicative ethics, both as a social practice and as a normative ideal, is what distinguishes the kind of self-consciously historical universalism I advocate from the stronger justification programs of Habermas and

Apel. Even in the face of this admission, a cultural relativist can still press that this ethics simply privileges the institutions and principles of secular, western democratic societies and parades them as constituents of the moral point of view. In my view, a serious engagement with the claims of cultural relativism would have to tackle at least three different types of issues. First are methodological and epistemological issues about the understanding and evaluation of historical cultures – both those with which we are contemporary and those which belong to the past. I reject radical incommensurability of conceptual frameworks and hold that the understanding of the past as well as of other cultures which are our contemporaries proceeds like a hermeneutic dialogue. In such a dialogue one brings one's own presuppositions to the conversation, adjusts them in the light of the answer of the other, reformulates yet another set of questions, and so on. Cf. Bernard Williams's very helpful reflections on "real" and "notional" confrontations with cultures in thinking about these issues, in *Ethics and the Limits of Philosophy* (Harvard University Press, Cambridge, Mass., 1985), pp. 160ff. Second are sociological questions about the worldwide relevance of modernity and its development on a world scale since the seventeenth century. Radical cultural relativism, which views other cultures as isolated islands of cultural autonomy, is poor sociology and history – this is a claim which I cannot fully argue for in this book but, simply put, the interaction of cultures and civilizations on a world scale has been going on throughout history, and we have still a very incomplete understanding of the processes through which cultures have interacted and have influenced one another. What we desparately need from history and the social sciences today are studies of such cross-cultural processes of interaction, influence and struggle. The story of a uniform western cultural imperialism, spreading itself like a disease in the world throughout the nineteenth century, is at the most a half-truth. The West and its "other(s)" met much earlier, and it is only with the development of capitalism and modern science and technology, that the "West" was able to assert itself as a world-historical reality. But to reduce this complex process to a linear story of western imperialism is a product of the political ideology of the late 1960s which believed in the "pure, innoncent" periphery surrounding the "corrupt" metropolis. This kind of nativist "third worldism" has been shown to be bankrupt at the latest since the nationalist wars among China and Vietnam. A sobering and penetrating analysis of the phenomenon of nationalism on a world scale is given by Benedict Anderson, *Imagined Communities: Reflections on the Origin and Spread of Nationalism* (Verso, London, 1983). Third, cultural relativists give an easy answer to the extremely complex legal, political and moral issues which arise as the world becomes one, and as humanity ceases to be just a regulative ideal and becomes increasingly a reality. My sense here is that the various international conventions, from the United Nations Declaration of Human Rights to the Charter 77 principles signed by European states, indicate a normative consciousness on a world scale which simply belies the isolationism of a radical relativist position. Armchair philosophers of cultural relativism would do well, I think, to consider the existing level of international cooperation and agreement when reflecting about the extent to which communication and collaboration across cultures have become a reality – a fact as well as a norm. The unfortunate confusion in some so-called left circles about these issues has produced the sad state of affairs that it was Margaret Thatcher who came sooner to the moral and political defense of Salman Rushdie than progressives who were seeking ways of appeasing the "culturally relative" sensitivities of tyrants, bigots and reactionaries hostile to the spirit and freedom of the mind. See the touching article on Salman Rushdie by James Fenton, "Keeping Up with Salman Rushdie," *New York Review of Books*, 38.6 (March 28, 1991), pp. 26ff.

49 Although Mantziaris writes of "political neutrality," it is more appropriate to name the issue under consideration one of "moral neutrality." I shall discuss political neutrality in chapter 3 below.

50 Christos Mantziaris, "On the Observation of Community: An Observation of Kymlicka and Benhabib," paper presented for discussion at the Philosophy Department of the J. W. Goethe Universität, Frankfurt am Main, June 18, 1990, p. 25.

51 The classical example here is Aristotle's critique of the institution of slavery among warring Greek city-states and his proposal that Greeks should not enslave each other, but that it is not morally reprehensible to enslave the "barbarians," i.e. the Persians, who are not Greeks, whose language and customs he does not understand. See Aristotle, *The Politics*, in *The Basic Works of Aristotle*, introd. and ed. McKeon, pp. 1134, 1255a29ff. If a conversation can be imagined between Aristotle and a communicative ethicist it would go as follows:

> *Communicative Ethicist*: Aristotle, I find your argument that it is just to enslave non-Greeks objectionable, because I cannot see how, and on which moral grounds, you can justify this practice. The fact that you finally defeated the Persians is certainly not enough justification for this; you accept that Priam, Hector and Electra should not have been enslaved. Why enslave Darius then?
> *Aristotle*: Slavery is just if it reflects distinctions of natural virtue among human beings. Just as reason must rule the will, and the will the appetites in the soul of a just and moderate man, so it is right that those who do not possess the deliberative capacity obey those who do.
> *Communicative Ethicist*: How do you know that they do not possess the deliberative capacity? They seem to speak just as we do, even though you call them "to Barbario," those who babble; they have also shown themselves quite capable of military planning, and they nearly beat you Greeks. Is not the possession of language and military strategic planning an indication that they possess deliberative faculty?

Aristotle: Yes they may, but for them it is "without authority."

Communicative Ethicist: What do you mean by this? That they do not or cannot exercise it?

Aristotle: I mean that if they really possessed the deliberative faculty, and deliberated rightly they would do things the way we do them. They have no constitutional government, their wives are like slaves, their gods are so different.

Communicative Ethicist: But is the way in which they are different from you so much more different than the way in which you Greeks are different from each other?

Aristotle: Yes, despite differences in our constitutions and some of our laws, we are all Greeks, share the same gods, the same language. They are Persians; they are so different that they cannot be considered quite human, for they do not do things the way we do them. And the way we do things is just and best because it corresponds to the order of nature.

Communicative Ethicist: Forgive me Aristotle but from where I stand today your claim that only the way Greeks do things is human because it corresponds to the order of nature is simply false. There is no "one order of nature," and "one way of doing things." We have learnt in the course of history that human languages are translatable, that the ancient Persians did not merely "babble" as you Greeks thought, that they spoke, that they had a culture, civilization and religion just like you did. The fact that they are different does not make them any less human; now you may not find the fact that their wives are slaves good and just. Neither do I (though let me add that your record on women in Ancient Greece is not something to be proud of either). If you want to demonstrate the superiority of your way of life, your *politeia* to them, you must convince them with reasons, just like Plato tries to convince others in his dialogues. Anyways, let me point out that even in your culture there were the Stoics who believed in the universal brotherhood of all man and who did not accept the claim that different meant non-human.

Humorous and preposterous as this dialogue may be in some respects, it seems to me to be an accurate characterization of a conventional moral point of view from the standpoint of which the limits of the social universe amount to the limits of the moral domain as such. Between us and Aristotle there is the undeniable hermeneutic horizon of modernity, the experience of those many wars, revolutions, revolts and struggles which have finally led to the establishment of universal human equality as a norm even if not as a fact.

52 See Karl Mannheim, *Ideology and Utopia*, trans. Louis Wirth and Edward Shils (Harcourt, Brace and World, New York, 1936), pp. 229ff., for the classic statement of the paradoxes of traditional and conventional world-views.

53 On April 9, 1991 the New York Times reported that polygamists, most of whom are fundamentalist Mormons, are beginning to go "public"

and pressing their case to receive wider tolerance, respect, a larger following, and ultimately legal protection. The state branch of the American Civil Liberties Union in Utah has petitioned "its parent organization to make legal recognition of polygamy a national cause like gay and lesbian rights." Dirk Johnson, "Polygamists Emerge from Secrecy, Seeking Not Just Peace but Respect," *New York Times*, April 9, 1991, A22. The argument used to support wider tolerance and ultimately legalization of polygamy, not just by the ACLU branch, but by practitioners (especially female ones) themselves is a "diversity of lifestyles" claim. Mayor Dan Barlow, who has five wives, is quoted as saying that "in this liberal age, with all the alternative life styles that are condoned, it is the height of folly to censure a man for having more than one family." And a female lawyer who is one of nine wives is quoted as saying that "it is the ideal way for a woman to have a career and children." Several points in this story are noteworthy. First, even polygamy itself is being justified to the public from a "postconventional" perspective. The fundamentalist Mormons have their private religious beliefs, but in the public arena of the liberal democratic state, they are using the secular language of moral tolerance, and the recognition of the civil rights of dissenting groups and minorities – they wish to be recognized by the state as "practitioners of a different lifestyle," accepting thereby the legitimate plurality of lifestyles in the liberal state. Second, the female lawyer uses an almost inverted feminist logic in praising polygamy as a way of life guaranteeing female solidarity in taking care of the children, running a household, etc. Obviously, this woman's self-esteem is so far removed from traditional biblical accounts of female weakness and dependence that she can conceive of polygamy as some version of a 1990s "Hippie commune!" We see here a very interesting example of the way in which private and public languages of morals intertwine, and how the conventional, religious private morality of individuals and sects gets infiltrated and influenced by the postconventional morality of the liberal democratic state to produce an amalgam which sociologically may be named "secondary traditionalism or religiosity." Even the practices and choices dictated by religion get presented in terms of the wholly secular language of "lifestyle choices."

54 G. W. F. Hegel, "The Positivity of the Christian Religion," in *Early Theological Writings*, p. 154.

55 *Hegel's Philosophy of Right*, trans. Knox, Addition to para. 270, pp. 168–9.

56 Cf. Robert Spaemann, "Die Utopie der Herrschaftsfreiheit," *Merkur*, no. 292 (August 1972), pp. 735–52; Niklas Luhmann and J. Habermas, *Theorie der Gesellschaft oder Sozialtechnologie – Was leistet die Systemforschung?* (Suhrkamp, Frankfurt, 1976).

57 Cf. Herman Lübbe's essay "Are Norms Methodically Justifiable? A Reconstruction of Max Weber's Reply," in *The Communicative Ethics Controversy*, ed. Benhabib and Dallmayr, pp. 256–70.

58 For a provocative consideration of the implications of discourse theory for a critical theory of new social movements in western and soviet-type societies, see Andrew Arato and Jean Cohen, *Civil Society and Political*

Theory (MIT Press, Cambridge, Mass., 1992).

59 I have dealt with the difficulties of the concept of the "suppressed generalizable interest" extensively in *Critique, Norm and Utopia* (Columbia University Press, New York, 1986), pp. 310ff.

60 See Nancy Fraser, "Toward a Discourse Ethic of Solidarity," *Praxis International*, 5.4 (Jan. 1986), p. 425.

61 Karl-Otto Apel, "Is the Ideal Communication Community a Utopia," in *The Communicative Ethics Controversy*, ed. Benhabib and Dallmayr, pp. 23ff.

62 Cf. Amelie Rorty, "Community as the Context of Character," part 4 in *Mind in Action: Essays in the Philosophy of Mind* (Beacon, Boston, 1988), pp. 271–347; Martha Nussbaum, *The Fragility of Goodness* (Cambridge University Press, Cambridge, 1986); Annette Baier, "What do Women Want in Moral Theory," *Nous*, no. 19 (1985), pp. 53–63, and "Hume: The Women's Moral Theorist?" in *Women and Moral Theory*, ed. E. F. Kittay and Diana T. Meyers (Rowman and Littlefield, New Jersey, 1987), pp. 37–56; Lawrence Blum, *Friendship, Altruism and Morality* (Routledge and Kegan Paul, London, 1980); Ursula Wolff, *Das Problem des moralischen Sollens* (de Gruyter, Berlin and New York, 1983); Virginia Held, "Feminism and Moral Theory," in *Women and Moral Theory*, ed. Kittay and Meyers; Sara Ruddick, *Maternal Thinking* (Beacon, Boston, 1989).

63 Virginia Held, "Feminism and Moral Theory,", pp. 114ff.

64 I discuss the gender bias of modern conceptions of autonomy in "The Generalized and the Concrete Other," chapter 5 below.

65 Cf. Amelie Rorty, "Virtues and the Vicissitudes," in *Mind in Action*, pp. 314ff.

66 See in particular Herbert Schnädelbach's reflections in "Remarks about Rationality and Language," in *The Communicative Ethics Controversy*, ed. Benhabib and Dallmayr, pp. 270ff.

67 In chapter 3, "Models of Public Space: Hannah Arendt, the Liberal Tradition and Jürgen Habermas," and chapter 4 "Judgment and the Moral Foundations of Politics in Hannah Arendt's Thought," I explore these issues further. My position is that to restrict discourse ethics to the standpoint of public issues of justice alone, as Habermas often does, is inadequate; on the other hand, neither do I think that an ethic restricted to the standpoint of the "concrete others," without the universalistic principles which sustain justice in modern societies, is defensible. I plead for a mediation of the perspectives of the "generalized" and "concrete" others by exploring how a postconventional, universalist standpoint could shape public norms of coexistence no less than private ones of love, care and friendship.

68 For a recent statement of the hermeneutic critique of ethical theory from this point of view, cf. Ronald Beiner, "Do We Need a Philosophical Ethics? Theory, Prudence and the Primacy of Ethos?" *Philosophical Forum*, 20.3 (Spring 1989), pp. 230ff.

69 Cf. Habermas, "Moralbewusstsein und kommunikatives Handeln," pp. 187ff., where the work of Norma Haan and Carol Gilligan is discussed; Apel, "Kann der postkantische Standpunkt der Moralität

noch einmal in substantielle Sittlichkeit 'aufgehoben' werden?",
pp. 103ff.
70   See Hannah Arendt, "The Crisis in Culture," in *Between Past and Future: Six Exercises in Political Thought* (Meridian, New York, 1961), pp. 21–2.

2 Autonomy, Modernity and Community

Communitarianism and Critical Social Theory in Dialogue

Political Theory and the Disenchantment with Modernity

Max Weber had characterized the emergence of modernity in the West as a process of "rationalization" and "disenchantment."[1] Particularly in the last decade this conception of modernity as a process of "disenchantment" has been replaced by a disenchantment with modernity itself. Whereas at one time the "modernized" western industrial democracies considered themselves the normative yardstick by which to measure the evolutionary development of other societies, today the view is spreading that modernity itself, far from being a normative yardstick, is a historical stage to be overcome on the way to a "postmodern" or "postindustrial" society.

As Claus Offe has suggested, this shift in perspective has altered the social-scientific context within which the term modernity nowadays stands. Max Weber's question, "which chain of circumstances has led to the fact that exactly in the West, and in the West alone, cultural phenomena have appeared, which nonetheless – or at least as we like to think – lie in a line of development having universal significance and validity?"[2] has been replaced by a more cautious and equivocal attitude toward one's own society. The irony of this change, as Claus Offe sees it,

> is not so much that the gaze is turned away from either "the others" or from history and toward one's own contemporary and structural conditions, but rather that the situation of "modern" societies appears just as blocked, just as burdened with myths, rigidities, and developmental constraints, as modernization theory had once diagnosed to be the case for "pre-modern" societies. In any case, "modernity" is no longer exclusively the desirable endpoint of the development of

others, but rather the precarious point of departure for the further development of one's own ("western") society.[3]

The current skepticism toward modernity and the developmental stage reached by modern societies alters significantly our understanding of two of the major political theories of the last decade. Liberalism and Marxism, as the two major political philosophies of the nineteenth century, have also been most closely identified with the project of modernity. They share the Promethean conception of humanity in that they view mankind as appropriating an essentially malleable nature, unfolding its talents and powers in the process, and coming to change itself through the process of changing external reality.

Within the present mood of disenchantment with modernity, this Promethean legacy of liberalism and Marxism has come under considerable attack. The communitarian critique of liberalism is rooted in the same sense of disenchantment with the project of modernity as is the postmodernist critique of Marxism. Faced with the myth of Promethean humanity, communitarians argue that the liberal conception of historical progress is illusory and that history has brought with it irreversible losses such as a coherent sense of community and a moral vocabulary which was part of a shared social universe. In a similar vein, postmodernists argue that there is no "meta-narrative" of history which recounts the tale of Geist or of the proletariat, of freedom and continuous human emancipation. Not only has Marxism failed to appreciate irreversibility in history, but as the ideology of many modernizing third world elites, it has been complicitous in the destruction of traditional communities and the lives of premodern peoples.[4] Unlike the communitarians, for the postmodernist the objectionable aspect of the Promethean concept of the subject is not the disregard for constitutive, communal ties which this view seems to imply but rather the repressiveness of this understanding of the subject. The Promethean self privileges mastery over *jouissance* (Lacan) and the joyful enjoyment of otherness; in its narcissistic search for the domination of nature, it is possessed by an instrumental logic and fails to appreciate the mode of being of the non-instrumental "others." The conception of a homogeneous humanity as the master of nature destroys those "others" whose subjectivity may precisely consist in their proximity to nature and in their denial of instrumentality. These others are the so-called "primitives", children, fools, and according to some, women.[5]

In their critique of modernity and liberalism, communitarians and postmodernists unwittingly echo many of the themes of the first generation of Frankfurt School thinkers and especially the words of Adorno and Horkheimer in *The Dialectic of Enlightenment*. The uncovering of the darker side of the liberal ideals of economic growth and scientific progress, the memory of non-instrumental human relations, and even the critique of the repressive subjectivity which is always thought to accompany the domination of nature are among the themes, by now well known, of this work.[6] Ironically today this revival of the themes of the *Dialectic of Enlightenment* occurs against the background of a paradigm shift in critical theory from "the critique of instrumental reason" to the "critique of communicative rationality." This paradigm shift initiated by the work of Jürgen Habermas has brought contemporary critical theory closer to the liberalism of John Rawls than to liberalism's critics. In the evolving debate between liberalism, communitarians and postmodernist critics, where is contemporary critical social theory to be situated? The purpose of this chapter is to answer this question by bringing communitarianism and critical social theory and in particular the project of communicative ethics into dialogue.

Communitarianism and contemporary critical social theory share some fundamental epistemological principles and political views. The rejection of ahistorical and atomistic conceptions of self and society is common to both, as is the critique of the loss of public spiritedness and participatory politics in contemporary societies. While the critical theory of Jürgen Habermas, and more specifically his analysis of the contradictions of modern societies, can provide communitarianism with a more differentiated vision of the social problems of our societies, the communitarian insistence that contemporary moral and political theory enrich its understanding of the self and base its vision of justice upon a more vibrant view of political community offers a corrective to the excessive formalism of justice-centered and deontological theories.

As a political theory, "communitarianism" must primarily be identified *via negativa*, that is less in terms of the positive social and political philosophy it offers than in light of the powerful critique of liberalism it has developed. It is on account of their shared critique of liberalism that thinkers like Alasdair MacIntyre, Charles Taylor, Michael Walzer and Michael Sandel have been called communitarians.[7]

The communitarian critique of liberalism can be distinguished into an epistemological and a political component. The epistemological critique focuses on the incoherence of the Enlightenment project of justifying morality and of providing normative foundations for politics via the device of a voluntary contract between free and autonomous agents. The political critique of liberalism developed by communitarians is more varied. In the following I shall isolate two major issues of contention between communitarianism and critical social theory: (1) The critique of the "Unencumbered Self" and the

Priority of the Right over the Good; (2) The Politics of Community and the Integrationist vs. Participatory Responses to Modernity.

The Critique of the "Unencumbered" Self and the Priority of the Right over the Good

The communitarians criticize the epistemic standpoint of the Enlightenment on the grounds that this standpoint and liberal political philosophies which proceed from it presuppose an incoherent and impoverished concept of the human self. In order to look at the world in the way suggested by those who believe in the Archimedean point of view, we must be certain kinds of people. But, argue communitarians, the kinds of people we are and the epistemic perspective required of us by Enlightenment liberalism are antithetical to each other. We can adopt "the view from nowhere" (Thomas Nagel) required of us by Kantian liberalism, only if we can also conceive of ourselves as "unencumbered" selves. In his influential critique of John Rawls, Michael Sandel has sought to link this view of the unencumbered self to the commitment within liberal thought to the priority of the right over the good.

I shall not be concerned here to discuss in detail this criticism, or to evaluate the responses which have been formulated against Sandel in Rawls's defense.[8] What interests me is the following issue: despite the fact that Habermas also rejects the vision of the unencumbered self, he has not drawn some of the consequences which communitarians assume to follow from this rejection.[9] The intersubjective constitution of the self and the evolution of self-identity through the communicative interaction with others has been a key insight of Habermas's work since his early essay on "Labor and Interaction: Remarks on Hegel's *Jena Philosophy of Mind*."[10] Habermas often formulates this insight concerning the intersubjective constitution of self-identity in the language of George Herbert Mead. The "I" becomes an "I" only among a "we," in a community of speech and action. Individuation does not precede association; rather it is the kinds of associations which we inhabit that define the kinds of individuals we will become.[11] Nonetheless, in his theory of communicative ethics Habermas follows Rawls and Kohlberg in defending a deontological outlook and the priority of the right over the good.[12] Is he being simply inconsistent or is it that, contrary to what Sandel assumes, a deontological ethical theory and a certain conception of the self stand in no relation of implication to each other?

The defense of a deontological outlook in Habermas's theory takes a different form than what we encounter in Rawls's *Theory of*

Justice. Whereas Rawls distinguishes between justice as the basic virtue of a social system and the domain of moral theory at large in which a full theory of the good is at work,[13] Habermas is committed to the stronger claim that after the transition to modernity and the destruction of the teleological world-view, moral theory in fact can only be deontological and must focus on questions of justice. Following Kohlberg, he insists that this is not merely a historically contingent evolution, but that "judgments of justice" do indeed constitute the hard core of all moral judgments. Habermas writes: "Such an ethic . . . stylises questions of the good life, and of the good life together into *questions of justice*, in order to render practical questions accessible to cognitive processing by way of this abstraction."[14] It is not that deontology describes a kind of moral theory juxtaposed to a teleological one; for Habermas, deontological judgments about justice and rights claims define the moral domain insofar as we can say anything cognitively meaningful about these phenomena.

How can we in fact defend the thesis that judgments of justice and right constitute *the moral domain*? I can see two distinct arguments in Habermas's work on this issue, but neither of them I consider satisfactory. First, Habermas assumes that only judgments of justice possess a clearly discernible formal structure and thus can be studied along an evolutionary model, whereas judgments concerning the good life are amorphous and do not lend themselves to the same kind of formal study.[15] Of course this observation, far from justifying the restriction of the moral domain to matters of justice, could also lead to the conclusion that one needed to develop a less formalistic ethical theory. This is a conclusion which has been successfully defended by Bernard Williams in his *Ethics and the Limits of Philosophy* and by Charles Taylor in various articles.[16]

Second, Habermas maintains that the evolution of judgments of justice is intimately tied to the evolution of self–other relations. Judgments of justice reflect various conceptions of self–other relations, which is to say that the formation of self-identity and moral judgments concerning justice are intimately linked. This is because justice is the social virtue par excellence.[17]

Again, it can be objected that the evolution of self–other relations is always accompanied by the development of self-understanding and self-evaluation, and if justice is the sum of *other-regarding* virtues par excellence, this still does not preclude the consideration of *self-regarding* virtues and their significance for moral theory. If one understands Habermas's defense of a deontological ethics as a claim concerning the appropriate object domain of moral theory, then I see no decisive arguments in favor of such a restrictive view of what moral theory can hope to accomplish.

Yet maybe it is not even necessary to cast the basic insight of communicative ethics in terms of a formalistic and justice-oriented theory. In other words, the *strong* deontological interpretation which Habermas gives to communicative ethics can be distinguished from the basic insight of this project. I understand this basic insight to be the following: the fairness of moral norms and the integrity of moral values can only be established via a process of practical argumentation,[18] which allows its participants full equality in initiating and continuing the debate and suggesting new subject matters for conversation. Thus understood, communicative ethics is a theory of moral justification. Justification in ethics should be considered a form of moral argumentation. What Thomas Scanlon has written in defense of his concept of contractualism can be applied to communicative ethics as well. "Moral argument of more or less the kind we have been familiar with may remain as the only form of justification in ethics . . . what a good philosophical theory should do is to give us a clearer understanding of what the best forms of moral argument amount to and what kind of truth it is that they can be a way of arriving at."[19]

In such a conversation of moral justification as envisaged by communicative ethics, individuals do not have to view themselves as "unencumbered" selves. It is not necessary for them to define themselves independently either of the ends they cherish or of the constitutive attachments which make them what they are. In entering practical discourses individuals are not entering an "original position." They are not being asked to define themselves in ways which are radically counterfactual to their everyday identities. This model of moral argumentation does not predefine the set of issues which can be legitimately raised in the conversation and neither does it proceed from an unencumbered concept of the self. In communicative ethics, individuals do not stand behind any "veil of ignorance."

Contrary to Sandel's critique of Rawls then, the very model of communicative ethics suggests that a procedural moral theory, which constrains what can be defined as the moral good in light of a conception of moral justification, need not subscribe to an "unencumbered" concept of the self. In one crucial respect, communicative ethics endorses the modern understanding of the self and contends that moral autonomy means not only the right of the self to challenge religion, tradition and social dogma, but also the right of the self to distance itself from social roles and their content or to assume "reflexive role-distance." In their critique of the "unencumbered self", communitarians often fail to distinguish between the significance of constitutive communities for the formation of one's self-identity and a conventionalist or role-conformist attitude which would consist in an uncritical recognition of "my station and its duties" (F. H. Bradley). Communitarians often seem to conflate the philosophical thesis concerning the significance of constitutive communities for the formation of one's identity with a socially conventionalist and morally conformist attitude. The specifically *modern* achievement of being able to criticize, challenge and question the content of these constitutive identities and the "prima facie" duties and obligations they impose upon us should not be rejected.[20] Otherwise communitarians are hard put to distinguish their emphasis upon constitutive communities from an endorsement of social conformism, authoritaranism and, from the standpoint of women, of patriarchalism.[21] By contrast, communicative ethics develops a view of the person which makes this insight central and attributes to individuals the *ability* and the *willingness* to assume reflexive role-distance and the ability and the willingness to take the standpoint of others involved in a controversy into account and reason from their point of view. Naturally, these assumptions concerning the self are not "weak" and uncontroversial. They presuppose that individuals have the psychic-moral *Bildung* or formation which will make it motivationally plausible as well as rationally acceptable for them to adopt the reflexivity and universalism of communicative ethics.

As a procedural theory of moral argumentation, communicative ethics is based on certain *substantive* presuppositions. In my view this is unavoidable. All procedural theories must presuppose some substantive commitments. The issue is whether these substantive commitments are presented as theoretical certainties whose status cannot be further questioned, or whether we can conceive of ethical discourse in such a radically reflexive fashion that even the presuppositions of discourse can themselves be challenged, called into question and debated (see pp. 30ff. above). Since practical discourses do not theoretically predefine the domain of moral debate and since individuals do not have to abstract from their everyday attachments and beliefs when they begin argumentation, we cannot preclude that it will be not only matters of justice but those of the good life as well that will become thematized in practical discourses or that the presuppositions of discourse themselves will be challenged. A model of communicative ethics, which views moral theory as a theory of argumentation, need not restrict itself to the priority of justice. I see no reason as to why questions of the good life as well cannot become subject matters of practical discourses. Surely discourses will not yield conceptions of the good life equally acceptable to all, nor is it desirable that they do so. Yet, contrary to what Habermas at times suggests, our conceptions of the good life just like our conceptions of justice are matters about which intersubjective debate and reflection is possible, even if consensus on these matters, let alone legislation, is not a goal. The line between matters of justice and those of the good life is not given by some moral dictionary, but evolves as a result of historical and cultural struggles. This is not to say that no such line needs to be drawn between matters of justice or those of the good life, between the public and the private spheres. As I will argue in chapters 3 and 6, it is not the moral classification of problems which will help in this task but the articulation of those normative principles and values which we would like to foster and cherish in a democratic polity.

In conclusion then I concur with critics of deontology like Williams, Taylor and Sandel that a strong deontological theory which views justice as the center of morality unnecessarily restricts the domain of moral theory, and distorts the nature of our moral experiences.[22] But a universalist and communicative model of ethics need not be so strongly construed. Such a theory can be understood as defending a "weak" deontology, according to which the argumentative establishment of norms is the central criterion of their validity. Such a theory can also allow moral debate about our conceptions of the good life, thus making them accessible to moral reflection and moral transformation. Of course, this is a far weaker result than may be preferred by a strong teleologist but it remains for such a teleologist to show that under conditions of modernity one can indeed formulate and defend a univocal conception of the human good. So far Habermas is right: under conditions of modernity and subsequent to the differentiation of the value spheres of science, aesthetics, jurisprudence, religion and morals we can no longer formulate an overarching vision of the human good. Indeed, as Alasdair MacIntyre's definition of the good life, namely "the life spent in seeking the good life for man,"[23] very well reveals, as moderns we have to live with varieties of goodness. Whether the good life is to be fulfilled as an African famine relief fighter, a Warsaw ghetto resistant, a Mother Teresa or a Rosa Luxemburg, ethical theory cannot prejudge; at the most, modern moral theory provides us with some very general criteria by which to assess our intuitions about the basic validity of certain courses of action and the integrity of certain kinds of values. I regard neither the plurality and variety of goodnesses with which we have to live in a disenchanted universe nor the loss of certainty in moral theory to be a cause of distress. Under conditions of value differentiation, we have to conceive of the unity of reason not in the image of a homogeneous, transparent glass sphere into which we can fit all our cognitive and value commitments, but more as bits and pieces of dispersed crystals whose contours shine out from under the rubble.

The Politics of Community: The Integrationist versus Participatory Responses to Modernity

The dispute over the concept of the self and deontology can be distinguished into a moral and a political aspect. In moral theory, deontology implies that conceptions of justice should precede those of the good life, both in the sense of limiting what can be legitimately defended as the good life and in the sense that conceptions of justice can be justified independently of *particular* conceptions of the good life. In the political realm, deontology means that the basic principles of a just order should be morally neutral, both in the sense of allowing many different conceptions of the good life to be freely pursued and cherished by citizens, and also in the sense that the basic liberties of citizens ought never to be curtailed for the sake of some specific conception of the social good or welfare. The arguments I have looked at so far concerned the moral claims for deontology only. Most communitarians reject deontology in the realm of moral theory, and argue that conceptions of justice necessarily imply certain conceptions of the good life. The political arguments for deontology usually weigh more heavily in the minds of liberal thinkers and it is around this issue that communitarian thinkers have been most severely criticized.

In their critique of Rawls, communitarians have neither focussed on the first principle of justice, namely the principle of the most extensive basic equal liberty,[24] nor have they questioned the ordering of the two principles of justice and the priority of liberty. It is partly this lack of explicitness on their part concerning the "priority of liberty" issue which has led their contemporary critics to assume that communitarians are advocates of small, homogeneous, undifferentiated social units, particularly prone to intolerance, exclusivism, and maybe even forms of racism, sexism and xenophobia.[25]

In his interesting analysis of these issues in *Patterns of Moral Complexity*, Charles Larmore maintains that communitarianism follows the tradition of "political romanticism" whose chief feature is the search for the reconciliation of personal and political ideals.[26] Defending a position which he names "modus vivendi" liberalism, Larmore writes:

> However, just this belongs at the core of the liberal tradition. Conceptions of what we should be as persons are an enduring object of

dispute, toward which the political order should try to remain neutral. We do better to recognize that liberalism is not a philosophy of man, but a philosophy of politics. . . . This means that we must adopt a more positive attitude toward the liberal "separation of domains" than either political romantics or some liberals themselves have shown.[27]

I have doubts that one can defend liberalism without recourse to a "philosophy of man" or on the basis of what John Rawls has recently called "overlapping consensus" alone.[28] What interests me is Larmore's claim that the "reconciliation" of personal and political ideals or of various social spheres is the mark of contemporary communitarianism as it has been the distinguishing characteristic of political romanticism since Herder and the conservative reaction to the French revolution. Communitarian political thought indeed contains two strains, a reconciliationist one or what I shall prefer to call an "integrationist strain" and a "participatory" one. It is the vacillation between these two strains that makes communitarian thought vulnerable to the charge of violating the priority of liberty.

According to the first conception, the problems of individualism, egotism, anomie and alienation in modern societies can only be solved by a recovery or a revitalization of some coherent value scheme. This coherent value scheme may be a religion, as Novalis and some German romantics had hoped for,[29] or it may be a "civic religion," the principles of which will inculcate citizen's virtue as Rousseau had dreamt of.[30] Then again one may view this value scheme as a "code of civility," which survives, on MacIntyre's view, in Orthodox Jewish, Greek and Irish communities;[31] or it may be a vision of friendship and solidarity which shapes moral character and lends it depth as Sandel evokes.[32] In each case, it is characteristic of the integrationist view that it emphasizes value revival, value reform, or value regeneration and neglects institutional solutions.

By contrast, the view that I shall name "participationist" sees the problems of modernity less in the loss of a sense of belonging, oneness and solidarity but more in the sense of a loss of *political agency and efficacy*. This loss of political agency is not a consequence of the separation of the personal from the political or of the differentiation of modern societies into the political, the economic, the civic and the familial-intimate realms. This loss may be a consequence of the contradiction between the various spheres which diminishes one's possibilities for agency in one sphere on the basis of one's position in another sphere (as for example when early bourgeois republics curtailed citizenship rights on the basis of income and occupation and denied wage-earners the vote). Or it may also result from the fact that membership in the various spheres becomes mutually exclusive because of the nature of the activities involved, while the mutual exclusivity of the spheres is reinforced by the system (take the duties of motherhood and the public aspirations of women in the economy, politics or science, and the fact that public funds are not used to support better, more readily available and more affordable forms of childcare).

The participationist view then does not see social differentiation as an aspect of modernity which needs to be overcome. Rather the participationist advocates the reduction of contradictions and irrationalities among the various spheres, and the encouragement of non-exclusive principles of membership among the spheres. Communitarian thinkers have not always been clear as to which perspective they want to emphasize in face of the problems of modern societies, and their liberal cirtics have been right to focus on this ambivalence.

Whether they focus upon the libertarianism of Nozick[33] or upon the welfare liberalism of Rawls, contemporary communitarians are concerned with the liberalism of the post World War II welfare state.[34] They focus upon a problem that is central to the welfare state as a political formation, namely the principles and criteria of distributive justice. Michael Walzer and Charles Taylor agree that there can be no single principle of distributive justice applicable to all social goods. As Walzer states: "different social goods ought to be distributed for different reasons, in accordance with different procedures, by different agents; and that all these differences derive from different understandings of the social goods themselves . . ."[35] Second, our societies operate on the basis of different and at times mutually exclusive principles of distribution, like need, membership, merit, contribution. "What all this means," writes Taylor, "is that we have to abandon the search for a single set of principles of distributive justice. On the contrary a modern society can be seen under different, mutually irreducible perspectives, and consequently can be judged by independent, mutually irreducible principles of distributive justice."[36] Third, the search for a single, overarching principle of distributive justice, applicable across spheres, appears plausible to contemporary liberals only because of the *philosophical framework* which they choose for stating the issue. Proceeding, in Taylor's words, from the perspective of the individual as bearer of rights, they claim to be able to frame the issue of distributive justice solely in terms of the conflicting rights claims of various individuals. Both Taylor and Walzer agree that if the issue is framed in this fashion, then indeed such individuals would choose something like the Rawlsian difference principle.[37] Taylor rejects this framework on the grounds of his moral critique of deontology and argues that different principles of distributive justice are related to different conceptions of the good, and these in turn, are related to different understandings of the nature of our human associations.[38] Similarly, for Walzer the political community itself has to be adopted as the "appropriate setting for justice" and not some "original position,"[39] for the community itself is also a good, and perhaps the most important one, which gets distributed.

These criticisms of the search for a unified theory of distributive justice can also be stated in an "integrationist" or a "participatory" language. When Taylor and Walzer emphasize that the appropriate setting for justice is the political association itself, and that it is on the basis of shared understandings entertained by members of such a community that we have to proceed to think about justice, they follow the integrationist line. Modern societies are not communities integrated around a single conception of the human good or even a shared understanding of the value of belonging to community itself. Issues of distributive justice arise precisely because there is no such shared understanding among the members of the political community, but as Taylor and Walzer also acknowledge, such societies are marked by a "plurality" of visions of the good and of the good of association itself. If this is so, the search for a publicly acceptable scheme of just distribution is not as ill-guided as they would have us believe, for the question as to how one can distribute goods, services, income, etc., across primary groups which do not share the same moral conceptions is neither irrelevant nor foolhardy. In their epistemic critique of the perspective of the "right-bearing individual," Taylor and Walzer at times hypostatize what Taylor himself describes as the "philosophical framework" of community,[40] and treat this as if it were not only a methodological framework but also a living political reality.

Although Michael Walzer's aim in *Spheres of Justice* is to further an egalitarian, participatory conception of justice, the main task of which is to allow complex equality and to prevent the "illegitimate" domination of one set of goods by another (of public offices and votes by money, for example), in his continuous appeal to "shared understandings" of social goods Walzer also slides into the integrationist language. Since his aim is to proceed "immanently and phenomenologically,"[41] available and shared definitions and understandings of social meaning have to be his starting point. This beginning point, though, at times leads him to underestimate the degree to which what he is doing is not just a phenomenological redescription of what agents in our kinds of societies think about various goods; rather, Walzer is practicing a "normative hermeneutic," which is not very far removed from Rawlsian "reflective equilibrium" in its intentions. Proceeding from shared views and understandings of certain goods like citizenship or healthcare, for example, Walzer is refining, systematizing, making coherent, criticizing and replacing by a "better" understanding the common views of these issues. *Spheres of Justice* abounds with such examples, but the most telling is Walzer's remarkable discussion of the issue of guest-workers in contemporary western societies. Walzer is not reluctant to go far beyond the prevailing political consensus on this issue both in Western Europe and in the United States to plead for the right to naturalization of such guest-workers, not just of the right to permanent residence but the right to citizenship. Walzer writes: "Democratic citizens, then, have a choice: if they want to bring in new workers, they must be prepared to enlarge their own membership; if they are unwilling to accept new members, they must find ways within the limits of the domestic labor market to get socially necessary work done."[42] Walzer does not contest the right of these communities to make one or the other choice but he makes it very clear what he, as a political theorist, believes is right: "Political justice is a bar to permanent alienage – either for particular individuals or for a class of changing individuals."[43] This last sentence in particular is a good example of the "participatory" nature of Walzer's argument.

The distinction between these two modes of approaching the problems of modernity and politics allows us to see more clearly the relation between Habermas's work and some contemporary communitarian projects. The defense of modernity in light of the principle of public participation has been an essential aspect of Habermas's work since his early essay on *The Structural Transformation of the Public Sphere.*[44] Reversing the pessimistic assessment of modernity as a "dialectic of Enlightenment," Habermas has emphasized the extent to which modernity does not only signify differentiation, individuation and bifurcation. The emergence of an autonomous public sphere of political reasoning and discussion is also central to the project of the moderns. The irrationalities of modern societies derive rather from several factors: first, access to the public sphere has always been limited by particularistic considerations of class, race, gender and religion; second, increasingly not the consensual generation of norms but money and power have become modes through which individuals define the social bond and distribute social goods. In Walzer's language, Habermas sees a trend in modern societies toward "simple equality" spurred on by the dominance of money and power as media of coordinating activities. Third, as money and power become increasingly autonomous principles of social life, individuals lose a sense of agency and efficacy. They can neither see the nature of the social bond nor can they comprehend its meaning. Political alienation, cynicism and anomie result. Fourth, the demands of increased role-distance and the continuing subjection of tradition to critique and revision in a disenchanted universe make it difficult for individuals to develop a coherent sense of self and community under conditions of modernity. These trends can only be counteracted by expanding individuals' cognitive participation in various branches of knowledge which today have become the monopoly of experts, and by increasing the possibilities for meaningful life-choices on the parts of individuals. In other words, in each instance the solution is to overcome the problems of modern societies by extending the principle of modernity, namely the unlimited and universally accessible participation of all in the consensual generation of the principles to govern public life.

Undoubtedly, Habermas has at times stated these insights in the language of traditional liberalism. Yet his participatory conception of public life and his insistence that only more democratization not less can solve the problems of modernity clearly transcend the traditional liberal preoccupation with negative and positive liberty in the direction of a participatory-communalist critique of contemporary welfare-state societies. In his view then, the task of distributive justice would be to enhance the citizen's possibilities for the more effective exercise of political agency and control. In fact, it is because the emphasis is on participatory rather than distributive justice that "practical discourses" are so empty and yield no determinate solutions in Habermas's theory. Like Walzer, Habermas sees the attempt of the political theorist to provide citizens with a normative yardstick as a preemption of their right to democratic politics.[45]

If communitarian political theory is understood then as advocating a participationist rather than an integrationist restructuring of our political life, it cannot be subject to the charge of political romanticism, for participationism does not entail dedifferentiation, value homogeneity, or even value reeducation. Participationism is not an answer to the dilemmas of modern identity, estrangement, anomie and homelessness. For on the participationist model, the public sentiment which is encouraged is not reconciliation and harmony, but rather political agency and efficacy, namely the sense that we have a say in the economic, political and civic arrangements which define our lives together, and that what one does makes a difference. This can be achieved without value homogeneity among individuals. Of course, it is likely that a very atomized society will undermine one's options and motivation for political agency, while a vibrant, participatory life can become central to the formation and flourishing of one's self-identity. Equally, while the prevalance of certain kinds of public value systems will make the participationist option more or less likely, an increased sense of public-political agency and efficacy will contribute to the revitalization of certain kinds of values.

This emphasis on political participation and the widest-reaching democratization of decision-making processes in social life, is one that Jürgen Habermas's critical theory shares with the tradition usually referred to as that of "republican or civic virtue," and which extends from Aristotle to Machiavelli, to the Renaissance humanists, to Jefferson, Rousseau and Hannah Arendt. Clearly, this tradition has been a source of inspiration for contemporary communitarians as well. The crucial distinction between the participatory vision of contemporary critical theory and that of the tradition of "civic virtue" is that thinkers of the latter tradition, more often than not, have formulated their views of participatory politics in express hostility toward the institutions of modern civil society, like the market. "Virtue" and "commerce" are thought to be antithetical principles. In Hannah Arendt's words, under conditions of modernity politics is reduced to administration. Participatory politics then is considered possible either for a land-based gentry of civic virtue or for the citizens of the Greek polis, but not for complex, modern societies with their highly differentiated spheres of the economy, the law, politics, civil and familial life.

We owe it to the work of Jürgen Habermas that it has enriched our understanding of the social and cultural possibilities of modernity in such a way that neither communities of virtue nor contracts of self-interest can be viewed as exhausting the modern project. His modernist and participatory vision distinguishes the politics of communicative ethics both from liberalism and from the republican tradition of "civic virtue." I shall refer to this model of politics as the "discourse model of legitimacy." The next chapter will explore the differences between the "discourse model of legitimacy," Hannah Arendt's civic republican view of politics, and Bruce Ackerman's conception of liberal dialogue.

Notes

This paper was originally delivered at the American Political Science Association convention in Chicago in 1987. It has appeared as my contribution to the Festschrift in honor of Jürgen Habermas's sixtieth birthday, published as *Cultural-Political Interventions in the Unfinished Project of Enlightenment*, ed. Axel Honneth, Thomas McCarthy, Claus Offe and Albrecht Wellmer (MIT Press, Cambridge, Mass., 1992). It has been revised for inclusion in this volume.

1   Max Weber, "Science as a Vocation," in *From Max Weber: Essays in Sociology*, ed. and trans. H. H. Gerth and C. W. Mills (Free Press, New York, 1974), p. 155.
2   Max Weber, *The Protestant Ethic and the Spirit of Capitalism*, trans. Talcott Parsons (Scribners, New York, 1958), P. 13. The ambivalence in Weber's

manner of posing this question can hardly be overlooked: on the one hand, he qualifies the "unavoidable and justifiable" nature of this query with the parenthetical remark that "we", the children of the European *Kulturwelt*, "would like to think" that these developments have universal significance and validity. He thereby suggests that this query is very much the consequence of *our perspective*, that it is only our "cultural interest" that motivates us to pose this question. On the other hand, this *perspectivalism* sharply contrasts with the *universalism* expressed in the main body of the text: it is "unavoidable and justifiable" that problems of universal history be examined in this light. The tension between the universalist and perspectivalist positions betrayed by this question runs through the corpus of Weber's writings on modernity and rationalization. I have also modified Talcott Parsons's translation in accordance with the German original, see Max Weber, "Die Protestantische Ethik und der Geist des Kapitalismus," in *Gesammelte Aufsätze zur Religionsoziologie*, ed. J. Winckelman (Mohr, Tübingen, 1922), p. 1.

3   Claus Offe, "Modernity and Modernization as Normative Political Principles," *Praxis International*, 7.1 (April 1987), pp. 2ff.

4   Jean Baudrillard, *The Mirror of Production*, trans. Mark Poster (Telos, St Louis, 1975).

5   Cf. Jean-François Lyotard, *The Postmodern Condition: A Report on Knowledge*, trans. Geoff Bennington and Brian Massumi (University of Minnesota Press, Minneapolis, 1984), p. 27. The view that all these groups of individuals represent the "other" of reason is fraught with difficulties, for in stating this, we are defining their identity only with regard to what they are not. I believe this kind of categorization of the "others" of reason is just as imperialistic in its cognitive attitude as the instrumental reason it criticizes. For any definition of a group's identity not in terms of its own constitutive experiences but in terms of its victimization by others reduces that group's subjectivity to the terms of the dominant discourse and does not allow for an appreciation of the way in which it may challenge that discourse. I think this is the Janus face of postmodernism as far as movements like feminism and cultural autonomy are concerned. The postmodernist appreciation of otherness is framed in terms of the "guilty conscience" of the dominant, western traditions of rationality. For a discussion of the implications of postmodernism for feminism, see chapter 7.

6   Max Horkheimer and Theodor Adorno, *Dialectic of Enlightenment*, trans. John Cumming (Herder and Herder, New York, 1972).

7   Of course, this approach should suggest neither that communitarianism is a school in the sense that one can speak of the Frankfurt School nor that there are no interesting and important differences among these thinkers. Since my goal is to establish *intraparadigmatic* dialogue, however, that is a dialogue across traditions, to some extent I shall have to minimize *interparadigmatic* differences.

Although all the philosophical elements of the critique of liberalism defined as communitarian were contained already in Roberto M. Unger's *Knowledge and Politics* (Free Press, New York, 1975), pp. 29ff., Unger's position is more complicated insofar as his diagnosis of the condition of modern societies is centered less around the loss of community than around the paradoxes of the welfare state and the decline of the rule of law; cf. *Law in Modern Society* (Free Press, New York, 1976). In this respect Unger stands much closer to the tradition of critical social theory than do other communitarians, and his position would have required independent treatment.

Two recent essays by Charles Taylor and Michael Walzer, written in response to various liberal critics and reflecting upon their own positions "après la lutte" (so to speak), are highly significant for assessing the current state of the debate. See Charles Taylor, "Cross-Purposes: The Liberal–Communitarian Debate," in *Liberalism and the Moral Life* ed. Nancy L. Rosenblum (Harvard University Press, Cambridge, Mass., 1989), pp. 159–83; Michael Walzer, "The Communitarian Critique of Liberalism," *Political Theory*, 18.1 (Feb. 1990), pp. 6–23.

8   See Amy Gutmann, "Communitarian Critics of Liberalism," *Philosophy and Public Affairs*, 14.3 (Summer 1985), pp. 311ff.; Charles Larmore, *Patterns of Moral Complexity* (Cambridge University Press, New York, 1987); Will Kymlicka, *Liberalism, Community and Culture* (Oxford University Press, Oxford, 1989).

9   Will Kymlicka's clear and trenchant treatment of this issue in "Liberalism and Communitarianism," shows that communitarians themselves (Taylor, Sandel and MacIntyre in particular) are inconsistent in their positions, insofar as they also accept in some sense that "the *person* is prior to her ends" and not just "constituted" by her attachments. In *Philosophy and Public Affairs*, 18.2 (June 1988), pp. 181–204, here p. 192, emphasis in the text. Arguing for liberalism, Kymlicka emphasizes precisely those qualities of autonomous individuality which critical theory also valorizes: reflexivity vis à vis the setting of one's goals in life and the determination of one's interests; the ability to stand back and question those constitutive commitments into which we are born or into which sometimes we are "thrown," and I would add the ability to "act from principle." Both liberalism and critical theory are committed to a vision of the autonomous self. Disagreements emerge around another issue: inasmuch as philosophical liberals try to reformulate conceptions of the self without involving assumptions drawn from a comprehensive philosophical theory but in the light of articulating publicly shared conceptions of personality and agency, they weaken their own moral vision and are led into conceptual incoherence. The conceptual framework via which liberals state their views of the person follow a dualistic logic. On the one hand, there is the world of "causative" influences like language, culture and community which shape a person; these are so to speak the givens of phenomenal agency in this world. On the other hand, there are "the rational grounds" through which individuals assume an attitude of choice and reflection toward the given characteristics of their lives, bodies and communities – the position of noumenal agency. Kymlicka repeats this view in that he writes: "In any event, this solution is in contrast with the liberal view, which desires a society that is transparently intelligible – where nothing works behind

the back of its members – *Where all causes are turned into reasons"* (ibid. pp. 196–7, my emphasis). Hegelians would argue that this contrast between "causes" and "reasons" is spurious in understanding the reality of language, culture, society and institutions. As MacIntyre and Taylor have emphasized very well, in the explanation of human action, culture and societies the language of causality reduces the interpretive relation of the self to its world to the external relation of two bodies to each other. But human action can only be understood by understanding the language of reasons and the interpretive framework within which agents themselves view their world. Of course, a "causal" explanation going beyond mere hermeneutic interpretation is possible and even desirable. Such explanations in the social sciences must begin with an "already always interpreted reality." Critical social theorists, like the neo-Hegelians MacIntyre and Taylor, proceed from the primacy of the interpretive framework over the empiricist language of causes. Whereas for Kymlicka the view of a society that is "transparently intelligible" becomes a moral imperative, critical theorists along with Hegelians insist that the very contrast between "causes" and "reasons" needs to be reformulated in the light of the interpretive dimensions of human actions, institutions and culture. For an early statement, see Charles Taylor, "Interpretation and the Sciences of Man," *Review of Metaphysics*, 25 (1971), pp. 3–51; Alasdair MacIntyre, *Against the Self-Images of the Age* (University of Notre Dame Press, Notre Dame, 1978), chs 18–22 in particular; Jürgen Habermas, *On the Logic of the Social Sciences*, trans. Shierry Weber Nicholsen and Jerry A. Stalk (MIT Press, Cambridge, Mass., 1989); Richard J. Bernstein, *Restructuring Social and Political Theory* (University of Pennsylvania Press, Philadelphia, 1978).

10 In *Theory and Practice*, trans. John Viertel (Beacon, Boston, 1973), pp. 142–70.

11 J. Habermas, "Moral Development and Ego Identity," in *Communication and the Evolution of Society*, trans. and introd. Thomas McCarthy (Beacon Boston, 1979), pp. 93ff.

12 Habermas, "Discourse Ethics: Notes on a Program of Philosophical Justification," in *Moral Consciousness and Communicative Action*, trans. Christian Lenhardt and Shierry Weber Nicholsen (MIT Press, Cambridge, Mass., 1990), pp. 43ff.

13 John Rawls, *A Theory of Justice* (Harvard University Press, Cambridge, Mass., 1972), pp. 398ff.

14 Habermas, "A Reply to My Critics," in *Habermas: Critical Debates*, ed. John Thompson and D. Held (MIT Press, Cambridge, Mass., 1982), p. 246.

15 For a recent statement in the context of the Kohlberg–Gilligan debate, see Habermas, "Moral Consciousness and Communicative Action," in *Moral Consciousness and Communicative Action*, p. 181; cf. my discussion of this distinction between "justice" and the "good life" in chapter 6.

16 See Bernard Williams, *Ethics and the Limits of Philosophy* (Harvard University Press, Cambridge, Mass., 1985); Charles Taylor, "The Diversity of Goods," in *Philosophy and the Human Sciences*, vol. 2 of *Philosophical Papers* (Cambridge University Press, Cambridge, 1985), pp. 230–47.

17   See Habermas, "Moral Consciousness and Communicative Action," p. 121.

18   Naturally, there are some constraints on practical argumentations, like equality and symmetry of chances to initiate discussion and debate, etc., which can be named "deontological" in nature. These are ground rules of argument which are intended to assure the "fairness" of the outcome by assuring the "fairness" of the process through which such an outcome is reached. In this sense, in communicative ethics the "good," as it might be agreed upon by participants in a practical discourse, is constrained by the "right", i.e. by conditions of fair argumentation and fair debate. This is why communicative ethics remains a deontological theory but, as distinguished from Habermas's version of it, I prefer to defend a "weak deontological" interpretation according to which questions of justice as well as of the good life, of norms as well as of values, can be subject to discursive debate and testing in an open-ended conversation which does not aim at consensus but at "reaching an understanding."

19   T. M. Scanlon, "Contractualism and Utilitarianism," in *Utilitarianism and Beyond*, ed. A. Sen and Bernard Williams (Cambridge University Press, Cambridge, 1984), p. 107.

20   Throughout history there have been exemplary moral individuals who in effect have become the moral heroes of our cultures and civilizations precisely because they could engage in such questioning and reflection: not only Socrates but Antigone as well, not only Buddha but Maimonides, not only the Stoics but the Prophet Amos have questioned the authority of conventional duties and obligations in their cultures and society. That they may have done so in the name of some other values which they held to be unquestionable precisely because they were embedded in their cultural universe and carried its moral authority is not damaging to my argument. The "rationalization of value spheres" (Max Weber) under conditions of modernity means that increasingly all the "moral givens" of tradition are called into question but that furthermore, the attitude of moral rebellion and questioning which was once the privilege and virtue of heroes, prophets and moral sages now becomes "routinized" in everyday life, as modern societies define the duties and obligations which follow from social roles in increasingly abstract, formal and impersonal rules and norms. Simply put, as a co-worker in a modern company you stand today under no relationship of personal gratitude and obedience to your superiors beyond that which is dictated by the functional division of labor in that company. As social obligations become more abstract, they allow individuals greater latitude to fill in the "cracks" for themselves. That many female secretaries, for example, frequently make coffee for their usually male bosses, arrange golf appointments for them, or call up the cleaners is not part of the functional division of labor in the firm. One criticizes these patterns of interaction precisely because they continue paternalistic, patrimonial and premodern forms of dependence. This, of course, does not mean that the logic of gender differences and social roles would not assert itself in other ways in the modern workplace.

Secretaries still continue to cook coffee, look pretty and presentable, and "mother" not only the boss but other co-workers as well. But a modern secretary who refuses to act in these ways and who questions what is expected of her is not being a moral sage or heroine, she is simply assuming one of the moral stances which life in the modern world allows her.

21 This point is cogently argued by Marilyn Friedman in "Feminism and Modern Friendship: Dislocating the Community," *Ethics*, 99.2 (Jan. 1989), pp. 275–90.

22 In his ethical theory, Habermas not only disregards self-regarding virtues, but restricts the sphere of justice to the public-institutional domain alone, thus disregarding *structures of informal justice* as they shape our everyday relations within the family and with friends. As I argue in chapter 5 below, one consequence of this bias in the theory is the exclusion of all *gender-related* issues from the domain of justice and their relegation to the private sphere. Cf. also Norma Haan, "An Interactional Morality of Everyday Life," in *Social Science as Moral Inquiry*, ed. N. Haan, R. Bellah, P. Rabinow and W. Sullivan (Columbia University Press, New York, 1983), pp. 218ff.

23 Alasdair MacIntyre, *After Virtue* (Notre Dame University Press, Notre Dame, Ind., 1981), p. 204.

24 See Rawls, *A Theory of Justice*, pp. 60ff.

25 See H. Hirsch, "The Threnody of Liberalism," in *Political Theory*, 14.3 (Aug. 1986), pp. 423–49; Iris Young, "The Ideal of Community and the Politics of Difference," in *Social Theory and Practice*, 12.1 (Spring 1986), pp. 2–25.

26 Charles Larmore, *Patterns of Moral Complexity* (Cambridge University Press, Cambridge, 1987), p. 119.

27 Ibid., p. 129.

28 John Rawls, "Justice as Fairness: Political, Not Metaphysical," *Philosophy and Public Affairs*, 14.3 (Summer 1985), pp. 223ff.

29 See Novalis, "Christendom or Europe," in *Hymns to the Night and Other Selected Writings*, trans. and introd. Charles E. Passage (Library of Liberal Arts, New York, 1960), pp. 45ff.

30 J. J. Rousseau, *Du Contrat Social*, first published 1762 (Garnier, Paris, 1962), pp. 327ff.

31 MacIntyre, *After Virtue*, pp. 234, 244–5.

32 Michael Sandel, "The Procedural Republic and the Unencumbered Self," *Political Theory*, 12.1 (1984), pp. 81ff.

33 Cf. Charles Taylor, "Legitimation Crisis?" and "The Nature and Scope of Distributive Justice," in *Philosophy and the Human Sciences*, pp. 248–318.

34 See Michael Walzer, *Spheres of Justice* (Basic Books, New York, 1983).

35 Ibid., p. 6.

36 Taylor, "The Nature and Scope of Distributive Justice," p. 312.

37 Walzer, *Spheres of Justice*, p. 79; Taylor, "The Nature and Scope of Distributive Justice," pp. 308ff.

38 Taylor, "The Nature and Scope of Distributive Justice," p. 291.

39 Walzer, *Spheres of Justice*, p. 29.

40   Taylor, "The Nature and Scope of Distributive Justice," pp. 297ff.
41   Walzer, *Spheres of Justice*, p. 26.
42   Ibid., p. 61.
43   Ibid.
44   An English translation of this work which was first published in 1962 is finally available, see J. Habermas, *The Structural Transformation of the Public Sphere*, trans. Thomas Burger (MIT Press, Cambridge, Mass., 1988).
45   See Michael Walzer, "Liberalism and the Art of Separation," *Political Theory* (Aug. 1984), pp. 315–30; J. Habermas, "Legitimation Problems in the Modern State," in *Communication and the Evolution of Society*, trans. T. McCarthy (Beacon Boston, 1979), pp. 179ff.

3   Models of Public Space

Hannah Arendt, the Liberal Tradition and Jürgen Habermas

The art of making distinctions is always a difficult and risky undertaking. Distinctions can enlighten as well as cloud an issue. One is always also vulnerable to objections concerning the correct classification of the thought of certain thinkers. This chapter will side-step questions of historical interpretation and classification in order to delineate three different conceptions of "public space" that correspond to three main currents of western political thought. The view of public space common to the "republican virtue" or "civic virtue" tradition is described as the "agonistic" one and the thought of Hannah Arendt will be the main point of reference. The second conception is provided by the liberal tradition, and particularly by those liberals who, beginning with Kant, make the problem of a "just and stable public order" the center of their political thinking. This will be named the "legalistic" model of public space. The final model of public space is the one implicit in Jürgen Habermas's work. This model, which envisages a democratic-socialist restructuring of late-capitalist societies, will be named "discursive public space."

By situating the concept of "public space" in this context, the discussion is restricted from the outset to normative political theory. The larger sense of the term *Öffentlichkeit*, which would include a literary, artistic and scientific public, will not be of concern here; for whatever other applications and resonances they might have, the terms "public," "public space," "res publica" will never lose their intimate rootedness in the domain of political life. This approach will help highlight certain very significant differences among political theories all of which on the surface appear to accord central place to "public space" or "publicity" in political life. Not only are there important differences among these three conceptions of public space, but two of these views are severely limited in their usefulness for analyzing and evaluating political discourse and legitimation problems in advanced capitalist, and possibly even in what is now being referred to as "soviet style," societies.[1] When compared with the Arendtian and liberal conceptions, the strength of the Habermasian model is that questions of democratic legitimacy in advanced capitalist societies are central to it. Nevertheless, whether this model is resourceful enough to help us think through the transformation of politics in our kinds of societies is an open question. Taking the women's movement and the feminist critique of the public/private distinction as a point of reference, the final sections of this chapter will probe the discourse model of public space from this point of view.

Hannah Arendt and the Agonistic Concept of Public Space

Hannah Arendt is the central political thinker of this century whose work has reminded us with great poignancy of the "lost treasures" of our tradition of political thought, and specifically of the "loss" of public space, of *der öffentliche Raum*, under conditions of modernity. Hannah Arendt's major theoretical work, *The Human Condition*, is usually, and not altogether unjustifiably, treated as an anti-modernist political work. By "the rise of the social" in this work, Arendt means the institutional differentiation of modern societies into the narrowly political realm on the one hand and the economic market and the family on the other. As a result of these transformations, economic processes which had hitherto been confined to the "shadowy realm of the household" emancipate themselves and become public matters. The same historical process which brought forth the modern constitutional state also brings forth "society," that realm of social interaction which interposes itself between the "household" on the one hand and the political state on the other.[2] A century ago, Hegel had described this process as the development in the midst of ethical life of a "system of needs" (*System der Bedürfnisse*), of a domain of economic activity governed by commodity exchange and the pursuit of economic self-interest. The expansion of this sphere meant the disappearance of the "universal", of the common concern for the political association, for the *res publica*, from the hearts and minds of men.[3] Arendt sees in this process the occluding of the political by the "social" and the transformation of the public space of politics into a psuedospace of interaction in which individuals no longer "act" but "merely behave" as economic producers, consumers and urban city dwellers.

This relentlessly negative account of the "rise of the social" and the decline of the public realm has been identified as the core of Arendt's political "anti-modernism."[4] Indeed, at one level Arendt's text is a panegyric to the agonistic political space of the Greek polis. What disturbs the contemporary reader is perhaps less the high-minded and highly idealized picture of Greek political life which Arendt draws but more her neglect of the following constellation of issues. The agonistic political space of the polis was only possible because large groups of human beings like women, slaves, laborers, non-citizen residents, and all non-Greeks were excluded from it and made possible through their "labor" for the daily necessities of life that "leisure for politics" which the few enjoyed; by contrast, the rise of the social was accompanied by the emancipation of these groups from the "shadowy interior of the household" and by their entry into public life; is Arendt's critique of this process also a critique of political universalism as such? Is the "recovery of the public space" under conditions of modernity necessarily an elitist and anti-democratic project which can hardly be reconciled with the demand for universal political emancipation and the universal extension of citizenship rights that have accompanied modernity since the American and French revolutions?[5]

Yet it is greatly misleading to read Hannah Arendt primarily as a nostalgic thinker. She devoted as much space in her work to analyzing the dilemmas and prospects of politics under conditions of modernity as she did to the decline of public space in modernity. If we are not to read her account of the disappearance of the public realm as a *Verfallsgeschichte* (a history of decline) then, how are we to interpret it? The key here is Arendt's odd methodology which conceives of political thought as "storytelling." Viewed in this light, her "story" of the transformation of public space is an "exercise" of thought. Such thought exercises dig under the rubble of history in order to recover those "pearls" of past experience, with their sedimented and hidden layers of meaning, such as to cull from them a story that can orient the mind in the future.[6] The vocation of the theorist as "story teller" is the unifying thread of Arendt's political and philosophical analyses from the origins of totalitarianism to her reflections on the French and American revolutions to her theory of public space and to her final words to the first volume of *The Life of the Mind* on "Thinking".

> I have clearly joined the ranks of those who for some time now have been attempting to dismantle metaphysics, and philosophy with all its categories, as we have known them from their beginning in Greece until today. Such dismantling is possible only on the assumption that the thread of tradition is broken and we shall not be able to renew it. Historically speaking, what actually has broken down is the Roman trinity that for thousands of years united religion, authority, and tradition. The loss of this trinity does not destroy the past . . .
> What has been lost is the continuity of the past . . . What you then are

left with is still the past, but a *fragmented* past, which has lost its certainty of evaluation.[7]

Read in this light, Arendt's account of the "rise of the social" and the decline of public space under conditions of modernity can be viewed not as a nostalgic *Verfallsgeschichte* but as the attempt to think through the human history sedimented in layers of language. We must learn to identify those moments of rupture, displacement and dislocation in history. At such moments language is the witness to the more profound transformations taking place in human life. Such a *Begriffsgeschichte* is a remembering, in the sense of a creative act of "re-membering", that is, of putting together the "members" of a whole, of a rethinking which sets free the lost potentials of the past. "The history of revolutions . . . could be told in a parable form as the tale of an age-old treasure which, under the most varied circumstances, appears abruptly, unexpectedly, and disappears again, under different mysterious conditions, as though it were a *fata morgana*."[8]

Nonetheless, Arendt's thought is not free of assumptions deriving from an *Ursprungsphilosophie* which posits an original state or temporal point as the privileged source to which one must trace back the phenomena such as to capture their "true" meaning. As opposed to rupture, displacement and dislocation, this view emphasizes the continuity between the past origin and the present condition, and seeks to uncover at the origin the lost and concealed essence of the phenomena. There are really two strains in Hannah Arendt's thought, one corresponding to the method of fragmentary historiography, and inspired by Walter Benjamin,[9] the other inspired by the phenomenology of Husserl and Heidegger, and according to which memory is the mimetic recollection of the lost origins of phenomena as contained in some fundamental human experience. In accordance with this latter approach, reminders abound in the *The Human Condition* of "the original meaning of politics" or of the "lost" distinction between the "private" and the "public."[10] The concept that perhaps best illustrates Arendt's equivocation between fragmentary history and *Ursprungsphilosophie* is that of "public space." This topographical figure of speech is suggested early on in her work, at the end of *The Origins of Totalitarianism*, to compare various forms of political rule. Constitutional government is likened to moving within a space where the law is like the hedges erected between the buildings and one orients oneself upon known territory. Tyranny is like a desert; under conditions of tyranny one moves in an unknown, vast, open space, where the will of the tyrant occasionally befalls one like the sandstorm overtaking the desert traveler. Totalitarianism has no spatial topology: it is like an iron band, compressing people increasingly together until they are formed into one.[11]

Indeed, if one locates Arendt's concept of "public space" in the context of her theory of totalitarianism, it acquires a rather different focus than the one dominant in *The Human Condition*. The terms "agonistic" and "associational" can capture this contrast. According to the "agonistic" view, the public realm represents that space of appearances in which moral and political greatness, heroism and preeminence are revealed, displayed, shared with others. This is a competitive space, in which one competes for recognition, precedence and acclaim; ultimately it is the space in which one seeks a guarantee against the futility and the passage of all things human: "For the *polis* was for the Greeks, as the *res publica* was for the Romans, first of all their guarantee against the futility of individual life, the space protected against this futility and reserved for the relative permanence, if not immortality, of mortals."[12]

By contrast, the "associational" view of public space suggests that such a space emerges whenever and wherever, in Arendt's words, "men act together in concert."[13] On this model, public space is the space "where freedom can appear."[14] It is not a space in any topographical or institutional sense: a town hall or a city square where people do not "act in concert" is not a public space in this Arendtian sense. But a private dining room in which people gather to hear a *Samizdat* or in which dissidents meet with foreigners become public spaces; just as a field or a forest can also become public space if they are the object and the location of an "action in concert," of a demonstration to stop the construction of a highway or a military airbase, for example. These diverse topographical locations become public spaces in that they become the "sites" of power, of common action coordinated through speech and persuasion. Violence can occur in private and in public, but its language is essentially private because it is the language of pain. Force, like violence, can be located in both realms. In a way, it has no language, and nature remains its quintessential source. It moves without having to persuade or to hurt. Power, however, is the only force that emanates from action, and it comes from the mutual action of a group of human beings: once in action, one can make things happen, thus becoming a source of a different kind of "force."

The distinction between the "agonal" and the "associational" models corresponds to the Greek as opposed to the modern experience of politics. The agonal space of the polis was made possible by a morally homogeneous and politically egalitarian, but exclusive community, in which action could also be a revelation of the self to others. Under conditions of moral and political homogeneity and lack of anonymity, the "agonal" dimension, the vying for excellence among peers, could take place. But for the moderns public space is essentially porous; neither access to it nor its agenda of debate can be predefined by criteria of moral and political homogeneity. With the entry of every new group into the public space of politics after the French and American revolutions, the scope of the public gets extended. The emancipation of workers made property relations into a public-political issue; the emancipation of women has meant that the family and the so-called private sphere become political issues; the attainment of rights by non-white and non-Christian peoples has put cultural questions of collective self- and other-representations on the "public" agenda. Not only is it the "lost treasure" of revolutions that eventually all can partake in them, but equally, when freedom emerges from action in concert, there can be no agenda to *predefine* the topic of public conversation. The struggle over what gets included in the public agenda is itself a struggle for justice and freedom. The distinction between the "social" and the "political" makes no sense in the modern world, not because all politics has become administration and because the economy has become the quintessential "public," as Hannah Arendt thought, but primarily because the struggle to make something public is a struggle for justice.

Perhaps the episode which best illustrates this blind spot in Hannah Arendt's thought is that of school desegregation in Little Rock, Arkansas. Arendt likened the demands of the black parents, upheld by the US Supreme Court, to have their children admitted into previously all-white schools, to the desire of the social parvenue to gain recognition in a society that did not care to admit her. This time around Arendt failed to make the "fine distinction" and confused an issue of public justice – equality of educational access – with an issue of social preference – who my friends are or whom I invite to dinner. It is to her credit, however, that after the intervention of the black novelist, Ralph Ellison, she had the grace to reverse her position.[15]

At the root of Arendt's vacillations on this issue lies a more important problem, namely her phenomenological essentialism. In accordance with essentialist assumptions, "public space" is defined either as that space in which only a certain *type of activity*, namely action as opposed to work or labor, takes place or it is delimited from other "social" spheres with reference to the *substantive content* of the public dialogue. Both strategies lead to dead-ends. Let us note that the differentiation of action types into labor, work and action, and the principle of public space operate on different levels. Different action-types, like work and labor, can become the locus of "public space" if they are reflexively challenged and placed into question from the standpoint of the asymmetrical power relations governing them. To give a few examples: obviously "productivity quotas" in the factory workshop, how many chips per hour a worker should produce, can become matters of "public concern," if the legitimacy of those setting the quotas, their right to do so, their reasons for doing so are challenged. Likewise, as recent experience has shown us, even the most intricate questions of nuclear strategy, like the number of nuclear warheads on a missile, the time required to diffuse them etc. can be "reclaimed" by a public under conditions of democratic legitimacy and become part of what our "res publica" is about. Arendt, by contrast, relegated certain types of activity like work and labor, and by extension most, if not all, issues of economics and technology to the "private" realm alone, ignoring that these activities and relations, insofar as they are based on power relations, could become matters of public dispute as well.

Likewise, the attempt to define "public space" by specifying the agenda of the public conversation is futile. Even on Arendtian terms, the effect of collective action in concert will be to put ever new and unexpected items on the agenda of public debate. Arendt herself in the "associational" model developed not a substantive but a *procedural* concept of public space, which is in fact compatible with this view. What is important here is not so much what public discourse is about as the way in which this discourse takes place: force and violence destroy the specificity of public discourse by introducing the "dumb" language of physical superiority and constraint and by silencing the voice of persuasion and conviction. Power alone is generated by public discourse and is sustained by it. From the standpoint of this procedural model, neither the distinction between the social and the political nor the distinction between work, labor or action are that relevant. At stake is the reflexive questioning of issues by all those affected by their foreseeable consequences and the recognition of their right to do so.

When compared to Hannah Arendt's reflections, the advantage of the liberal concept of public space is that the link between power, legitimacy and public discourse is made most explicit by it. Yet this model is also more sterile than the Arendtian one in that it conceives of politics too closely along the analogy of juridical relations, thereby losing that emphasis on spontaneity, imagination, participation and empowerment which Arendt saw to be the mark of authentic politics whenever and wherever it occurred.

The Liberal Model of Public Space as "Public Dialogue"

With his model of "liberal dialogue," Bruce Ackerman expresses a fundamental tenet of contemporary liberalism: liberalism is a form of political culture in which the question of legitimacy is paramount.[16]

Liberalism is a way of talking about and publicly justifying power, a political culture of *public dialogue* based on certain kinds of *conversational constraints*. The most significant conversational constraint in liberalism is *neutrality*, which rules that no reason advanced within a discourse of legitimation can be a good reason if it requires the power holder to assert two claims: (a) that his conception of the good is better than that asserted by his fellow citizens; or that (b) regardless of his conception of the good, he is intrinsically superior to one or more of his fellow citizens.[17]

Bruce Ackerman bases his case for public dialogue "not on some general feature of the moral life, but upon the distinctive way liberalism conceives of the problem of public order."[18] His question is how different primary groups, about whom we only know that they do not share the same conception of the good, can "resolve the problem of coexistence in a *reasonable* way."[19] Ackerman believes that citizens in a liberal state must be guided by a Supreme Pragmatic Imperative (SPI) which states that they must be willing to participate in an ongoing dialogue about their conception of the good with others who are not members of their primary group.

Ackerman is concerned to find a justification of this imperative that will not fall into the three traps which traditionally affect moral philosophies of liberalism. One must find a justification of the SPI that is not based on trumping, that is, already asserting as supreme one moral view over others. Furthermore, one cannot assume, as utilitarians do, that there is a translation manual neutral enough in its language and in terms of which all our various moral commitments can be stated. According to Ackerman, such a translation manual would violate the sense of the good of one of the parties. Finally, one cannot ask the parties to assume a "transcendental perspective" as the precondition for entering into dialogue. Such a transcendental perspective, let us say the point of view of the "original position" or that of the "ideal speech situation," abstracts so radically from the condition of existing differences that it forces the parties to the public dialogue to assent to moral truths which they do not hold.

The way out is the path of "conversational restraint."

> When you and I learn that we disagree about one or another dimension of the moral truth, we should not search for some common value that will trump this disagreement; nor should we try to translate our moral disagreement into some putatively neutral framework; nor should we seek to transcend our disagreement by talking about how some hypothetical creature would resolve it. We should simply say *nothing at all* about this disagreement and try to solve our problem by invoking premises that we *do* agree upon. In restraining ourselves in this way, we need *not* lose the chance to talk to one another about our

deepest, moral disagreements in countless other, *more private, contexts.* Having constrained the conversation in this way, we may instead use dialogue for pragmatically productive purposes: to identify normative premises all political participants find reasonable (or, at least, not unreasonable.[20] (Emphasis added)

The pragmatic justification of "conversational restraint" is not morally neutral; this justification trumps certain conceptions of the good life in that it privatizes them and pushes them out of the agenda of public debate in the liberal state.[21] Not only members of certain religious groups, who may still seek to convert others to their faith, but also all groups working for the radical change of the social structure would then have to withdraw from the public arena of the liberal state into other more "private" contexts. The difference between my defense of a communicative ethic which also "trumps" certain conventional views of morality and Bruce Ackerman's defense of conversational restraints is that on the model of practical discourse following from communicative ethics, no issues of debate and no conceptions of the good life are precluded from being voiced in the public arena of the liberal state. Ackerman and I agree that conventional views of morality are not likely to be impartial and comprehensive enough to allow the public coexistence of differing and competing conceptions of the good life. Thus they cannot serve as the moral foundations of a liberal-democratic state. Yet they should be allowed to exist in such a state as partial conceptions of the good which enjoy an equal public forum with other more comprehensive views.[22]

The pragmatic justification not only trumps but also "transcends" for it asks the parties to the conversation to agree to "say nothing at all about" fundamental disagreements. It is unclear why this agreement *not to talk* about fundamental disagreements in public is any less loaded or controversial an assumption than the idea of a "veil of ignorance" which asks us to feign ignorance about our conception of the good. If I am deeply committed to the belief that prevalent conceptions of sexual division of labor in our societies are morally wrong because they oppress women and hinder their full expression of themselves as human beings, why should I agree not to do the best I can to make this a public issue and to convince others of my point of view? Or suppose I am a member of the Israeli opposition to the occupation of the West Bank and Gaza territories. I consider this occupation wrong not on pragmatic grounds but on moral grounds, because I believe that the occupation is corrupting the ethical values of the Jewish people. I may well be aware that under current conditions, public opinion is so divided that I stand no chance of winning assent; nevertheless is it unreasonable of me to

seek the widest possible forum of public discussion and participation
to air my views, rather than to agree with you, as Ackerman advocates, not to talk about what is of most concern to me. Either
Ackerman's justification of the SPI is based on stronger moral
grounds than he admits to or it cannot claim the supreme status it is
supposed to enjoy.[23]

But is the path of conversational restraint indeed so arbitrary?
Why not regard it as one of those procedural constraints on dialogue
that we all have to agree to on reasonable, moral grounds, even if
not wholly pragmatic ones? The idea of conversational restraint, as
it has been presented so far, presupposes a questionable moral
epistemology which implicitly justifies a separation between the
public and the private that is oppressive to the concerns of certain groups. On these grounds as well its moral persuasiveness is
limited.

By the "moral epistemology" of the conversational restraint
model I mean the following. The liberal theorist of conversational
restraint presupposes that the primary groups to the conversation
already know what their deepest disagreements are even before
they have engaged in the conversation. These groups already seem
convinced that a particular problem is a moral, religious or aesthetic
issue as opposed to an issue of distributive justice or public policy.
While we can legitimately discuss the second, says the liberal
theorist, let us abstract from the first. Take, however, issues like
abortion, pornography and domestic violence. What kinds of issues
are they? Are they questions of "justice" or of the "good life"? The
moral or political theorist is in possession of no moral dictionary or
moral geometry in this matter such as would allow her to classify
these issues as being matters of "justice" or of the "good life." In
part it is the unconstrained public dialogue that will help us define
the nature of the issues we are debating. Certainly, as citizens and
as theorists we enter the public fray with a set of more or less
atriculated, more or less preformed opinions, principles and values.
As democratic citizens and theorists we are participants in a debate,
but we should not seek to define the agenda of the debate. We may,
on the basis of more or less well supported principles and values,
wish to maintain that abortion should be considered a matter of
individual choice for the women involved; but it is not a (non-
existent) consensus about the kind of issue this is that leads us to
this position. Rather principles of moral autonomy and moral
choice, the right of women to self-realization, and some sensitivity
to the often tragic and irreconcilable aspects of our value commitments inform our views. Indeed citizens must feel free to introduce, in Bruce Ackerman's words, "any and all moral arguments
into the conversational field." For it is only after the dialogue has

been opened in this radical fashion that we can be sure that we have come to agree upon a mutually acceptable definition of the problem rather than reaching some compromise consensus.

The issue of pornography illustrates my point well. This question has been so divisive and has created such strange and unholy alliances – as between Andrea Dworkin and Jerry Falwell for example – that it is the paradigm example of the kind of moral disagreement that the modus vivendi liberal may urge us to agree not to publicly disagree about. This, however, is precisely what we should not do at this stage of the debate. Whether pornography is to be defined as a question of the reasonable limitations to be imposed upon the First Amendment right of free speech; whether pornography is to be thought of as a private, moral issue concerning matters of sexual taste and style; whether pornography is to be thought of as a matter of aesthetic-cultural sensibility and as a question of artistic fantasy – we simply cannot know before the process of unconstrained public dialogue has run its course. I no more want to live in a society which cannot distinguish between *Hustler* magazine and Salinger's *Catcher in the Rye* than Ackerman does, or in a society that would place Henry Miller and D. H. Lawrence in the company of *Deep Throat*. As sensitive as one may be to the traditional liberal fear that unlimited public conversation might erode those few constitutional guarantees we can rely upon, the reprivatization of issues that have become public only generates conceptual confusion, political resentment and moral outrage. I consider limitations upon the content and scope of public dialogue, other than constitutional guarantees of free speech, to be unnecessary. A normative theory of such conversational constraints fails to become a critical model of legitimation.

An additional limitation of the liberal model of public space is that it conceives of political relations all too often narrowly along the model of juridical ones. The chief concern expressed by the idea of "dialogic neutrality" is that of the rightful coexistence of different groups, each subscribing to a different conception of the good, in a pluralistic society. The just in modern societies, it is said, should be neutral vis-à-vis fundamental assumptions concerning the good life. Neutrality is indeed one of the fundamental cornerstones of the modern legal system: modern, promulgated law, unlike ancient and customary law, should not "ethically" mold character but should provide the space within which autonomous individuals can pursue and develop various conceptions of the good life. Even under conditions of a modern, pluralist, democratic society, however, politics is about something other than "neutrality." Democratic politics challenges, redefines and renegotiates the divisions between the good and the just, the moral and the legal, the private and the public. For these distinctions, as they have been established by modern states at the end of social and historical struggles, contain within them the result of historical power compromises.

To illustrate. Before the emergence of strong working-class movements and the eventual establishment of social-welfare type measures in European countries and North America, questions relating to the health of workers in the workplace, problems of accidents on the job, and in our days, the harmful side-effects of certain chemicals, were frequently construed by employers as issues of "trade secrets" and "business privacy." As a result of political struggles the definition of these issues were transformed from trade secrets and private business practices to major issues of "public concern." The principle of liberal neutrality is not helpful in guiding our thoughts on such matters. All it says is that once this redefinition and political renegotiation of the right and the good has occurred, then the law should be neutral; that is OSHA (Office of Safety and Health Administration) should be neutral in applying this legislation to Chinese laundromats, Italian restaurants or the Lockheed corporation. But public dialogue is not about what all the Chinese laundromats, Italian restaurants and the Lockheed corporation know they agree to, even before they have entered the public foray; rather public dialogue means challenging and redefining the collective good, and one's sense of justice as a result of the public foray. The liberal principle of dialogic neutrality, while it expresses one of the main principles of the modern legal system, is too restrictive and frozen in application to the dynamics of power struggles in actual political processes. A public life, conducted according to the principle of liberal dialogic neutrality, would not only lack the agonistic dimension of politics, in Arendtian terms, but perhaps more severely, it would restrict the scope of the public conversation in a way which would be inimical to the interests of oppressed groups. All struggles against oppression in the modern world begin by redefining what had previously been considered "private", non-public and non-political issues as matters of public concern, as issues of justice, as sites of power which need discursive legitimation. In this respect, the women's movement, the peace movement, the ecology movements, and new ethnic identity movements follow a similar logic. There is little room in the liberal model of neutrality for thinking about the logic of such struggles and social movements. In Arendtian language, liberalism ignores the "agonistic" dimension of public-political life.

Given the historical concerns out of which political liberalism has emerged and to which it has sought an answer, like the limits of absolutist state power and the problems of religious tolerance, this is hardly surprising. The search for a just, stable and tolerant political order has been the distinguishing mark of liberal political theory. This search has also led to an excessive focus in contemporary liberalism upon the limits and justification of state power and other public agencies to the neglect of other dimensions of political life, like life in political associations, movements, citizens' groups, town meetings, and public fora. In Benjamin Barber's perspicacious words, among the cognitive requirements of contemporary liberalism appears to be "an antipathy to democracy and its sustaining institutional structures (participation, civic education, political activism) and a preference for 'thin' rather than strong versions of political life in which citizens are spectators and clients while politicians are professionals who do the actual governing . . ."[24] Certainly, this is no place to settle the old conflict between liberalism and democracy. Benjamin Barber's observation is quite to the point insofar as it might help us see why the concept of "public space," as a space of political deliberation, action and exchange plays such a minimal role in contemporary liberalism. It is as if once the "constitutional assembly" in which we select principles of a just political association is over, the citizens of the liberal state retire into their private abodes and quit the democratic arena of political give and take.

The contrast between democratic deliberation, of the sort envisaged by Arendt and Barber, and the liberal conception of public dialogue can be well captured when juxtaposed to John Rawls's idea of "free public reason." Rawls specifies this principle as follows:

> Just as a political conception of justice needs certain principles of justice for the basic structure to specify its content, it also needs certain guidelines of enquiry and publicly recognized rules of assessing evidence to govern its application. Otherwise, there is no agreed way for determining whether these principles are satisfied, and for settling what they require of particular institutions, or in particular situations. . . . And given the fact of pluralism, there is, I think, no better practical alternative than to limit ourselves to the shared methods of, and the public knowledge available to common sense, and the procedures and conclusions of science when these are not controversial.[25]

Rawls adds the very important observation that "The maxim that justice must not only be done, but be seen to be done, holds good not only in law but in free public reason."[26]

The idea that the justice of institutions be "in the public's eye," so to speak, for the public to scrutinize, to examine and reflect upon is fundamental. That it recognizes the legitimation of power or the examination of the justice of institutions to be a public process, open to all citizens to partake in, is one of the central tenets of liberalism and one which has its roots in the political primacy of consent in social contract theories. From the standpoint of a discourse model of legitimacy as well this is crucial. Note, however, that for Rawls "free public reason" does not describe the kind of reasoning used by citizens and their representatives in the polity. Undoubtedly, Rawls would like them to exercise their "free public reason" in this way. But as the idea of free public reason has been formulated it applies less to a process of democratic discussion or parliamentary debate than to the reasoning of a parliamentary investigative body or the kind of investigation a federal agency may conduct when determining whether a hospital which has received public funds has also complied with affirmative action regulations. In Rawls's view, free public reason is the manner in which public associations account for their doings and conduct their affairs in a polity.[27]

While there is little doubt that this principle of free public reason expresses a governing normative rule for the public accountability of the major institutions of a liberal-democratic society, consider also what is missing from it. All contestatory, rhetorical, affective, impassioned elements of public discourse, with all their excesses and virtues, are absent from this view. Free public reason is not freely wielded public reasoning, with all the infuriating ideological and rhetorical mess that this may involve. Again in his comment on Ackerman, Benjamin Barber captures this point well. "It is neutrality that destroys dialogue, for the power of political talk lies in its creativity, its variety, its openness and flexibility, its inventiveness, its capacity for discovery, its subtlety and complexity, its potential for empathetic and affective expression – in other words, in its deeply paradoxical, some would say, dialectical, character."[28] Certainly, one cannot only focus on the speeches of Abraham Lincoln, Adlai Stevenson and Jesse Jackson to the exclusion of the less ennobling outbursts of a Richard Nixon, Fidel Castro or Nikita Khrushchev. What Barber's observation captures nonetheless is the open-ended, contestatory, affective dimension of the political through which free public reason can assume the character of "shared reasoning."

To this conception of contestatory public speech[29] or shared reasoning, the liberal theorist will respond that, lofty and ennobling as its vision may be, the agonistic view of the political leaves the flood gates open for the whim of majoritarian decisions. What if less than noble majorities challenge the principles of neutrality and the lines between the right and the good in such ways as to lead to religious fanaticism, persecution of unpopular minorities, intrusion of the state into the domain of private life, or even the political condoning of surveillance by children of parents, by spouses of each other, all in the name of some shared good? In response to such concerns John Rawls suggests that certain matters be taken off the political agenda of the liberal state insofar as "They are part of the public charter of a constitutional regime and not a suitable topic for on-going public debate and legislation, as if they can be changed at any time, one way or the other."[30] The rejection of slavery and serfdom and the guarantee for all religions of equal liberty of conscience are among the topics which should be taken off the political agenda of the liberal state for Rawls. He adds: 'Of course, that certain matters are taken off the political agenda does not mean that a political conception of justice should not explain why this is done. Indeed, as I note above, a political conception should do precisely this."[31]

This standard liberal concern about the corrosive effect of unbridled majoritarian politics upon civil and political liberties is, I believe, incontrovertible. Agonistic visions of the political are often inattentive to the institutional preconditions which must be fulfilled for such a politics to unfold. But for complex, democratic societies the contrast between "the agonistic" and "the legalistic" conceptions of public space may be overly simplistic to the extent that a liberal, legal-constitutional framework guaranteeing equal civil, political rights as well as rights of conscience is a precondition for universal citizenship participation. As I shall explore in the next chapter, in her reflections on Kant's concept of judgment Hannah Arendt confronted the question of what the liberal theorist would name fundamental rights and liberties, and what I name the normative foundations of the political. She was unable to offer a satisfactory resolution to this problem and the question of the normative presuppositions of the political runs through her work like a red thread from her melancholy reflections on "the right to have rights" in *The Origins of Totalitarianism* to her ruminations on constitutions in *On Revolution.*[32]

If both the agonistic and the legalistic models of public space are insufficiently complex to deal with the realities of highly differentiated and pluralistic modern societies, and must be viewed as complementing rather than excluding one another, then it is plausible to assume that a more adequate conception of the public space should combine both dimensions. Although it has not been often presented in this way, the Habermasian principle of "Öffentlichkeit" can fulfill this requirement. The discursive public space is the essential sociological correlate of the discourse concept of legitimacy. It is in such discursive spaces that such dialogues of legitimacy expire. In the next section, I will explore these features of Habermas's concept of "Öffentlichkeit," but I also would like to show how the contestatory dimension of public discourse gets overridden in this model by Habermas's rigid separations between "justice" and "the good life," "needs" and "interests," "values" and "norms."

The Discursive Model of Public Space

Since the *Structural Transformation of the Public Sphere*, Habermas has analyzed the development of modern societies in light of the extension of the sphere of public participation.[33] Along with social differentiation and the creation of independent value spheres, modernity brings with it a threefold possibility.[34] In the realm of institutions, the consensual generation of general norms of action through practical discourses moves to the fore. In the realm of personality formation, the development of individual identities becomes increasingly more dependent on the reflexive and critical attitudes of individuals in weaving together a coherent life story beyond conventional role and gender definitions. Self-definitions, who one is, become increasingly autonomous vis-à-vis established social practices and fluid when compared to rigid role understandings. Likewise the appropriation of cultural tradition becomes more dependent upon the creative hermeneutic of contemporary interpreters. Tradition in the modern world loses its legitimacy of simply being valid because it is the way of the past. The legitimacy of tradition rests now with resourceful and creative appropriations of it in view of the problems of meaning in the present. Viewed in this threefold fashion, the principle of participation, far from being antithetical to modernity, is one of its chief prerequisites. In each realm – society, personality and culture – in the functioning of institutional life, the formation of stable personalities over time and the continuity of cultural tradition, the reflective effort and contribution of individuals becomes crucial.

Placed in this broader sociological context, the meaning of participation is altered. The exclusive focus on "political" participation is shifted toward a much more inclusively understood concept of "discursive will formation." Participation is not seen as an activity that is only and most truly possible in a narrowly defined political realm, but as an activity that can be realized in the social and cultural spheres as well. Participating in a citizen's initiative to clean up a polluted harbor is no less political than debating in cultural journals the pejorative presentation of certain groups in terms of stereotypical images (combating sexism and racism in the media). This conception of participation, which emphasizes the determination of norms of action through the practical debate of all affected by them, has the distinctive advantage over the republican or civic virtue conception that it articulates a vision of the political true to the realities of complex, modern societies.

This modernist understanding of participation yields a novel conception of public space. Public space is not understood *agonistically* as a space of competition for acclaim and immortality among a political elite; it is viewed democratically as the creation of procedures whereby those affected by general social norms and by collective political decisions can have a say in their formulation, stipulation and adoption. This conception of the public is also different than the liberal one; for although Habermas and liberal thinkers believe that legitimation in a democratic society can only result from a public dialogue, in the Habermasian model this dialogue does not stand under the constraint of neutrality, but is judged according to the criteria represented by the idea of a "practical discourse." The public sphere comes into existence whenever and wherever all affected by general social and political norms of action engage in a practical discourse, evaluating their validity. In effect, there may be as many publics as there are controversial general debates about the validity of norms. Democratization in contemporary societies can be viewed as the increase and growth of autonomous public spheres among participants. As Jean Cohen has astutely observed:

> Both the complexity and the diversity within contemporary civil societies call for the posing of the issue of democratization in terms of a variety of differentiated processes, forms, and *loci* depending on the axis of division considered. Indeed, there is an elective affinity between the discourse ethic and modern civil society as the terrain on which an institutionalized plurality of democracies can emerge.[35]

Now this model of a plurality of public spaces emerging in modern societies around contested issues of general concern transcends the dichotomy of majoritarian politics versus constitutional guarantees of civil liberties discussed in the previous section. As explained previously, the discourse model of legitimacy and the discursive view of public space are radically proceduralist. They present normative dialogue as a conversation of justification taking place under the constraints of an "ideal speech situation." The normative constraints of the ideal speech situation or of practical discourses have been specified as the conditions of *universal moral respect* and *egalitarian reciprocity*. The presence of these constraints avoids the dilemmas of simple majoritarian political outcomes. Kenneth Baynes has explained this issue well: "If there are no substantive constraints on what can be introduced into a practical discourse, what is to prevent the outcome from conflicting with some of our most deeply held moral convictions? What is to prevent the participants agreeing to anything, or perhaps, more plausibly, never reaching any general agreement at all?"[36] Baynes suggests that the imposition of certain constraints on discourses is the only way to avoid this dilemma. Yet he also stresses, quite in line with a suggestion made above, that the "constraints imposed on discourse are subject to discursive vindication,"[37] themselves and he further adds:

> At a less fundamental level, many other constraints may well be imposed on discourses in view of the issues or tasks at hand. It is reasonable to assume, for example, that the basic rights and liberties specified in Rawls's first principle and contained in the U.S. Constitution would serve as constraints on most public debates, *removing topics from the agenda because of their deeply personal nature or close connection with recognized spheres of privacy. However, discussion about the nature and scope of these rights is always something that can become the subject of public debate.* As arguments about rights become more closely tied to specific interpretations of social goods, what counts as a good argument will no doubt depend more heavily on the shared meanings and practices that make up the everyday life-world . . .[38] (Emphasis added)

As the above quote reveals, there is a tension for most communicative or discourse theorists between the desire for unconstrained dialogue not to be subject to traditional liberal constraints on the one hand and not to have majoritarian decision procedures corrode civil liberties and rights on the other. I concur with Baynes that formulating the "normative constraints of discourses," as constraints whose fairness and appropriateness can themselves become topics of debate, is plausible. The normative constraints of practical discourses would occupy the same place in discourse theories of legitimacy and public space as the Rawlsian basic liberties and rights specified under the first principle of justice occupy in his theory.[39]

Where I would differ both from Rawls's formulation about keeping certain topics "off limits" and Baynes's desire to remove them from the agenda of discourse is in the matter of procedure. Basic human, civil and political rights, as guaranteed by the Bill of Rights to the US Constitution and as embodied in the constitutions of most democratic governments, are never "off the agenda" of public discussion and debate. They are simply constitutive and regulative institutional norms of debate in democratic societies which cannot be transformed and abrogated by simple majority decisions. The language of keeping these rights off the agenda mischaracterizes the nature of democratic debate in our kinds of societies: although we cannot change these rights without extremely elaborate political and juridical procedures, we are always disputing their meaning, their extent and their jurisdiction. Democratic debate is like a ball game where there is no umpire to definitively interpret the rules of the game and their application. Rather in the game of democracy the rules of the game no less than their interpretation and even the position of the umpire are essentially contestable. But contestation means neither the complete abrogation of these rules nor silence about them. When basic rights and liberties are violated, the game of democracy is suspended and becomes either martial rule, civil war or dictatorship; when democratic politics is in full session the debate about the meaning of these rights, what they do or do not entitle us to, their scope and enforcement is what politics is all about. In communicative ethics and in democratic politics we assume critical and reflexive distance precisely toward those rules and practices which we also cannot avoid but uphold. One cannot challenge the specific interpretation of basic rights and liberties in a democracy without taking these also absolutely seriously; likewise one cannot question the texture and nature of our everyday moral commitments in communicative ethics without permanent and continuous embroilment in them on a day-to-day level.

The discourse theory of legitimacy and public space then transcends the traditional opposition of majoritarian politics versus liberal guarantees of basic rights and liberties to the extent that the normative conditions of discourses are, like basic rights and liberties, rules of the game which can be contested within the game but only insofar as one first accepts to abide by them and play the game at all. This formulation seems to me to correspond to the reality of democratic debate and public speech in real democracies much more than the liberal model of constitutional conventions. In democratic politics nothing is really off the agenda of public debate, but there are fundamental rules of discourse which are both constitutive and regulatory in such a manner that, although what they mean for democratic give and take is itself always contested, the rules themselves cannot be suspended or abrogated by simple majoritarian procedures.

Having argued that the discourse model of legitimacy and the discourse model of public space capture the role of democratic debate more successfully than the Arendtian and the liberal versions, I would now like to turn to an issue which will allow me to explore some of the limitations of the discourse model more specifically.

Feminist Critiques of the Public/Private Distinction

Any theory of publicity, public space and public dialogue must presuppose some distinction between the private and the public. In the tradition of western political thought and down to our own days, the way in which the distinction between the public and the private spheres has been drawn has served to confine women and typically female spheres of activity like housework, reproduction, nurturance and care for the young, the sick and the elderly to the "private" domain, and to keep them off the public agenda in the liberal state. These issues have often been considered matters of the good life, of values, of non-generalizable interests. Along with their relegation, in Arendt's terms, to the "shadowy interior of the household," they have been treated, until recently, as "natural" and "immutable" aspects of human relations. They have remained pre-reflexive and inaccessible to discursive analysis. Much of our tradition, when it considers the autonomous individual or the moral point of view, implicitly defines this as the standpoint of the *homo politicus* or the *homo economicus* but hardly ever as the female self.[40] Challenging the distinction of contemporary moral and political discourse, to the extent that they privatize these issues, is central to women's struggles which intend to make these issues "public."

"Privacy," "privacy rights" and the "private sphere," as invoked by the modern tradition of political thought, have included at least three distinct dimensions: first and foremost, privacy has been understood as the sphere of moral and religious conscience. As a result of the historical separation of church and state in Western European and North American countries, and as a consequence of developments in modern philosophy and science, matters of ultimate faith concerning the meaning of life, of the highest good, of the most binding principles in accordance with which we should conduct our lives, come to be viewed as rationally "irresolvable" and as issues about which individuals themselves should decide according to the dictates of their own consciences and world-views.

In the emergence of western modernity, a second set of privacy rights accompany the eventual establishment of the liberal separation of the church and state. These are privacy rights pertaining to *economic liberties*. The development of commodity relations in the market-place and of capitalism does not only mean "the rise of the social," in Arendtian terms. Along with the socialization of the economy, that is along with the decline of subsistence-type household economies and the eventual emergence of national markets, a parallel development establishing the "privacy" of economic markets takes place. In this context, "privacy" means first and foremost non-interference by the political state in the free flow of commodity relations, and in particular non-intervention in the free market of labor-power.

The final meaning of "privacy" and "privacy rights" is that of the "intimate sphere." This is the domain of the household, of meeting the daily needs of life, of sexuality and reproduction, of care for the young, the sick and the elderly. As Lawrence Stone's pathbreaking study on the origins and transformations of the early bourgeois family shows,[41] from the beginning there were tensions between the continuing patriarchal authority of the father in the bourgeois family and developing conceptions of equality and consent in the political world. As the male bourgeois citizen was battling for his rights to autonomy in the religious and economic spheres against the absolutist state, his relations in the household were defined by non-consensual, non-egalitarian assumptions. Questions of justice were from the beginning restricted to the "public sphere," whereas the private sphere was considered outside the realm of justice.

To be sure, with the emergence of autonomous women's movements in the nineteenth and twentieth centuries, with women's massive entry into the labor force in this century, and their gain of the right to vote, this picture has been transformed. Contemporary moral and political theory, however, continues to neglect these issues, and ignores the transformations of the private sphere resulting from massive changes in women's and men's lives. While conceptually matters of justice and those of the good life are distinct from the sociological distinction between the public and private spheres, the frequent conflation of religious and economic freedoms with the freedom of intimacy, under the one title of "privacy" or of "private questions of the good life," has had two consequences: first, contemporary normative moral and political theory, Habermas's discourse ethics not excluded, has been "gender blind," that is, these theories have ignored the issue of "difference," the difference in the experiences of male versus female subjects in all domains of life. Second, power relations in the "intimate sphere" have been treated as though they did not even exist. The idealizing lens of concepts like "intimacy" does not allow one to see that women's work in the private sphere, like care for the young and the running of the household, has been unrenumerated. Consequently, the rules governing the sexual division of labor in the family have been placed beyond the scope of justice. As with any modern liberation movement, the contemporary women's movement is making what were hitherto considered "private" matters of the good life into "public" issues of justice by thematizing the asymmetrical power relations on which the sexual division of labor between the genders has rested. In this process, the line between the private and the public, between issues of justice and matters of the good life is being renegotiated.

Certainly, a normative theory, and in particular a critical social theory, cannot take the aspirations of any social actors at face value and fit its critical criteria to meet the demands of a particular social movement. Commitment to social transformation, and yet a certain critical distance, even from the demands of those with whom one identifies, are essential to the vocation of the theorist as social critic. For this reason, the purpose of these final considerations is not to criticize the critical theory of Habermas simply by confronting it with the demands of the women's movement. Rather, my goal is to point to an area of conceptual unclarity as well as political contestation in contemporary debates. Any theory of the public, public sphere, and publicity presupposes a distinction between the public and the private. These are the terms of a binary opposition. What the women's movement and feminist theorists in the last two decades have shown is that traditional modes of drawing this distinction have been part of a discourse of domination which legitimizes women's oppression and exploitation in the private realm. But the discourse model, precisely because it proceeds from a fundamental norm of egalitarian reciprocity and precisely because it projects the democratization of all social norms, cannot preclude the democratization of familial norms and of norms governing the gender division of labor in the family as well.[42] If in discourses the agenda of the conversation is radically open, if participants can bring any and all matters under critical scrutiny and questioning, then there is no way to predefine the nature of the issues discussed as being public ones of justice versus private ones of the good life. Distinctions such as between justice and the good life, norms and values, interests and needs are "subsequent" and not prior to the process of discursive will formation. As long as these distinctions are renegotiated, reinterpreted and rearticulated as a result of a radically open and procedurally fair discourse, they can be drawn in any of a number of ways. Thus there is both an "elective affinity" and a certain tension between the demands of social movements like the women's movement and the discourse ethic. Let me explain:

The elective affinity, to use Max Weber's felicitous phrase, between discourse ethics and social movements like the women's movement derives from the fact that both project the extension of a postconventional and egalitarian morality into spheres of life which were hitherto controlled by tradition, custom, rigid role expectations and outright inegalitarian exploitation of women and their work. Discourse ethics, like the women's movement, has argued that only relations of egalitarian reciprocity, based upon the mutual respect and sharing of the parties involved, can be fair from a moral point of view. Conventional relations and role expectations as between the "wife" and the "husband," the "parents" and the "children" are thus opened to questioning, renegotiation and redefinition. As I shall argue in chapter 6 below, there is also an elective affinity between the commitment to an ethics of dialogue and feminist ideals. In many ways, the contemporary women's movement is the culmination of the logic of modernity which projects the discursive negotiation of societal norms, the flexible appropriation of tradition and the formation of fluid and reflexive self-identities and life histories.

The tension between discourse ethics and the models of legitimacy and public space deriving from it on the one hand and the claims of the women's movement on the other rests primarily[43] upon the overly rigid boundaries which Habermas has attempted to establish between matters of justice and those of the good life, public interests versus private needs, privately held values and publicly shared norms. But as I suggested above it is only the unconstrained process of discourse and not some moral calculus which will allow us to reestablish these boundaries once their traditional meaning has been contested.

Faced with this claim, Habermas as well as the liberal political theorist might respond that this position invites the corrosion of rights of privacy and the total intrusion of the state into the domain of the individual. The issue, they will argue, is not that these distinctions must be reconceptualized but where the line between the private and the public will be situated as a result of this discursive reconceptualization. Put in more familiar terms, does discourse theory allow for a theory of individual rights guaranteeing privacy, or is it simply a theory of democratic participation which does not respect the legal boundaries of individual liberty? The tension between democratic politics and liberal guarantees of constitutional rights, which I have claimed discourse theory to have solved, returns once more. Let me suggest, and ironically against Habermas himself, why the kind of discourse about the family and the gender division of labor initiated by the women's movement is both an instance of the democratization of the public sphere and why the discourse model can accommodate such challenges to the public/private distinction.

In principle, the discourse model is based upon a strong assumption of individual autonomy and consent; thus even in discourses which renegotiate the boundaries between the private and the public the respect for the individuals' consent and the necessity of their voluntarily gained insight into the validity of general norms guarantees that this distinction cannot be redrawn in ways that jeopardize, damage and restrict this autonomy of choice and insight. I agree with Cohen who writes:

> Although in this case, too, processes of discursive will formation decide the boundary between the private and the public, they cannot entirely abolish the private. Indeed, the meta-norms of discourse themselves provide for the autonomy of the individual moral conscience. If all those affected must have an equal chance to assume

dialogue roles, if the dialogue must be free and unconstrained, and if each individual can shift the level of the discourse, then practical discourse presupposes autonomous individuals with the capacity to challenge any given consensus from a *principled* standpoint. The very rules which underlie argument and the cooperative search for consensus predicate the distinction between morality and legality. By articulating the meta-norms of the principle of democratic legitimacy and rights, the discourse ethic provides the justification for the autonomy of morality, grounding, as it were, its own self-limitation.[44]

I concur with Cohen that the very logic of discourses permits us to challenge the traditionalist understandings of the public/private split but that the very resources of the discourse model of publicity also prohibit the drawing of these distinction in ways which jeopardize the autonomy and insight of individuals involved. Having argued this far, one has suggested why the discourse model can serve as a norm of democratic legitimacy and public speech in societies like ours where the line between the private and the public is being hotly contested. But it is not only discourse theory which must be confronted with the claims of feminists; feminist theory itself sorely needs a model of public space and public speech which returns it to the politics of empowerment. The feminist critique of Habermas's model of the public sphere must be complemented by the appropriation by feminists of a critical theory of the public sphere.

Undoubtedly, our societies are undergoing tremendous transformations at the present. In western democracies, under the impact of corporatization, the mass media and the growth of business-style political associations, like PAC's (Political Action Committees) and other lobbying groups, the public sphere of democratic legitimacy has shrunk. In the last US presidential campaign of 1988, the level of public discourse and debate, both in terms of substance and style, had sunk so low that major networks like CBS and ABC felt compelled to run sessions of self-reflexive anlaysis on their own contributions as the electronic media to the decline of public discourse. The autonomous citizen, whose reasoned judgement and participation was the sine qua non of the public sphere has been transformed into the "citizen consumer" of packaged images and messages, or the "electronic mail target" of large lobbying groups and organizations.[45] This impoverishment of public life has been accompanied by the growth of the society of surveillance and voyeurism on the one hand (Foucault) and the "colonization of the lifeworld" on the other (Habermas). Not only has public life been transformed, private life as well has undergone tremendous changes, only some of which can be welcome for furthering the values of democratic legitimacy and discursive will formation.

As the sociologist Helga Maria Hernes has remarked, in some ways, welfare state societies are ones in which "reproduction" has gone public.[46] When, however, issues like childrearing, care for the sick, the young and the elderly, reproductive freedoms, domestic violence, child abuse and the constitution of sexual identities go "public" in our societies, more often than not a "patriarchal-capitalist-disciplinary bureaucracy" has resulted.[47] These bureaucracies have frequently disempowered women and have set the agenda for public debate and participation. In reflecting about these issues as feminists we have lacked a *critical model of public space and public discourse.* Here is where as feminists we should not only criticize Habermas's social theory, but enter into a dialectical alliance with it. A critical model of public space is necessary to enable us to draw the line between "juridification," "Verrechtlichung" in Habermas's terms, on the one hand, and making "public," in the sense of making accessible to debate, reflection, action and moral-political transformation on the other. To make issues of common concern public in this second sense means making them increasingly accessible to discursive will formation; it means to democratize them; it means bringing them to the standards of moral reflection compatible with autonomous postconventional identities. As feminists, we have lacked a critical model which could distinguish between the bureaucratic administration of needs and collective democratic empowerment over them. More often than not, debates among feminists have been blocked by the alternatives of a legalistic liberal reformism (the NOW (National Organization for Women) agenda; ACLU (American Civil Liberties Union) positions) and a radical feminism which can hardly conceal its own political and moral authoritarianism.[48]

For reasons which I have already explored, some of the models of public space discussed in this essay are severely limited to help us cope with this task. Arendt's agonistic model is at odds with the sociological reality of modernity, as well as with modern political struggles for justice. The liberal model of public space transforms the political dialogue of empowerment far too quickly into a juridical discourse about basic rights and liberties. The discourse model is the only one which is compatible both with the general social trends of our societies and with the emancipatory aspirations of new social movements like the women's movement. The radical proceduralism of this model is a powerful criterion for demystifying discourses of power and their implicit agendas. In a society where "reproduction" is going public, practical discourse will have to be "feminized." Such feminization of practical discourse will mean first and foremost challenging unexamined normative dualisms as between justice and the good life, norms and values, interests and needs, from the standpoint of their gender context and subtext.

Notes

This paper was first delivered at the conference on Habermas and the Public Sphere at the University of North Carolina at Chapel Hill, which took place in September 1989, and published in *Habermas and the Public Sphere*, ed. Craig Calhoun (MIT Press, Cambridge, Mass., 1992), pp. 73–98. It has been revised for this volume.

1   See Andrew Arato, "Civil Society Against the State: Poland 1980–81," *Telos*, 47 (1981), pp. 23–47, and "Empire vs. Civil Society: Poland 1981–82," *Telos*, 50 (1981–2), pp. 19–48; Andrew Arato and Jean Cohen, *Civil Society and Political Theory* (MIT Press, Cambridge, Mass., 1992); John Keane, ed., *Civil Society and the State: New European Perspectives* and *Democracy and Civil Society* (both Verso, London, 1988).

2   H. Arendt, *The Human Condition* (8th edn, University of Chicago Press, Chicago, 1973), pp. 38–49.

3   See G. W. F. Hegel, *Rechtsphilosophie* (1821), pp. 189ff.; trans. by T. M. Knox as *Hegel's Philosophy of Right* (Clarendon, London, 1973), pp. 126ff.

4   Cf. Christopher Lasch's introduction to the special Hannah Arendt issue of *Salmagundi*, no. 60 (1983), pp. vff.; Jürgen Habermas, "Hannah Arendt's Communications Concept of Power," *Social Research, Hannah Arendt Memorial Issue*, no. 44 (1977), pp 3–24.

5   For a sympathetic critique of Arendt along these lines, cf. Hannah Pitkin, "Justice: On Relating Public and Private," *Political Theory*, 9.3 (1981), pp. 327–52.

6   See Hannah Arendt, *Men in Dark Times*, (Harcourt, Brace and Jovanovich, New York and London, 1968), p. 22; "Preface," in *Between Past and Future: Six Exercises in Political Thought* (Meridian, Cleveland and New York, 1961), p. 14. There is an excellent essay by David Luban, which is one of the few discussions in the literature dealing with Hannah Arendt's methodology of storytelling, cf. D. Luban, "Explaining Dark Times: Hannah Arendt's Theory of Theory," *Social Research*, 5.1, pp. 215–47; see also E. Young-Bruehl, "Hannah Arendt als Geschichtenerzaehlerin," in *Hannah Arendt: Materialien zu Ihrem Werk* (Europaverlog, Munich, 1979), pp. 319–27.

7   H. Arendt, *The Life of the Mind*, vol. 1: *Thinking* (Harcourt, Brace and Jovanovich, New York, 1977), p. 212.

8   Arendt, "Preface," in *Between Past and Future*, p. 5.

9   Cf. Arendt's statement with Note A appended to the English edition of Benjamin's "Theses on the Philosophy of History" (which Arendt edited in English): "Historicism contents itself with establishing a causal connection between various moments in history. But no fact that is cause is for that very reason historical. It became historical posthumously, as it were, through the events that may be separated from it by thousands of years. A historian who takes this as his point of departure stops telling the sequence of events like the beads of a rosary. Instead, he grasps the constellation which his own era has formed with a definite earlier one. Thus he establishes a conception of the present as

the 'time of the now' which is shot through with chips of Messianic time." In Walter Benjamin, *Illuminations*, ed. and introd. H. Arendt (Schocken, New York, 1969).

10 Arendt, *The Human Condition*, pp. 23, 31ff.

11 Arendt, *The Origins of Totalitarianism* (Harcourt, Brace and Jovanovich, New York, 1968), ch. 13, p. 466.

12 Arendt, *The Human Condition*, p. 56.

13 Hannah Arendt's persistent denial of the "women's issue," and her inability to link together the exclusion of women from politics and this agonistic and male-dominated conception of public space, is astounding. The "absence" of women as collective political actors in Arendt's theory – individuals like Rosa Luxemburg are present – is a difficult question, but to begin thinking about this means first challenging the private–public split in her thought as this corresponds to the traditional separation of spheres between the sexes (men = public life; women = private sphere). I explore this issues more extensively in *The Reluctant Modernism of Hannah Arendt* (Sage, Beverly Hills, in preparation).

14 Arendt, "Preface," in *Between Past and Future*, p. 4.

15 See Hannah Arendt, "Reflections on Little Rock," *Dissent*, 6.1 (Winter 1959), pp. 45–56; Ralph Ellison in *Who Speaks for the Negro?*, ed. R. P. Warren (Random House, New York, 1965), pp. 342–4; and Arendt to Ralph Ellison in a letter of July 29, 1965 as cited by Young-Breuhl, *Hannah Arendt. For Love of the World* (Yale University Press, New Haven, 1982), p. 316.

16 Bruce Ackerman, *Social Justice in the Liberal State* (Yale University Press, New Haven, 1980), p. 4.

17 Ibid., p. 11.

18 "Why Dialogue?" *Journal of Philosophy*, 86 (Jan. 1989), here at p. 8.

19 Ibid., p. 9.

20 Ibid., pp. 16–17. Ackerman is unclear if by the principle of "conversational restraint" and "neutrality" he means the version stated in this more recent article, which actually *removes* controversial moral conceptions from the public agenda of debate in the liberal state or if he means the version advocated in *Social Justice in the Liberal State*, which *constrains* the kinds of grounds one can put forward in justifying one's conception of the good without, however, excluding such conceptions from being aired in public, see *Social Justice in the Liberal State*, p. 11. I have no difficulties in accepting the latter argument for reasons explained in chapter 2 above and pertaining to the logic of moral argumentations. It is his most recent version which I find indefensible. Ackerman's reply to his critics, "What is Neutral About Neutrality?" does not clarify the matter further either, see *Ethics*, 93 (Jan. 1983), pp. 372–90.

21 I have modified this paragraph in this version of this article. My original argument which maintained that Ackerman's position "trumped" the views of those primary groups who did not regard "public peace and order" as the supreme good was not quite to the point. Since all of us, the communicative ethicist no less than the liberal theorist, are concerned with peaceful and civil coexistence in complex, modern

societies, the views of groups who reject such principles of coexistence clearly present a limit case in our considerations. Their views, however, can hardly be considered the representative case from which to proceed in deliberating about such matters. The issue of political, cultural and moral marginalization is an extremely difficult one to solve in societies which are increasingly multinational, multiracial and multicultural. My assumption is that the radically open and egalitarian model of public space which I am advocating has more of a chance to give the marginals access to the agenda of the public dialogue, thus eliminating some of the causes of their marginality.

22   Part of the difficulty in Ackerman's position derives from a lack of precision as to what constitutes the "agenda of the liberal state." Does Ackerman mean by this phrase the constitution and debates at the Supreme Court level, or does he mean the electronic and the printed media, or other public fora like mailings, open meetings, etc.? The same constraints of neutrality may not automatically hold for all public fora in our societies; this is why conflicts between the constitutional right of free speech and the actual practice of associations and citizens are likely to be such a recurrent feature of a liberal-democratic society. For example, should racism in the media be allowed? Does artistic freedom allow us to stage plays some may consider "anti-semitic?" I whole-heartedly agree with Ackerman that certain forms of conversational constraints may be wholly appropriate and desirable for the legal system in modern societies. As I have argued in chapter 2, in this context what is meant by the term "neutrality" is that the norms embodied in the legal and public institutions of our societies should be so abstract and general as to permit the flourishing of many different ways of life and many different conceptions of the good. It is plurality, tolerance and diversity in culture, religion, lifestyles, aesthetic taste and personal expression which are to be encouraged. In a situation of conflict among diverse conceptions of the good, appeal must be made to the principles embodied in the constitutions of liberal democracies like basic civil and political rights. The modern legal system mediates among the conflicting claims of various life-forms, lifestyles and visions of the good. In cases of a conflict between the principles of right which make coexistence possible among adherents of divergent conceptions of the good and principles of other more partial conceptions of the good, of which we know that they cannot be generalized beyond their specific adherents, the right trumps over that particular conception of the good. This seems to me to be the only defensible conception of "neutrality" in the liberal state; but the model of conversational restraints which Ackerman has in view does not only limit the *forms of justification* to be used by the major public institutions in our societies, like the Supreme Court, the Congress and the like; instead it limits the *range of debate* in the liberal state which may very well involve divergent, incompatible and even hostile conceptions of the good. As long as this agonistic conversation does not lead to the imposition of one understanding of the good upon all others as the officially sanctioned way of life, there is no reason why these partial conceptions of the good cannot

be out there, competing and arguing with each other, in the public space of the liberal state.

23   It is not inconceivable that there will be situations when restraining public dialogue in a polity may be a morally desirable option. The most frequently cited instances are national security considerations or what the tradition used to describe as "raison d'état." I must admit that I am extremely skeptical even about such prima facie morally plausible cases which would lead to the imposition of "gag rules" in a society. Take the case of the suppression by the State Department and some officials of the media of the news of the extermination of the Jews and the building of concentration camps in Europe during World War II. In order not to exacerbate public pressure for the United States to enter the war, the government temporarily censored this news. Is it so clear, however, which is the better argument in such an instance? Were the national security considerations of the US at that point in time so clearly superior to the moral claims of the European Jews to demand help and an end to their extermination from any source? And may it not have been desirable on moral grounds for the American public to be informed right away and as fully as possible of these circumstances rather than under conditions of a carefully orchestrated war effort? (Cf. David S. Wyman, *The Abandonment of the Jews* (Pantheon, New York, 1984). Ironically, as these lines are being written the military command of the Allied forces in the Persian Gulf and the news media are struggling over the justification for and the extent of the military censorship on coverage of events in the Gulf. No party to this controversy challenges the principle that in a situation of war, in order not to violate the safety of troops or reveal information about logistics, transportation and sensitive equipment certain restraints should be respected. Beyond this self-imposed rules of journalistic restraint, the exercise of military censorship violates the public's right to know and to form an opinion on a matter as crucial as war and peace. The situation in the Persian Gulf shows once more the incompatibility of democracy and "gag rules" in a society. I believe that the moral burden of proof in cases when such restrictions on free speech and the free flow of information are imposed is almost always on the shoulders of the advocates of "gag rules." Nonetheless, every polity in which political discourse is an institution respects certain constraints of the use of free speech; furthermore, individuals and associations may be guided by a certain sense of what is appropriate "public speech." A philosophical and moral theory of public dialogue, which views this as a procedure for moral legitimation, accepts constitutional guarantees to free speech as well as suggesting some norms of public dialogue. But insofar as it is also critical of existing relations such a view may challenge both existing legal practices and cultural codes of speech from the standpoint of a moral norm.

24   Benjamin Barber, *The Conquest of Politics: Liberal Philosophy in Democratic Times* (Princeton University Press, Princeton, NJ, 1988), p. 18.

25   John Rawls, "The Idea of an Overlapping Consensus," *Oxford Journal of Legal Studies*, 7.1 (1987), p. 8.

26 Ibid., p. 21.

27 This connection between the model of reasoning appropriate for corporate bodies and the idea of free public reason is more clear in John Rawls, "On the Idea of Free Public Reason," lecture delivered at the conference on Liberalism and the Moral Life at the City University of New York in April 1988.

28 Barber, *The Conquest of Politics*, p. 151.

29 I owe this phrase to Nancy Fraser who introduces it in the context of her discussion of discourses in the welfare state, cf. Nancy Fraser, *Unruly Practices: Power, Discourse and Gender in Contemporary Social Theory* (Polity, Cambridge, 1989), pp. 144ff.

30 John Rawls, "The Idea of an Overlapping Consensus," p. 14, note 22.

31 Ibid.

32 See Hannah Arendt, *The Origins of Totalitarianism*, part 2, ch. 5, and *On Revolution* (Viking, New York, 1969), pp. 147ff.

33 J. Habermas, *Structural Transformation of the Public Sphere*, trans. Thomas Burger (MIT Press, Boston, 1989); originally appeared as *Strukturwandel der Öffentlichkeit* (Luchterland, Darmstadt and Neuwied 1962).

34 The following is a condensed summary of the argument of the second volume of *The Theory of Communicative Action*, and in particular of the chapter on the "Dialectics of Rationalization" (Beacon, Boston, 1985).

35 Jean Cohen, "Discourse Ethics and Civil Society," *Philosophy and Social Criticism*, 14.3–4 (1988), p. 328.

36 Kenneth Baynes, "The Liberal/Communitarian Controversy and Communicative Ethics," *Philosophy and Social Criticism*, 14.3–4 (1988), p. 304.

37 Ibid. See my discussion of this issue above, pp. 32–3.

38 Ibid., p. 305.

39 The step leading from the norms of "universal moral respect" and "egalitarian reciprocity" to basic rights and liberties is not a very big one, but one which will not be undertaken in this essay. Suffice it to say that a discourse theory of basic rights and liberties needs to be developed.

40 Cf. below, "The Generalized and the Concrete Other: The Kohlberg-Gilligan Controversy and Moral Theory."

41 L. Stone, *The Family, Sex and Marriage in England*, abridged edn (Harper and Row, New York, 1979).

42 Nancy Fraser has raised these considerations pointedly in her, "What's Critical about Critical Theory? The Case of Habermas and Gender," in *Feminism as Critique*, ed. Seyla Benhabib and Drucilla Cornell (University of Minnesota Press, Minneapolis, 1987), pp. 31–56.

43 Nancy Fraser has argued that Habermas's model of public space is also incompatible with feminist aspirations insofar as it is unitary as opposed to being multiple, dispersed and plural; is overly rationalistic and privileges rational speech over more evocative and rhetorical modes of public speech; and is prudish in that it minimizes the role of the body and the carnivalesque elements in public self-presentation. I agree with Fraser about the last two criticisms although in my opinion these do not affect the *principle* of the public sphere itself, that is the

necessity of discursive justification of democratic politics; these observations only highlight the need to give a less rationalistic formulation of
this principle than Habermas himself has done. As far as the charge of
monism versus plurality of public spaces is concerned, I believe that
Fraser here misreads Habermas and that in principle there can be as
many publics as there are discourses concerning controversial norms.
Thus there is today in the USA a "public" on the pornography debate
in which lawmakers, the art community, the various religious institutions, the women's movement with its theorists and activists are
participants. The "public sphere" of the pornography debate is not
necessarily coextensive with the public sphere of the foreign policy
debate in which all of us as citizens are more or less involved. I see no
evidence, textual or otherwise, that Habermas's concept of the public
sphere must be monistic. See Nancy Fraser, "Rethinking the Public
Sphere: A Contribution to the Critique of Actually Existing Democracy," in *Habermas and the Public Sphere*, ed. Calhoun, pp. 109–42; for
Habermas's recent formulations on the issue, see the statement: "The
idea of people's sovereignty is dematerialized (*entsubstantialisiert*) in this
process. Even the suggestion that a network of associations can assume
the place of the now displaced body of the people remains too con-
cretistic. Sovereignty which is now completely dispersed does not even
embody itself in the minds of the associated members [of the polity –
S.B.], rather – if we can still use the term embodiment at all – it is in
those subjectless forms of communication that regulate the flow of
discursive opinion and will-formation that such sovereignty finds
its place. The regulation of opinion and will-formation through such
subjectless networks of communication gives rise to fallibilistic conclusions which we can presume to incorporate practical reason. When
popular sovereignty becomes subjectless and anonymous and is dissolved into processes of intersubjectivity, it limits itself to democratic
procedures and to the ambitious communicative presuppositions of
their implementation." J. Habermas, "Ist der Herzschlag der Revolution
zum Stillstand gekommen? Volkssouveränität als Verfahren. Ein nor-
mativer Begriff der Öffentlichkeit?" in *Die Ideen von 1789 in der deutschen
Rezeption*, ed. Forum für Philosophie Bad Homburg (Suhrkamp,
Frankfurt am Main, 1989), pp. 7–37, here pp. 30–1.

44 Jean Cohen, "Discourse Ethics and Civil Society," p. 321. Cf. also
Cohen's suggestion: "In point of fact, however, discourse ethics logi-
cally presupposes *both* classes of rights. By basing rights not on an
individualistic ontology, as classical liberals have done, but on the
theory of communicative interaction, we have strong reason to emphasize the cluster of rights of communication. . . . The rights of privacy
would be affirmed because of the need to reproduce autonomous
personalities without which rational discourse would be impossible. . . .
From this point of view, the rights of communication point us to the
legitimate domain for formulating and defending rights. The rights
of the personality identify the subjects who have the rights to have
rights." Ibid., p. 327. Cf. also Baynes, "The Liberal/Communitarian
Controversy and Communicative Ethics," pp. 304ff.

45   Kiku Adatto has provided an impressive empirical study on the trans-
     formations of the television coverage of presidential elections by the
     three major evening newscasts of ABC, CBS and NBC from 1968 to
     1988. Two empirical findings stand out most saliently and indicate why
     "the democratic public space" is increasingly less a reality in American
     political life. Adatto reports that: "The average 'sound bite,' or block of
     uninterrupted speech, fell from 42.3 seconds for presidential candidates
     in 1968 to only 9.8 seconds in 1988. In 1968, almost half of all sound
     bites were 40 seconds or more, compared to less than one percent in
     1988. . . . In 1968, most of the time we saw the candidates on the
     evening news, we also heard them speaking. In 1988 the reverse was
     true; most of the time we saw the candidates, someone else, usually a
     reporter, was doing the talking." Adatto observes that in this process
     "television displaced politics as the focus of coverage . . . the images
     that once formed the background of political events – the setting
     and the stagecraft – now occupied the foreground." See Kiku Adatto,
     "Sound Bite Democracy: Network Evening News Presidential
     Campaign Coverage," Research Paper R-2, Joan Shorenstein Barone
     Center on Press, Politics and Public Policy (June 1990), pp. 4–5.
46   Helga Maria Hernes, *Welfare State and Woman Power. Essays in State
     Feminism* (Norwegian University Press, London, 1987).
47   Cf. Nancy Fraser, *Unruly Practices: Power, Discourse and Gender in Late-
     Capitalist Social Theory*, ch. 7, "Women, Welfare, and the Politics of
     Need Interpretation."
48   For a very good example of the first trend, see Rosemarie Tong, *Women,
     Sex and the Law* (Rowman and Littlefield, Totowa, NJ, 1984); for the
     second trend see Catharine MacKinnon's work, and the amazing
     "return of the repressed" Marxist orthodoxy of the state and the law in
     her writings, cf. her early article, "Feminism, Marxism, Method and
     the State: An Agenda for Theory", *Signs* 7.3 (Spring 1982), pp. 514ff.;
     "Feminism, Marxism, Method and the State: Towards a Feminist Juris-
     prudence," *Signs*, 8 (Summer 1983), pp. 645ff.; and the more recent
     Feminism Unmodified: Discourses on Life and Law (Harvard University
     Press, Cambridge, Mass., 1987).

4   Judgment and the Moral Foundations of Politics in Hannah Arendt's Thought

In a democratic polity agreement among citizens generated through processes of public dialogue is central to the legitimacy of basic institutions. Such dialogues submit the rationale behind the major power arrangements of societies to the test. Insight into the justice or injustice, fairness or unfairness of these arrangements gained as a result of such dialogic exchanges results in public knowledge won through public deliberation. Even when such processes of dialogue convince us that these power structures need alteration, when we reach this judgment as a result of participatory politics we not only have the assurance that we can support our position by principled argument but also, and more importantly, we form a judgment having submitted our opinion to the test of the judgment of others. Perhaps the most valuable outcome of such authentic processes of public dialogue when compared to the mere exchange of information or the mere circulation of images is that, when and if they occur, such public conversations result in the cultivation of the faculty of judgment and the formation of an "enlarged mentality." This chapter explores judgment as a moral and political faculty by taking its cue from Hannah Arendt's rereading of Kant's *Critique of Judgment*.

Judgment and Moral Considerations

Hannah Arendt's incomplete reflections on judgment, intended to be the third volume of her work, *The Life of the Mind*, are puzzling. The perplexing quality of these reflections derives less from the burden on contemporary students of her thought to seek to understand and imaginatively complete what an author might have intended to but was unable to say in her lifetime. This hermeneutic puzzle arises from three sets of claims which Arendt makes about judgment and which stand in tension to each other.

First, in the introduction to the first volume of *The Life of the Mind* Arendt clarifies that her preoccupation with the mental activities of thinking, willing and judging had two different origins.[1] The immediate impulse came from her attending the Eichmann trial in Jerusalem; the additional, but equally important, prompting was provided by her desire to explore the counterpart of the *Vita Activa* (which in English translation misleadingly appeared as *The Human Condition*) in the *Vita Contemplativa*. In coining the phrase "the banality of evil" and in explaining the moral quality of Eichmann's deeds in terms other than the monstrous or demonic nature of the doer, Arendt became aware of going counter to the tradition of western thought that saw evil in metaphysical terms as ultimate depravity, corruption or sinfulness. The most striking quality of Eichmann, she claimed, was not stupidity or wickedness or depravity but one she described as "thoughtlessness." This in turn led her to the question:

> Might the problem of good and evil, our faculty for telling right from wrong, be connected with our faculty of thought? . . . Could the activity of thinking as such, the habit of examining whatever happens to come to pass or attract attention, regardless of results and specific contents, could this activity be among the conditions that make men abstain from evil-doing or even actually "condition" them against it?[2]

Arendt pursued this question in a lecture on "Thinking and Moral Considerations" published in *Social Research* in 1971, around the same time that she was composing the volume on *Thinking*. Again she asked: "Is our ability to judge, to tell right from wrong, beautiful from ugly, dependent upon our faculty of thought? Does the inability to think and a disastrous failure of what we commonly call conscience coincide?"[3]

As these passages indicate, in approaching the problem of judgment Arendt was primarily interested in the interrelationships between thinking and judging as moral faculties. She was concerned with judgment as the faculty of "telling right from wrong."

In the second place, and in contrast to her interest in judgment as a moral faculty, Arendt also focussed on judgment as the retrospective faculty of culling meaning from the past, as a faculty essential to the art of storytelling. In the Postscriptum to the volume on *Thinking*, she briefly outlines how she proposes to handle the problem of judgment in volume 3. She still intends to discuss judgment as it is related to "the problem of theory and practice and to all attempts to arrive at a halfway plausible theory of ethics."[4] But her last paragraph to the Postscriptum turns from ethics to the problem of history. She intends to deny history's right of being the ultimate judge – "Die Weltgeschichte ist das Weltgericht" (Hegel) – without denying history's importance. As Richard Bernstein and Ronald Beiner have observed, in these subsequent reflections Arendt's interest appears to have shifted from the standpoint of the actor, judging in order to act, to that of the spectator, judging in order to cull meaning from the past.[5]

Third, Arendt's reflections on judgment do not only vacillate between judgment as a moral faculty, guiding action, versus judgment as a retrospective faculty, guiding the spectator or the story teller. There is an even deeper philosophical perplexity about the status of judgment in her work. This concerns her attempt to bring together the Aristotelian conception of judgment as an aspect of phronesis with the Kantian understanding of judgment as the faculty of "enlarged thought" or "representative thinking." As Christopher Lasch has observed:

> On the one hand, Arendt's defense of judgment as the quintessential political virtue seems to lead to an Aristotelian conception of politics as a branch of practical reason. On the other hand, her appeal to Kant as the source of her ideas about judgment appeals to a very different conception of politics, in which political action has to be grounded not in the practical arts but in universal moral principles. . . . Arendt's discussion of judgment, instead of clarifiying the difference between ancient and modern conceptions of morality and politics, seems to confuse the two.[6]

In this chapter I propose to examine some of these hermeneutical puzzles by focussing on one aspect of Arendt's reflections on judgment in particular. Although Arendt herself never made good on the "attempt to arrive at a halfway plausible theory of ethics" and instead called judgment "the most political" of all our cognitive faculties, I intend to argue that Arendt's characterization of action through the categories of natality, plurality and narrativity provides us with an illuminating framework for analyzing judgment not only as a political but as a moral faculty; furthermore, although Arendt provided us with an intriguing beginning point for thinking about the interrelationship of morality and politics, she herself was misled in these matters by a quasi-intuitionist concept of moral conscience on the one hand and an unusually narrow concept of morality on the other.

My purpose is to think with Arendt against Arendt. I will follow her inconclusive reflections on judgment to develop a phenomenological analysis of judgment as a moral faculty, but at the same time I will criticize her own problematic separation of morality from politics. However, I will also place Arendt's ruminations on this matter in the context of some contemporary debates in practical philosophy between neo-Aristotelians and neo-Kantians. This line of analysis will allow me to address the difficulty raised by Christopher Lasch. It may be that Arendt's attempt to bring together the Aristotelian concern with particulars in practical matters with a principled, universalist moral standpoint is not simply confusing but contains an insight very much worth developing. Arendt's incomplete doctrine of judgment, by weakening the opposition between contextual judgment and a universalist morality, could help us see through some false fronts in contemporary moral and political theory.

Judgment and Action

Let me begin with a general observation. We speak of judgment in many domains. Legal, aesthetic, medical, therapeutic, musical, military, interpretive-hermeneutic judgments are as much a part of our common vocabulary as are moral and political judgment. Moral and political judgments differ from these other exercises of judgment in one respect. Prima facie in the domains of law, aesthetics, medicine, therapy, music, the military, and the hermeneutic interpretation of texts we seem ready to admit that those exercising judgment are in possession of a special body of knowledge, and of a particular expertise or experience related to the frequent exercise of this body of knowledge. The exercise of judgment in these domains evokes immediately a distinction between the experts or the practitioners and a lay public that is neither in possession of this specialized body of knowledge nor experienced in its exercise.

In the case of moral and political judgment matters are different. Since I take moral judgment to be fundamentally distinct from all other forms of judgment in one crucial respect, which I will explain below, let me deal with political judgment first. At first sight, there appears to be no reason as to why we should not ascribe the expertise of political judgment to certain special individuals like statespersons, diplomats, elected representatives, administrative officers and the like. In fact, we might assume that ideally, even when not in practice, one reason for these individuals to hold the offices they do is their ability to exercise the kinds of judgments demanded from them by their tasks.

This model of political judgment, which views it as a form of expert opinion, is inadequate from the standpoint of a theory of democracy. Even if we abstract for a moment from the question of representative versus participatory democracy, the exercise of political judgment in a democratic polity cannot be relegated only to experts. Even in narrow models of representative democracy, the public, the citizens, are still expected to exercise their political judgment at least on election day. Citizens in a democratic polity are capable of exercising judgment in several areas. First, they have to be able to judge the relation between the possible in a social and political system and the desirable from some normative standpoint of justice, fairness, equality and freedom. Second, they have to be able to judge the capacity of this specific individual and organization to carry out their mandate. Finally they have to be able to judge the forseeable consequences of their choices from the standpoint of the past, present and future of their polity.

Participatory models of democracy see participation as a good in itself, to be extended as widely as possible. In these theories, both the domains in which the public is entitled to exercise political judgment and their institutional possibilities for doing so become political issues. A critique of the culture of experts, and the transfer of the power and prerogative of judgment from experts to the public are thus viewed as essential to the constitution of a democratic ethos. In other words, the very definition of political judgment – what it is, who is entitled to exercise it, and how people can be further enabled to exercise it – is itself a political and normative question, invoking principles of the politically desirable as well as crucial assessments of the politically feasible. There can be no value-neutral theory of political judgment; a theory of political judgment is itself a normative theory of the most desirable political order.

This contestable and contested quality of political judgment sheds new light upon all other domains of judgment – legal, aesthetic, therapeutic, military and medical. In each of these domains, judgment, as a social process of appropriating and exercising knowledge, can become a political question that involves debate and contestation about the limits, duties and capacities of expert authority in relation to the lay public.

Moral judgment differs from these other domains in one crucial respect: the exercise of moral judgment is pervasive and unavoidable; in fact, this exercise is coextensive with relations of social interaction in the lifeworld in general. *Moral judgment is what we "always already" exercise in virtue of being immersed in a network of human relationships that constitute our life together.* Whereas there can be reasonable debate about whether or not to exercise juridical, military, therapeutic, aesthetic, or even political judgment, in the case of moral judgment this option is not there. The domain of the moral is so deeply enmeshed with those interactions that constitute our lifeworld that to withdraw from moral judgment is tantamount to ceasing to interact, to talk and act in the human community.

To justify my claim that moral judgment is what we "always already" exercise in virtue of being immersed in a network of human relations, I want to begin by recalling the most salient features of action as Arendt introduces them in *The Human Condition*.[7] These are natality, plurality and the immersion of action in a web of interpretations which I shall call "narrativity." Natality is like a "second birth," according to Arendt. It is that quality through which we insert ourselves into the world, this time not through the mere fact of being born but through the initiation of words and deeds. This initiation of words and deeds, which Arendt names "the principle of beginning" (HC, p. 177), can no more be avoided than the fact of birth itself. The child becomes a member of a human community in that it learns to initiate speech and action. Although an unavoidable aspect of human acculturation, the condition of natality implies no determinism. Just as every speaker of a language has a capacity to generate an infinite number of grammatically well-formed sentences, the doer of deeds has a capacity to initiate always the unexpected and the improbable which nonetheless belongs to the possible repertoire of human action and conduct.

Whereas action corresponds to the fact of birth, "speech corresponds to the fact of distinctness and is the actualization of the human condition of plurality, that is, of living as a distinct and unique being among equals" (HC, p. 178). Plurality, which is revealed in speech, is rooted in the fact of human equality, which in this context does not mean moral and political equality but rather a generic equality of the human constitution that allows humans to understand each other (HC, p. 175). Whereas in the case of other species, this generic equality defines the individuality of each member of a species, in the case of humans the distinctness of individuals from one another is revealed through speech. We can say that the human capacity to use speech leads to a differentiation of the repertoire of activities beyond those which are species specific as well as allowing the emergence of a differentiated subjectivity in the inner life of the self. Speech differentiates action from mere behavior; the one who speaks is also the one who thinks, feels and experiences in a certain way. The individuation of the human self is simultaneously the process whereby this self becomes capable of action and of expressing the subjectivity of the doer.

Speech and action are fundamentally related, and "many, and even most acts," observes Arendt, "are performed in the manner of speech" (HC, p. 178). Speech and action have a revelatory quality: they reveal the "whoness" of the doer. This revelation of the whoness of the actor is always a revealing to somebody who is like oneself. Only if somebody else is able to understand the meaning of our words as well as the whatness of our deeds can the identity of the self be said to be revealed. Action and speech, therefore, are essentially interaction. They take place between humans.

Narrativity, or the immersion of action in a web of human relationships, is the mode through which the self is individuated and acts are identified. Both the whatness of the act and the whoness of the self are disclosed to agents capable of communicative understanding. Actions are identified narratively. Somebody has always done such-and-such at some point in time. To identify an action is to tell the story of its initiation, of its unfolding, and of its immersion in a web of relations constituted through the actions and narratives of others. Likewise, the whoness of the self is constituted by the story of a life – a coherent narrative of which we are always the protagonist, but not always the author or the producer. Narrativity is the mode through which actions are individuated and the identity of the self constituted.

Of course, these claims concerning the role of narrative in the individuation of actions and the constitution of self-identity are not uncontested. The tendency in the philosophical tradition has been to view these phenomena along the models of substance and accidents or a thing and its properties. The self becomes the "I know not what" underlying or suspending its actions. These, in turn, are not considered as meaningful deeds that reveal something to someone but rather as properties of bodies. The self whom Hume stumbles upon while ruminating in his consciousness, or the Kantian "I" that accompanies all my representations is not the self in the human community, the acting or interacting self, but the self qua thinker, qua subject of consciousness withdrawn from the world.

There is a fundamental connection between the tradition's ignoring of the question of judgment in moral life and the neglect of the specificity of action as speech and action or communicative interaction. Once we see moral action as interaction, performed toward others and in the company of others, the role of judgment emerges in at least three relevant areas of moral interaction.[8] These are the assessment of one's duties, the assessment of one's actions as fulfilling these duties, and the assessment of one's maxims as embodied, expressed or revealed in actions.

Toward a Phenomenology of Moral Judgment

Although the clash of moral duties is a frequently acknowledged topic in moral philosophy, the exercise of judgment concerned with the assessment of one's duties in particular situations arises even when there is no such clash. Consider a moral duty like generosity. How does an agent recognize *this particular situation* as being one that calls for the duty of generosity? Suppose through some circumstances, the details of which are not exactly clear, a friend in the publishing business manages to squander the family fortune, and is heavily in debt. We must first determine whether these particular circumstances are ones in which such a duty of generosity has a claim on what we are to do. But how do we determine the claims of the circumstances upon us? Note that this question does not concern the moral duty an agent acknowledges to be generous. It concerns the interpretation of the duty of generosity in this particular case. Is an individual who squanders the family fortune through her own deeds one that deserves my generosity? If I know from the previous history of the person her tendency to be reckless with money, would or should this influence my deliberations in the matter? The general rule of generosity – to help those in need – does not aid here, for the issue is whether this particular situation is one in which this rule leads to a moral claim upon me. My first thesis is: *The exercise of moral judgment that is concerned with the epistemic identification of human situations and circumstances as morally relevant does not proceed according to the model of the subsumption of a particular under a universal.* By "morally relevant" I mean a situation or a circumstance so defined that it would lead to the formulation of a prima facie moral duty among those involved.

What about the assessment of one's action then? Suppose I resolve the above situation by deciding in favor of helping my friend. How should this act of generosity be exercised? Whereas in the first instance we were asking, is this situation morally relevant for me because it imposes upon me the duty of generosity, now we are asking, what is it that I must do to fulfill this duty? Suppose, after deciding to help this friend, I go up to her in the midst of a crowded cocktail party and say that I know she is broke and here is a certain amount of money which I hope she will use better next time. Have I acted generously? Have I humiliated this individual? Have I simply exhibited my egotistic desire for praise from others? In other words, what I do, which course of action I decide upon, involves some interpretive ability to see my act not only as it relates to me but as it will be perceived and understood by others. I must have enough moral imagination to know the possible act descriptions or narratives that my action can be subsumed under. My second thesis is: *The identity of a moral action is not one that can be construed in light of a general rule governing particular instances but entails the exercise of moral imagination which activates our capacity for thinking of possible narratives and act descriptions in light of which our actions can be understood by others.*

Finally, let me turn to the assessment of one's maxim. It might appear that this area of moral considerations at least should be immune to the interpretive indeterminacy of moral judgment and imagination. I know what I want to do, it might be said, what my intentions are, even though my capacity to understand and to foresee what others think or might think, how they might construe my actions, may be limited or simply of no great interest to me. Indeed, there is often a clash between the whatness of a deed in the eyes of others and the whoness of the agent performing it. Actors are also sufferers; they not only act but become the object of the tale of others. Despite this oft-noted and unavoidable cleavage between intention and action, once they become a part of the world, actions reveal our intentions, and sometimes we do not know what our intentions are or may have been until our actions have become a part of the world. In formulating intentions, we project ourselves, our narrative history into the world and we want to be recognized as the doer of such and such. We identify our intentions in terms of a narrative of which we ourselves are the author. This narrative entails both knowledge of our past, and self-projection, desires for our future. It also anticipates the meaning that this past and future may have and will have in the eyes of others. The self is not only an I but a me, one that is perceived by others, interpreted and judged by others. The perspectives of the I and the me must somehow be integrated to succeed in making our intentions communicable. My third thesis is this. *The assessment of the maxim of one's intentions, as these embody moral principles, requires understanding the narrative history of the self who is the actor; this understanding discloses both self-knowledge and knowledge of oneself as viewed by others.*

What I have described so far may be considered a phenomenology of moral judgment. I have argued that if one proceeds from the model of moral action as communicative interaction, as speech and deed, moral judgment is relevant in three domains: in the assessment of morally relevant situations, in the identification of morally correct actions, and in the interpretation of the intentions and maxims of the moral agent. The assessment of morally relevant situations cannot be explained in light of the subsumptive model of judgment; the identification of morally correct actions requires moral imagination of possible act descriptions and narratives under which they fall; and the interpretation of one's intentions and maxims entails comprehension of narrative histories – both one's own and those of others.

Judgment in Kant's Moral Philosophy

Arendt's characterization of human action in terms of natality, plurality and narrativity provides us with an excellent beginning point for developing a phenomenology of moral judgment. I now would like to turn briefly to the status of judgment in Kant's moral philosophy. For as Richard Bernstein has also noted, one of the most perplexing aspects of Arendt's discussion of judgment consists of the following: "Arendt well knew that, even though she invokes the name of Kant, she was radically departing from Kant. There is no question in Kant that the 'ability of tell right from wrong' is a matter of practical reason and not the faculty of reflective judgment which ascends from particulars to generals or universals."[9] The question is whether the rather perfunctory role that moral judgment plays in Kant's practical philosophy is not related to his two-world metaphysics and to the denigration of action that follows from it. In explaining Arendt's relation to Kant on these matters, one must first consider Kant's theory of action.

Kant, in fact, did not completely ignore the role of judgment in practical philosophy. Judgment, "as the faculty of thinking the particular under the universal," is determinant when the universal is given and the particular is merely to be subsumed under it.[10] It is reflective, if only the particular is given and the universal has to be found for it. Since according to Kant, the moral law, as the universal guiding moral action, is in all circumstances given, moral judgment is determinant rather than reflective. Let me ask whether, even according to Kant's own reasoning, moral judgments can be merely determinant, that is whether they merely entail the subsumption of the particular under the universal law.

In the section "Of the Topic of Pure Practical Reason" in the *Critique of Practical Reason* Kant writes: "To decide whether an action which is possible for us in the sensuous world is or is not a case under the rule requires practical judgment, which applies what is asserted universally in the rule (in abstracto) to an action in concreto."[11] This problem presents special difficulties. Since an action determined by the law of practical reason must contain no other ground for its occurrence than the conception of the moral law, and since "all instances of possible action," according to Kant, "are only empirical and can belong only to experience and nature," it is absurd to wish to find an instance in the world of sense which allows the application of the law of freedom to it.[12] Kant sums up the difficulty:

> The morally good, on the contrary, is something which, by its object, is supersensuous; nothing corresponding to it can be found in sen-

suous intuition; consequently, judgment under laws of pure practical reason seems to be subject to special difficulties, which result from the fact that a law of freedom is to be applied to actions which are events occurring in the world of sense and thus, to this extent, belonging to nature.[13]

In this discussion Kant assumes that every action is an event in the world falling under natural laws. Yet for freedom to be possible, he also has to admit that although all actions, once performed, become events in the world, some actions must be caused by the idea of the moral law alone. What distinguishes a moral from a non-moral action is the ground of its determination, that is the nature of the principles governing one's maxims alone. Furthermore, only such actions can be morally good.

As is often the case, in his considerations on this matter Kant conflates two issues. First is a question we may name the epistemology of human actions. How can they be identified and individuated? Kant's metaphysics of two worlds, the noumenal and the phenomenal, leads him to the view that all actions once they become deeds in the world are events. But the problem is not whether actions are not also events, but whether the language of natural events is epistemologically adequate to describe human actions. Even as events in the world, human actions can only be understood with reference to reasons, that is with reference to the meaningful grounds or principles which act as their causes. Reasons are of such a kind that they require to be understood; they can only be described from the participants' or actors' own perspectives. I am not suggesting that an objectivating science of human action is not possible, but only that understanding – *Verstehen* – is an essential component of any such science of human action as well. Under the spell of the exaggerated promises of Newtonian science, Kant dissolves all distinction between natural, human and the social sciences, and simply takes it for granted that a natural, Newtonian science of human action is possible.

The second question which guides Kant is the distinction between the morally right and the morally good. Actions that are morally right are in conformity with the moral law; but only those that have the duty to conform to the moral law as their sole ground or motivational purpose are morally good. The distinction between the morally right and the morally good is not counter-intuitive; for it is possible to do the right thing for the wrong reasons. The intentions of the doer are obviously an essential, though by no means the sole, component of the moral quality or virtue of an action. Where Kant seems to go wrong though is in his insistence that we can never know if an action was morally virtuous in this sense at all, since the

morally good defies embodiment in the phenomenal world. We
might say with Hegel that "the purity of heart" becomes a chimera
in Kant's moral philosophy. As soon as it is embodied in action and
becomes a part of the world, it becomes impure; yet to embody the
good will in action is the only mark of freedom and moral dignity.
Thus we seem to be free only when we act, yet become unfree as
soon as we act. The way out of this quandary, I want to suggest,
is not to deny the distinction between the morally good and the
morally right but to reject the two-world metaphysics of Kantian
theory in favor of a social epistemology which can do justice to the
description and explanation of human action and interaction.[14]
Thus, although Kant does not ignore the role of judgment in practical philosophy, his reflections on this matter get mired in the
problem of his two-world metaphysics and preclude a closer examination of what may be involved in the exercise of moral judgment. I
have already argued that the assessment of one's duties in a concrete case depends upon the recognition of certain situations as
being morally relevant, and that this judgment cannot be explained
in light of the subsumptive model. Furthermore, the identification of
morally correct actions requires – *pace* Kant – the exercise of imagination in the articulation of possible narratives and act-descriptions
under which our deeds might fall; finally the interpretation of one's
actions and maxims entail the understanding of the narrative history
of the self and of others. These hermeneutic-interpretive operations
constitute an aspect of the contextualization of all moral principles in
specific instances. Judgment is not the faculty of subsuming a particular under a universal but the faculty of contextualizing the universal such that it comes to bear upon the particular.

Are we now in a position to answer the question why Arendt,
who repeatedly emphasized that judgment was a faculty of "telling
right from wrong" and not just the beautiful from the ugly, continued to appeal to Kant's doctrine of reflective judgment as a model
for judgment in general?[15] Clearly, Arendt had no use for Kant's
two-world metaphysics and for the denigration of human action
which resulted from it. In this respect, Kant only shared the contempt for the vita activa characteristic of the philosophical tradition as a whole. What Arendt saw in Kant's doctrine of aesthetic
judgment was something else. In Kant's conception of reflective
judgment, restricted by Kant himself – erroneously in Arendt's
eyes – to the aesthetic realm alone, Arendt discovered a procedure
for ascertaining intersubjective validity in the public realm. This
kind of intersubjective validity clearly transcended the expression of
simple preference while falling short of the a priori and certain
validity demanded by Kantian reason. Let us recall Kant's description of "reflective judgment":[16]

by the name sensus communis is to be understood the idea of a public sense, i.e. a critical faculty which in its reflective act takes account (a priori) of the mode of representation of everyone else, in order, as it were, to weigh its judgment with the collective reason of mankind, and thereby avoid the illusion arising from subjective and personal conditions which could readily be taken for objective . . . This is accomplished by weighing the judgment, not so much with actual, as rather with the merely possible, judgments of others, and by putting ourselves in the position of every one else.

In her early essay on "The Crisis in Culture," Arendt provides an illuminating gloss on this passage. She writes:

The power of judgment rests on a potential agreement with others, and the thinking process which is active in judging something is not, like the thought process of pure reasoning, a dialogue between me and myself, but finds itself always and primarily, even if I am quite alone in making up my mind, in an anticipated communication with others with whom I know I must finally come to some agreement. From this potential agreement judgment derives its specific validity. This means, on the one hand, that such judgment must liberate itself from the "subjective private conditions", that is, from the idiosyncracies which naturally determine the outlook of each individual in his privacy and are legitimate as long as they are only privately held opinions but which are not fit to enter the market place, and lack all validity in the public realm. And this enlarged way of thinking, which as judgment knows how to transcend its individual limitations, cannot function in strict isolation or solitude; it needs the presence of others "in whose place" it must think, whose perspective it must take into consideration, and without whom it never has the opportunity to operate at all.[17]

The answer then to the question as to why Arendt did not explore her departure from Kant in these matters is primarily that in Kant's discovery of the "enlarged mentality" Arendt saw the model for the kind of intersubjective validity we could hope to attain in the public realm. Why she saw such an "enlarged mentality" as specifically political rather than moral, however, has to do with her own rather narrow conception of the moral domain.

Neo-Kantian and Neo-Aristotelian Perspectives on Judgment

Prior to exploring the relationship between the moral and the political in Arendt's thought, we must consider the following objection to what has been said so far: Is it in fact possible to combine a phenomenology of moral judgment, based upon an Arendtian conception of action, with a Kantian model of intersubjective validity? While the first line of thinking is more characteristic of the Aristotelian tradition with its emphasis on context and narrative-bound particulars, the Kantian model of reflective judgment makes no such reference to contextuality and enjoins us abstractly "to think from the standpoint of everyone else." Whereas in the Aristotelian model it is the exemplary quality of the judgment of the *phronimos* which grants it validity, in the Kantian model the ground of the validity of our (aesthetic) judgments is their universal communicability with the hope of winning the assent of all.

Clearly to suggest that Arendt or anybody could simply combine or integrate these modes of thought into a frictionless unity would be equivalent to wanting to square the circle. There are fundamental metaphysical assumptions dividing Aristotle and Kant, and these underlie their theories of ethics and politics. Yet in contemporary debates among Kantians and Aristotelians, these metaphysical assumptions play hardly a role. Neo-Aristotelians like Gadamer, Taylor and MacIntyre base their practical philosophies neither upon an Aristotelian metaphysical teleology nor on an Aristotelian theory of form and matter. Equally, neo-Kantians like Rawls, Gewirth, Apel and Habermas reject Kant's two-world metaphysics as well as his Newtonian theory of action. A central issue in the current debate is whether a universalist moral standpoint must be formalistic, a prioristic and context insensitive or whether moral universalism can be reconciled with contextual sensitivity.[18]

It is at this juncture that Arendt's prima facie implausible synthesis of Aristotelian and Kantian elements proves fruitful. Here I can only suggest what an Arendtian contribution to this debate might be. Arendt intimated that intrinsic to Kant's model of "reflective judgment" may be a conception of rationality and intersubjective validity which would allow us to retain a principled universalist moral standpoint while acknowledging the role of contextual moral judgment in human affairs. Let me expand. Consider first a Kantian objection to the phenomenology of moral judgment presented above. What you have described, a Kantian might object, is an art of cleverness in human matters, "eine Geschicklichkeit auf Menschen und ihren Willen Einfluss zu haben" – a certain skill in influencing others and their will.[19] Certainly, the objection continues, the hermeneutic and interpretive abilities you describe are relevant in human company and for human sociability, but what lends them their moral quality is that they are guided by moral principles. In the absence of such moral principles, these hermeneutic-interpretive skills can be utilized to manipulate people, or to produce the semblance of virtue without its existence. As Kant pointedly writes:

"Ebenso gibt es Sitten (Conduite) ohne Tugend, Hoeflichkeit ohne Wohlwollen, Anstaendigkeit ohne Ehrbarkeit, usw." ("Likewise, there can be ethical conduct (conduite in French) without virtue, politeness without good will, and decency without honorableness."[20]

This Kantian objection applies to all variants of neo-Aristotelian theories in which the relationship of moral judgment to moral principles, and the grounds of the validity of the latter are left unclear. As the debate over the narrow or wider meaning of Aristotle's concept of prudence, phronesis shows, there are some crucial ambiguities in this concept.[21] At times phronesis is interpreted in the narrow sense as entailing the choice of means to a given end whose validity itself is not further investigated. Others, like Gadamer, interpret phronesis more widely as entailing not only knowledge of means but also of ends that constitute our life as a whole.[22] Yet compare the following statement from *Truth and Method* in which Gadamer himself reverts to the Aristotelian language of "seeing" and "the archer hitting the mark"[23] in describing the activities of the phronimos.

> From this it follows that ultimately all moral actions require taste – not as if this most individual balancing of decisions is the only thing that governs them, but it is an indispensable element. It is truly an act of undemonstrable tact to hit the target and give the application of the universal, the moral law (Kant), a discipline, which reason itself cannot. Thus taste is not the ground, but the supreme perfection of the moral judgment.[24]

Gadamer does not altogether collapse the distinction between taste and morality since he admits that taste is not the ground of the validity of moral judgment. But he does not tell us what the ground of the validity of moral judgment is either. Moral principles are viewed as embodied in the horizon of our traditions that constitute our ethical community. Of course, Gadamer does not have in mind a mechanical application of these principles or blind obedience to habits. All application involves interpretation and all interpretation involves understanding. In continuing a tradition we do not merely apply it, we co-interpret it, co-define it, and reinterpret it. However, there must be some principles, the Kantian would insist, for distinguishing between traditions worth preserving and those that are not, ethical practices worth sharing in and those we must reject even when they are our very own. We can concede to Gadamer that such criteria themselves are going to be embodied in some or another tradition or in some or another practice, may be handed down from the past, may be inspired by utopian hopes for the future.

From a Kantian standpoint, the crucial issue is whether the

exercise of judgment is guided by moral principles, which themselves reflect a universalistic morality, or whether such exercise
takes no bearings from moral principles and is instead governed by
a situational casuistic. In other words, a contemporary Kantian may
admit that Kant's claims about moral judgment being merely subsumptive as well as Kant's theory of action are inadequate and must
be rejected. Yet such a Kantian could also insist that a distinction
needs to be made between moral judgment and moral principle, and
the latter must be guided by a universalist morality considering all
humans as ends in themselves. Along these lines, Barbara Herman
has argued that Kantian morality lacks "rules of moral salience,"
enabling agents to identify morally relevant situations, maxims and
act-descriptions.[25] She contends nonetheless that such rules of moral
salience could well be formulated from within a Kantian framework,
insisting that moral judgment all the same needs to be guided by
universalistic moral principles.

This distinction between moral judgment and moral principles,
between general rules which guide and govern our moral action and
conduct and the specific form these rules assume in specific actions,
event and situations, helps us see how room may be made in
Kantian theory for the exercise of moral judgment. This distinction alone does not suffice though to establish that a universalistic
morality and contextual judgment are indeed compatible. If, as
is usually assumed to be the case, the moral law enjoins us to
abstract from situational detail and to think of what could be valid
for all rational beings *simpliciter*, then indeed there is no such
compatability. For the Kantian principle would enjoin exactly the
opposite of what moral judgment would require.

It is in this context that Kant's formula for reflective judgment the
only ground of whose validity is its universal communicability with
the hope of winning the assent of all, and Arendt's reading of this as
a procedure of "enlarged thought" become relevant. "Act in such a
way that the maxim of your actions can always be a universal law of
nature" can be reformulated as "Act in such a way that the maxim
of your actions takes into account the perspective of everyone else in
such a way that you would be in a position to 'woo their consent'."
Such a procedure of enlarged thought and contextual moral judgment are not at all incompatible. The moral principle of enlarged
thought enjoins us to view each person as one to whom I owe the
moral respect to consider their standpoint. This is the universalist-
egalitarian kernel of Kantian morality. Yet "to think from the standpoint of everyone else" requires precisely the exercise of contextual
moral judgment.

I isolated above three respects in which the exercise of moral
judgment was crucial: first, the recognition of morally relevant situa-

tions; second, the exercise of the moral imagination in the articulation of possible act-descriptions through which our deeds would be construed; third, the interpretation of one's action and maxims in light of the narrative history of the self and others. Each of these aspects of moral judgment requires for its successful exercise the ability to take the standpoint of the other. The more human perspectives we can bring to bear upon our understanding of a situation, all the more likely are we to recognize its moral relevance or salience. The more perspectives we are able to make present to ourselves, all the more are we likely to appreciate the possible act-descriptions through which others will identify our deeds. Finally, the more we are able to think from the perspective of others, all the more can we make vivid to ourselves the narrative histories of others involved. Moral judgment, whatever other cognitive abilities it may entail, certainly must involve the ability for "enlarged thought," or the ability to make up my mind "in an anticipated communication with others with whom I know I must finally come to some agreement" (Arendt).

Such capacity for judgment is not empathy, as Arendt also observes,[26] for it does not mean emotionally assuming or accepting the point of view of the other. It means merely making present to oneself what the perspectives of others involved are or could be, and whether I could "woo their consent" in acting the way I do. If such thinking from the standpoint of everyone else is to be distinguished from empathy, then how else are we to understand it? For Kant this was not an issue since he assumed that, thinking for one, a pure rational being could think for all. If we reject Kantian a priorism, and his assumption that as moral selves we are all somehow identical; if, in other words, we distinguish a universalist morality of principles from Kant's doctrine of a priori rationality, then I want to suggest we must think of such enlarged thought as a condition of actual or simulated dialogue. To "think from the perspective of everyone else" is to know "how to listen" to what the other is saying, or when the voices of others are absent, to imagine to oneself a conversation with the other as my dialogue partner. "Enlarged thought" is best realized through a dialogic or discursive ethic.

The Moral Foundations of Politics in Arendt's Work

Is there any reason to assume that this procedural model of enlarged thought, which enjoins us actually to engage in or simulate in thought a moral dialogue with all concerned, helps us recover that thread among thinking, judgment and moral considerations which

Hannah Arendt sought for? It is again one of the perplexities of Arendtian thinking on these matters that while she readily acknowledged the relevance of "enlarged thought" as a principle in the public-political realm, in her considerations on morality she reverted to the Platonic model of the unity of the soul with itself. In her 1971 essay on "Thinking and Moral Considerations," following Socrates in the *Gorgias*, she described conscience as the harmony or oneness of the soul with itself.[27] While I would not want to deny the relevance of this experience for moral considerations, I think Arendt was too quick in assuming that out of the self's desire for unity and consistency a principled moral standpoint could emerge. Let me simply remind you of Walt Whitman's famous lines: "Do I contradict myself? Very well then I contradict myself, I am large, I contain multitudes."[28]

While Arendt emphasized *harmony* as the morally relevant experience, she regarded *plurality* as the politicial principle par excellence. But through this emphasis on unity or harmony she presented a quasi-intuitionist conception of moral judgment. For if the basis of the validity of our moral judgments is that they allow us "to be at home with ourselves," are we not in fact making validity a matter of the idiosyncracies of the individual psyche? Was not one of the most perplexing characteristics of Eichmann in Arendt's eyes precisely the fact that he was "at home" with himself? Arendt fails to convince that an attitude of moral reflection and probing, such as enjoined by the procedure of enlarged thought, and the Platonic emphasis on unity or harmony of the soul with itself can be reconciled. In fact, the capacity for enlarged thought may well lead to moral conflict and alienation, but in a world in disarray an attitude of moral alienation may be more at home in the world than an attitude of simple harmony with oneself.

There is an irony in these reflections. The kinds of historical situations which led Arendt to her ruminations on thinking and moral considerations, most notably National Socialism and Stalinism in our century, are precisely instances when the intersubjectivity constitutive of the social world has been so dirempted and damaged that the motivation as well as the capacity to engage in enlarged thought disappears. In other words, one possible Arendtian objection to the model of actual or simulated dialogue I have presented may be that it reveals the utopianism of moral thought in the extreme. For these kinds of moral attitudes seem to disappear precisely when we most need them, that is in those situations of moral and political upheaval when the fabric of moral interactions which constitute everyday life are so destroyed that the moral obligation to think of the other as one whose perspective I must weigh equally alongside my own disappears from the conscience of individuals.

There is indeed a cleavage between moral principle and historical reality. The question when a principled moral standpoint of enlarged thought can become or fails to become the *moral culture* of a society cannot be answered by philosophical arguments concerning its validity and desirability. However, this admission is not equivalent to the acceptance of impotence in the face of history which the old Hegel, at least, always viewed as the price a Kantian ethics had to pay for formalism. We can name this issue the problem of the mediation of moral principles and moral culture. It is at this point when we are precisely concerned with mediating a principled moral standpoint with actual historical and social practices that the issue of a political ethic arises. A *political ethic* concerns the creation of institutions, the formation of practices, and the sustaining of civic values that cultivate the ability of enlarged thought and the universalist-egalitarian commitment which inspires them. Here I must depart from Arendt.

Arendt herself radically separated moral considerations from political action. Although her own political theory of the public space, community, power and participation seem to me to be inconceivable without an implicit political ethic of enlarged thought, in her book *On Revolution* she proceeded from a remarkably narrow conception of morality. As is well known, one of her major criticisms of the French revolutionaries was that in attempting to establish a republic of virtue they only succeeded in establishing one of terror.[29] "Purity of heart" in her view has no room in politics. Arendt here did not distinguish between the morally good and the morally right. The moral good, virtue, concerns indeed those dispositions, traits of character, emotions and intentions that lead to virtuous conduct. The morally right concerns our public actions and interactions which affect, influence and reflect upon the moral dignity and worth of the other as a public being. Thus one possible answer to Arendt's separation of morality and politics is to argue with Kant and with modern liberal political theory that there is a moral foundation to politics insofar as any political system embodies principles of justice. In Kantian theory this domain covers the *Rechtslehre*, namely those human rights and public principles of legislation that embody respect for the moral worth and dignity of another. This is what John Rawls reformulates in his theory of justice as the fundamental principles of justice that are to govern the basic institutions of societies. Between a "republic of terror" and a "republic of virtue," we might say, lies the conception of a "well-ordered and just society," embodying basic moral principles in its macropolitical and economic institutions.[30]

It is possible to go one step further in exploring the topic of a political ethic without altogether collapsing the distinction between the right and the good. This additional step would involve the encouragement and cultivation of a public ethos of democratic participation. Between the basic institutions of a polity, embodying principles of the morally right, and the domain of moral interactions in the lifeworld, in which virtue often comes to the fore, lie the civic practices and associations of a society in which individuals face each other neither as pure legal subjects nor as moral agents standing under ties of ethical obligations to each other but as public agents in a political space. The gap between the demands of justice, as it articulates the morally right, and the demands of virtue, as it defines the quality of our relations to others in the everyday lifeworld, can be bridged by cultivating qualities of civic friendship and solidarity. These moral attitudes of civic friendship and solidarity involve the extension of the sympathy and affection we naturally feel toward those closest to us unto larger human groups and thus personalize justice. Whereas it is customary particularly from a Kantian perspective to see a rupture here between the public virtue of impersonal justice and the private virtue of goodness, it is possible to envisage not their identity but their mediation.

The discourse model of ethics which enjoins enlarged thought, by making the perspective of all involved in a dialogue situation the sine qua non of the moral standpoint, allows us to think of this continuity and mediation. For the articulation of the perspectives of all involved requires, in fact, a civic and public life in which the right to opinion and action is guaranteed.[31] The articulation of differences through civic and political associations is essential for us to comprehend and to come to appreciate the perspective of others. The feelings of friendship and solidarity result precisely through the extension of our moral and political imagination not in vacuo, or via a Rawlsian thought experiment, but through the actual confrontation in public life with the point of view of those who are otherwise strangers to us but who become known to us through their public presence as voices and perspectives we have to take into account.

There is thus a fundamental link between a civic culture of public participation and the moral quality of enlarged thought. Enlarged thought, which morally obligates us to think from the standpoint of everyone else, politically requires the creation of institutions and practices whereby the voice and the perspective of others, often unknown to us, can become expressed in their own right. A major mistake of Kantian moral theory is to assume that the principles of enlarged thought can be realized via the isolated thought experiments of a thinker. These solitary thought experiments often substitute the standpoint of one privileged part for that of the whole. Indeed, it can hardly be otherwise. For "to think from the standpoint of everyone else" in Kantian moral philosophy is equivalent to thinking from the standpoint of one who is like all others in virtue of being a pure rational and autonomous agent. Once we reject the two-world metaphysics of Kantian theory, as well as the definition of our moral identities in purely rational terms, and we proceed to the perspectives of natality, plurality and the narrativity of action, we have to see that "to think from the standpoint of everyone else" entails sharing a public culture such that everyone else can articulate indeed what they think and what their perspectives are. The cultivation of one's moral imagination flourishes in such a culture in which the self-centered perspective of the individual is constantly challenged by the multiplicity and diversity of perspectives that constitute public life.

In this sense, Hannah Arendt was right in maintaining that judgment is the most political of all human faculties, for it leads to the recovery of the perspectival quality of the public world in which action unfolds. Where I depart from Arendt though is in her attempt to restrict this quality of mind to the political realm alone, thereby ignoring judgment as a moral faculty. The consequences of her position are on the one hand a reduction of principled moral reasoning to the standpoint of conscience, which is identified with the perspective of the unitary self, and on the other hand, a radical disjunction between morality and politics which ignores precisely the normative principles that seem to be embodied in the fundamental concepts of her own political theory like public space, power and political community. I have attempted to show that her own theory of action can be made fruitful for the exploration of moral judgment and that furthermore this theory of action leads to a reformulation of the essence of Kantian moral theory in terms of a dialogic procedure of enlarged thought. My final reflections have attempted to mediate between this perspective of enlarged thought and its political embodiment in a public culture of democratic ethos.

Notes

This article was originally delivered at the Hannah Arendt Memorial Symposium on Political Judgment, held at the New School for Social Research in the fall of 1985. I would like to thank Albrecht Wellmer and Charles Taylor for their comments on this lecture and the anonymous reader of the journal *Political Theory* for helpful criticism. I have revised and expanded the published version which appeared in *Political Theory*, 16.1 (Feb. 1988), pp. 29–51; reprinted by permission of Sage Publications, Inc.

1 Hannah Arendt, *The Life of the Mind*, vol. 1: *Thinking* (Harcourt, Brace and Jovanovich, New York and London, 1977), p. 3; volume 2 of *The Life of the Mind* is *Willing* (1978).
2 Ibid., p. 5.

3 Hannah Arendt, "Thinking and Moral Considerations: A Lecture," reprinted in *Social Research*, fiftieth anniversary issue (Spring/Summer 1984), p. 8.

4 Arendt, *Thinking*, p. 216.

5 Ronald Beiner, "Hannah Arendt on Judging," in Hannah Arendt, *Lectures on Kant's Political Philosophy* (University of Chicago Press, Chicago, 1982), pp. 117ff; R. J. Bernstein, "Judging – the Actor and the Spectator," in *Philosophical Profiles* (University of Pennsylvania Press, Philadelphia, 1986), pp. 221–38. Cf. also Arendt's discussion of Kant's distinction between the standpoint of the actor and that of the spectator in these lectures, pp. 44ff., 54ff.

6 Christopher Lasch, "Introduction," *Salmagundi*, special Hannah Arendt issue ed. Christopher Lasch, no. 60 (1983), p. xi.

7 H. Arendt, *The Human Condition* (University of Chicago Press, Chicago, 1958), 1973 edn used here. Abbreviated in text as HC.

8 For an illuminating discussion of moral judgment, see Charles Larmore, "Moral Judgment," *Review of Metaphysics*, 35 (Dec. 1981), pp. 275–96.

9 Bernstein, "Judging – the Actor and the Spectator," pp. 232–3.

10 Immanuel Kant, *The Critique of Judgment*, trans. and with an analytical index by J. C. Meredith (Clarendon, Oxford, 1964), p. 18. This edition will be abbreviated in the text as CrJ. I have also consulted *Kritik der Urteilskraft*, in *Kants Werke, Akademie-Textausgabe*, vol. 5 (Walter de Gruyter, Berlin, 1968).

11 I. Kant, "Critique of Practical Reason," in *Critique of Practical Reason and other Writings in Moral Philosophy*, trans. and introd. L. W. Beck (Garland, New York and London, 1976), p. 176.

12 Ibid.

13 Ibid., p. 177.

14 Kant returns to the question of moral judgment in the *Metaphysik der Sitten*, this time in the context of distinguishing perfect from imperfect duties. Perfect duties like telling the truth, keeping promises are ones where the action itself is directly determined by the moral law; imperfect duties, like generosity and benevolence, are ones whose maxims alone are determined by the moral law (pp. 230ff., 250ff.). This distinction between perfect and imperfect duties corresponds to that between the morally right and the morally good; whereas the first are subsumed under the "Rechtslehre" (doctrine of right), the second are subsumed under the "Tugendlehre" (doctrine of virtue). Kant admits that in virtue of the latitude allowed to imperfect duties – strive for your own perfection and the well-being of others – these require the exercise of the faculty of judgment. This faculty ought to determine how a "maxim is to be applied in specific cases;" this in turn requires another subsidiary maxim of application, and we thus land in a "moral casuistic" (p. 256). On Kant's view, the broader the domain of an imperfect duty the broader the scope for the exercise of the faculty of judgment. Kant ends these deliberations rather promptly with the observation that ethics is concerned not so much with judgment as with reason (p. 256). See Immanuel Kant, *Metaphysik der Sitten*, ed. K. Vorlaender, Philosophische Bibliothek, vol. 42 (4th edn, Felix Meiner, Hamburg, 1966).

15 Cf. Arendt, "Introduction," *Thinking*, p. 5; Arendt, "Thinking and Moral Considerations," p. 8. We also know from the notes of her students who attended her course on Kant's *Critique of Judgment* at the University of Chicago in 1971 that "Although Kant withheld questions of right and wrong from the sphere of reflective (aesthetic) judgment . . . Arendt herself was convinced that in doing so he had made a major mistake." Michael Denneny, "The Privilege of Ourselves: Hannah Arendt on Judgment," in *Hannah Arendt: The Recovery of the Public World*, ed. M. A. Hill (St Martin's, New York, 1979), p. 266.

16 Kant, *Critique of Judgment*, p. 151; Cf. Arendt's discussion of this passage in her *Lectures on Kant's Political Philosophy*, pp. 71ff.

17 Arendt, "Crisis in Culture," in *Between Past and Future: Six Exercises in Political Thought* (Meridian, New York, 1961), pp. 220–1.

18 For a recent attempt to reconcile universalism and moral judgment, see the instructive essay by Otfried Höffe, "Universalistische Ethik und Urteilskraft: ein Aristotelisher Blick auf Kant," *Zeitschrift für philosophische Forschung*, 44.4 (1990), pp. 539–63.

19 Kant, *Critique of Judgment*, p. 9.

20 Ibid., p. 50.

21 See R. Sorabji, "Aristotle on the Role of Intellect and Virtue," and David Wiggins, "Deliberation and Practical Reason," both in *Essays on Aristotle's Ethics*, ed. A. O. Rorty (University of California Press, Berkeley, 1980), pp. 201–21 and 221–41 respectively.

22 H. G. Gadamer, *Truth and Method*, trans. G. Barden and J. Cumming (Seabury, New York, 1975), p. 287.

23 Cf. Aristotle, *Nicomachean Ethics*, in *Basic Works of Aristotle*, ed. and introd. R. McKeon (Random House, New York, 1966), pp. 1114b5ff., 1142a25ff.

24 Gadamer, *Truth and Method*, pp. 37–8.

25 Barbara Herman, "The Practice of Moral Judgment," *Journal of Philosophy* (Aug. 1985), pp. 414–36.

26 Arendt, "Crisis in Culture," p. 221.

27 Arendt, "Thinking and Moral Considerations," p. 30. The passage discussed by Arendt is the following: "It would be better for me that my lyre or a chorus I directed should be out of tune and loud with discord, and that multitudes of men should disagree with me rather than that I, *being one*, should be out of harmony with myself and contradict *me*" (translation and emphases by Arendt). Cf. *Gorgias*, in *The Collected Dialogues of Plato*, ed. Edith Hamilton and Huntington Cairns, Bollingen Series 71 (Princeton University Press, Princeton, NJ, 1973), p. 265.

28 Walt Whitman, "Song of Myself," in *Leaves of Grass and Selected Prose*, ed. and introd. John Kouwenhoven (Modern Library, New York, 1950), stanza 51, p. 74.

29 Hannah Arendt, *On Revolution* (Viking, New York, 1969), pp. 68ff., 81ff. For a similar concern with the relation of morality and politics in Hannah Arendt's thought, cf. J. Habermas, "Hannah Arendt's Communications Concept of Power," *Social Research*, 44 (1977), pp. 3–25. I am in agreement with George Kateb who writes: "My fear is that judging is too frail a support for the hope of keeping an only slightly

altered Greek conception of action while reducing the dangers of its countenancing immorality... All that the faculty of judging can guarantee is that those one recognizes as one's equal will be taken into account. The demand that all be recognized as one's equals, that one not equate humanity with one's group, does not necessarily follow from the activity of judging." In *Hannah Arendt: Politics, Conscience, Evil* (Rowman and Allanheld, Totowa, NJ, 1983), pp. 38–9. Precisely for this reason, it is important to distinguish between moral judgment and moral principles as well as making explicit the foundations of one's concept of the political.

30   J. Rawls, *A Theory of Justice* (Harvard University Press, Cambridge, Mass., 1971) pp. 51ff.

31   On the rights of opinion and action, which Arendt describes as the "right to have rights," see Arendt, *Imperialism*, in *The Origins of Totalitarianism*, part 2 (Harcourt, Brace and Jovanovich, New York, 1968), pp. 176–7. For a provocative essay that explores and argues against the antidemocratic strain in Arendt's thought, cf. Sheldon Wolin, "Hannah Arendt: Democracy and the Political," *Salmagundi*, special H. Arendt issue ed. Christopher Lasch, no. 60 (1983), pp. 3–19. The alternative conception of the political which Wolin outlines in this essay is nonetheless much indebted to Arendt's views in *The Human Condition*; cf. Wolin, pp. 17–19.

PART II

Autonomy, Feminism and Postmodernism

The first half of this book has dealt primarily with the justification, scope and institutional implications of communicative or discourse ethics. I have explored the relations between communicative ethics on the one hand, communitarianism, liberalism and an Arendtian conception of "civic virtue" on the other. By eliminating some of the excessively rationalistic formulations given to communicative ethics by Jürgen Habermas, I have placed at the center of discourse ethics less the telos of a rationally motivated consensus but more the open-ended procedure of an "enlarged mentality," namely the capacity to reverse perspectives in practical disputes in general and the ability to reason from the standpoint of others involved. This principle of "reversibility of perspectives," which is also central to Lawrence Kohlberg's cognitive-developmental moral psychology, has not always been given the prominence it deserves in formulations of communicative ethics. Consequently, the project of communicative ethics has frequently been cast in the mold of a rationalistic con-sensus theory of Rousseauian ilk or it has been identified with the transcendental illusions of Kantian moral theory in general.[1] My explorations in part I have sought to militate against such inter-pretations by stressing the situatedness of the program of com-municative ethics within the hermeneutic horizon of modernity, and by emphasizing the contigent cultural, institutional and emotive presuppositions of the ability to take the "standpoint of others" and to reverse perspectives in moral reasoning. In the last chapter, I have suggested that good moral judgment, whatever else it entails, must also involve the ability to judge from the standpoint of the other.

The following two chapters which deal with the Kohlberg–Gilligan controversy in recent moral theory and moral psychology are crucial for the overall argument developed in this book for a number of reasons. First, if the universalizability procedure in ethics is reformulated along the lines of a reversibility of perspectives and the cultivation of "enlarged thinking," then more needs to be said about those "others" whose standpoint we are asked to understand and to represent to ourselves. In this chapter, borrowing from some insights of Carol Gilligan and expanding their implications for moral epistemology, I suggest that we think of the moral self not just as the "generalized" but also as the "concrete" other. Second, Carol Gilligan's critique of Lawrence Kolhberg's cognitive-developmental moral psychology in many ways parallels my own misgivings about the rationalistic biases and exclusive justice orientation of the Habermasian version of discourse theory. Furthermore, Gilligan's work also echoes some communitarian concerns about the strict lines dividing justice and the good life, an ethics of universalist principles and one of virtue and character. Gilligan's critique of Kohlberg radically questions the "juridical" or "justice bias" of universalist moral theories; this critique can allow us to reexamine a suggestion made in the introduction to this book that the central insights of universalist morality today could be recast as the search for a "postconventional Sittlichkeit" rather than as a justice-centered moral pespective alone. As I shall argue in the next two chapters, Gilligan's work provides us with fresh insights in this respect. Finally, Carol Gilligan's research in general has fascinating implications about the "women's question" in science and philosophy. What, if anything, changes in science and philosophy if women not only do theory but also become the "objects" of science and philosophy? How does the discovery of "gender" as an analytical category of research influence standard interpretations of morality and justice? Is it possible to reconcile the insight of feminist theory that gender difference is both central and ubiquitous in our lives with the kind of interactive universalism advocated in this book? Is not universalism of any sort, whether Kantian or Habermasian, incompatible with the goals and insights of feminism? These are the central issues to be examined in Part II.

Note

1   Unfortunately, a number of very thoughtful commentators insist on interpreting Habermas's moral theory first by abstracting it wholly from his social theory of modernity, and second, by failing to appreciate the degree to which Habermas has accepted Hegel's critique of Kant. One point that is persistently lost in such commentaries is how Habermas has tried to concretize Hegel's insight about the social and cultural constitution of self-identity by returning to George Herbert Mead's "symbolic interactionism." As representative of these positions, cf. Raymond

Geuss, *The Idea of a Critical Theory: Habermas and the Frankfurt School* (Cambridge University Press, Cambridge, 1981), pp. 65 ff., and most recently, Jeffrey Stout, *Ethics after Babel: The Language of Morals and their Discontents* (Beacon, Boston, 1988), pp. 166, 263. Since Stout is himself interested in "social criticism with both eyes open" (see *Ethics After Babel*, pp. 266 ff.), I think a more serious engagement with Habermas's theory of communicative action as a sociological theory and as a critique of our societies would have revealed many points of commonality, as well as giving Stout's concluding observations a firmer basis in contemporary social theory.

5   The Generalized and the Concrete Other

The Kohlberg–Gilligan Controversy and Moral Theory

Can there be a feminist contribution to moral philosophy? That is to say, can those men and women who view the gender-sex system of our societies as oppressive, and who regard women's emancipation as essential to human liberation, criticize, analyze and when necessary replace the traditional categories of moral philosophy in order to contribute to women's emancipation and human liberation? By focussing on the controversy generated by Carol Gilligan's work, this chapter seeks to outline such a feminist contribution to moral philosophy.

1   The Kohlberg–Gilligan Controversy

Carol Gilligan's research in cognitive, developmental moral psychology recapitulates a pattern made familiar to us by Thomas Kuhn.[1] Noting a discrepancy between the claims of the original research paradigm and the data, Gilligan and her co-workers first extend this paradigm to accommodate anomalous results. This extension then allows them to see some other problems in a new light; subsequently, the basic paradigm, namely the study of the development of moral judgment, according to Lawrence Kohlberg's model, is fundamentally revised. Gilligan and her co-workers now maintain that Kohlbergian theory is valid only for measuring the development of one aspect of moral orientation, which focusses on justice and rights.

In a 1980 article on "Moral Development in Late Adolesence and Adulthood: A Critique and Reconstruction of Kohlberg's Theory," Murphy and Gilligan note that moral-judgment data from a longitudinal study of 26 undergraduates scored by Kohlberg's revised manual replicate his original findings that a significant percentage of subjects appear to regress from adolescence to adulthood.[2] The persistence of this relativistic regression suggests a need to revise the theory. In this article they propose a distinction between "postconventional formalism" and "postconventional contextualism." While the postconventional type of reasoning solves the problem of relativism by constructing a system that derives a solution to all moral problems from concepts like social contract or natural rights, the second approach finds the solution in that "while no answer may be objectively right in the sense of being context-free, some answers and some ways of thinking are better than others" (ibid., p. 83). The extension of the original paradigm from postconventional formalist to postconventional contextual then leads Gilligan to see some other discrepancies in the theory in a new light, and most notably among these, women's persistently low score when compared with their male peers. Distinguishing between the ethical orientation of justice and rights and the ethical orientation of care and responsibility allows her to account for women's moral development and the cognitive skills they show in a new way. Women's moral judgement is more contextual, more immersed in the details of relationships and narratives. It shows a greater propensity to take the standpoint of the "particular other," and women appear more adept at revealing feelings of empathy and sympathy required by this. Once these cognitive characteristics are seen not as deficiencies, but as essential components of adult moral reasoning at the postconventional stage, then women's apparent moral confusion of judgment becomes a sign of their strength. Agreeing with Piaget that a developmental theory hangs from its vertex of maturity, "the point towards which progress is traced," a change in "the definition of maturity," writes Gilligan, "does not simply alter the description of the highest stage but recasts the understanding of development, changing the entire account."[3] The contextuality, narrativity and specificity of women's moral judgment is not a sign of weakness or deficiency, but a manifestation of a vision of moral maturity that views the self as a being immersed in a network of relationships with others. According to this vision, the respect for each other's needs and the mutuality of effort to satisfy them sustain moral growth and development.

When confronted with such a challenge, it is common that adherents of an old research paradigm respond by arguing

(a) that the data base does not support the conclusions drawn by revisionists;

(b) that some of the new conclusions can be accommodated by the old theory; and

(c) that the new and old paradigms have different object

domains and are not concerned with explaining the same phenomena after all.

In his response to Gilligan, Kohlberg has followed all three alternatives.

(a)   The data base

In his 1984 "Synopses and Detailed Replies to Critics," Kohlberg argues that available data on cognitive moral development does not report differences among children and adolescents of both sexes with respect to justice reasoning.[4] "The only studies," he writes, "showing fairly frequent sex differences are those of adults, usually of spouse housewives. Many of the studies comparing adult males and females without controlling for education and job differences . . . do report sex differences in favor of males" (p. 347). Kohlberg maintains that these latter findings are not incompatible with his theory.[5] For, according to this theory, the attainment of stages four and five depends upon experiences of participation, responsibility and role taking in the secondary institutions of society such as the workplace and government, from which women have been and still are to a large extent excluded. The data, he concludes, does not damage the validity of his theory but shows the necessity for controlling for such factors as education and employment when assessing sex differences in adult moral reasoning.

(b)   Accommodation within the old theory

Kohlberg now agrees with Gilligan that "the acknowledgement of an orientation of care and response usefully enlarges the moral domain" (Kohlberg, "Synopses," p. 340). In his view, though, justice and rights, care and responsibility, are not two *tracks* of moral development, but two moral *orientations*. The rights orientation and the care orientation are not bipolar or dichotomous. Rather, the care-and-response orientation is directed primarily to relations of special obligation to family, friends and group members, "relations which often include or presuppose general obligations of respect, fairness and contract" (p. 349). Kohlberg resists the conclusion that these differences are strongly "sex related;" instead, he views the choice of orientation "to be primarily a function of setting and dilemma, not sex" (p. 350).

(c)   Object domain of the two theories

In an earlier response to Gilligan, Kohlberg had argued as follows:

> Carol Gilligan's ideas, while interesting, were not really welcome to us, for two reasons . . . The latter, we thought, was grist for Jane Loewinger's mill in studying stages of ego development, but not for studying the specifically moral dimension in reasoning . . . Following Piaget, my colleagues and I have had the greatest confidence that reasoning about justice would lend itself to a formal structuralist or rationalist analysis . . . whereas questions about the nature of the "good life" have not been as amenable to this type of statement.[6]

In his 1984 reply to his critics, this distinction between moral and ego development is refined further. Kohlberg divides the ego domain into the cognitive, interpersonal and moral functions ("Synopses," p. 398). Since, however, ego development is a necessary but not sufficient condition for moral development, in his view the latter can be studied independently of the former. In light of this clarification, Kohlberg regards Murphy's and Gilligan's stage of "postconventional contextualism" to be more concerned with questions of ego as opposed to moral development. While not wanting to maintain that the acquisition of moral competencies ends with reaching adulthood, Kohlberg nevertheless insists that adult moral and ego development studies only reveal the presence of "soft" as opposed to "hard" stages. The latter are irreversible in sequence and integrally related to one another in the sense that a subsequent stage grows out of, and presents a better solution to problems confronted at, an earlier stage.[7]

It will be up to latter-day historians of science to decide whether with these admissions and qualification, Kohlbergian theory has entered the phase of "ad-hocism," in Imre Lakatos's words,[8] or whether Gilligan's challenge, as well as that of other critics, has moved this research paradigm to a new phase, in which new problems and conceptualizations will lead to more fruitful results.

What concerns me in this chapter is the question: what can feminist theory contribute to this debate? Since Kohlberg himself regards an interaction between normative philosophy and the empirical study of moral development as essential to his theory, the insights of contemporary feminist theory and philosophy can be brought to bear upon some aspects of his theory. I want to define two premises as constituents of feminist theorizing. First, for feminist theory the gender-sex system is not a contingent but an essential way in which social reality is organized, symbolically divided and lived through experientially. By the "gender-sex" system I understand the social-historical, symbolic constitution, and interpretation of the anatomical differences of the sexes. The gender-sex system is the grid through which the self develops an *embodied* identity, a certain mode of being in one's body and of living the body. The self becomes an I in that it appropriates from the human community a mode of psychically, socially and symbolically experiencing its bodily identity. The gender-sex system is the grid through which societies and cultures reproduce embodied individuals.[9]

Second, the historically known gender-sex systems have contributed to the oppression and exploitation of women. The task of feminist critical theory is to uncover this fact, and to develop a theory that is emancipatory and reflective, and which can aid women in their struggles to overcome oppression and exploitation. Feminist theory can contribute to this task in two ways: by developing an *explanatory-diagnostic analysis* of women's oppression across history, culture and societies, and by articulating an *anticipatory-utopian critique* of the norms and values of our current society and culture, such as to project new modes of togetherness, of relating to ourselves and to nature in the future. Whereas the first aspect of feminist theory requires critical, social-scientific research, the second is primarily normative and philosophical: it involves the clarification of moral and political principles, both at the meta-ethical level with respect to their logic of justification and at the substantive, normative level with reference to their concrete content.[10]

In this chapter I shall be concerned with articulating such an anticipatory-utopian critique of universalistic moral theories from a feminist perspective. I want to argue that the definition of the moral domain, as well as the ideal of moral autonomy, not only in Kohlberg's theory but in universalistic, contractarian theories from Hobbes to Rawls, lead to a *privatization* of women's experience and to the exclusion of its consideration from a moral point of view (part 2). In this tradition, the moral self is viewed as a *disembedded* and *disembodied* being. This conception of the self reflects aspects of male experience; the "relevant other" in this theory is never the sister but always the brother. This vision of the self, I want to claim, is incompatible with the very criteria of reversibility and universalizability advocated by defenders of universalism. A universalistic moral theory restricted to the standpoint of the "generalized other" falls into epistemic incoherencies that jeopardize its claim to adequately fulfill reversibility and universalizability (part 3).

Universalistic moral theories in the Western tradition from Hobbes to Rawls are substitutionalist, in the sense that the universalism they defend is defined surreptitiously by identifying the experiences of a specific group of subjects as the paradigmatic case of the human as such. These subjects are invariably white, male adults who are propertied or at least professional. I want to distinguish *substitutionalist* from *interactive* universalism. Interactive universalism acknowledges the plurality of modes of being human, and differences among humans, without endorsing all these pluralities and differences as morally and politically valid. While agreeing that normative disputes can be settled rationally, and that fairness, reciprocity and some procedure of universalizability are constituents, that is, necessary conditions of the moral standpoint, interactive universalism regards difference as a starting point for reflection and action. In this sense, "universality" is a regulative ideal that does not deny our embodied and embedded identity, but aims at developing moral attitudes and encouraging political transformations that can yield a point of view acceptable to all. Universality is not the ideal consensus of fictitiously defined selves, but the concrete process in politics and morals of the struggle of concrete, embodied selves, striving for autonomy.

2   Justice and the Autonomous Self in Social Contract Theories

Kohlberg defines the privileged object domain of moral philosophy and psychology as follows:

> We say that *moral* judgments or principles have the central function of resolving interpersonal or social conflicts, that is, conflicts of claims or rights . . . Thus moral judgments and principles imply a notion of equilibrium, or reversibility of claims. In this sense they ultimately involve some reference to justice, at least insofar as they define "hard" structural stages. ("Synopses," p. 216)

Kohlberg's conception of the moral domain is based upon a strong differentiation between justice and the good life.[11] This is also one of the cornerstones of his critique of Gilligan. Although acknowledging that Gilligan's elucidation of a care-and-responsibility orientation "usefully enlarges the moral domain" ("Synopses," p. 340), Kohlberg defines the domain of *special relationships of obligation* to which care and responsibility are oriented as follows: "the spheres of kinship, love, friendship, and sex that elicit considerations of care are usually understood to be spheres of personal decision-making, as are, for instance, the problems of marriage and divorce" (pp. 229–30). The care orientation is said thus to concern domains that are more "personal" than "moral in the sense of the formal point of view" (p. 360). Questions of the good life, pertaining to the nature of our relationships of kinship, love, friendship and sex, on the one hand, are included in the moral domain but, on the other hand, are named "personal" as opposed to "moral" issues.

Kohlberg proceeds from a definition of morality that begins with Hobbes, in the wake of the dissolution of the Aristotelian-Christian world-view. Ancient and medieval moral systems, by contrast, show the following structure: a definition of man-as-he-ought-to-be, a definition of man-as-he-is, and the articulation of a set of rules or precepts that can lead man as he is into what he ought to be.[12] In such moral systems, the rules which govern just relations among the human community are embedded in a more encompassing conception of the good life. This good life, the telos of man, is defined ontologically with reference to man's place in the cosmos.

The destruction of the ancient and medieval teleological conception of nature through the attack of medieval nominalism and modern science, the emergence of capitalist exchange relations and the subsequent division of the social structure into the economy, the polity, civil associations and the domestic-intimate sphere, radically alter moral theory. Modern theorists claim that the ultimate purposes of nature are unknown. Morality is thus emancipated from cosmology and from an all-encompassing worldview that normatively limits man's relation to nature. The distinction between justice and the good life, as it is formulated by early contract theorists, aims at defending this privacy and autonomy of the self, first in the religious sphere and then in the scientific and philosophical spheres of "free thought" as well.

Justice alone becomes the center of moral theory when bourgeois individuals in a disenchanted universe face the task of creating the legitimate basis of the social order for themselves. What "ought" to be is now defined as what all would have rationally to agree to in order to ensure civil peace and prosperity (Hobbes, Locke), or the "ought" is derived from the rational form of the moral law alone (Rousseau, Kant). As long as the social bases of cooperation and the rights claims of individuals are respected, the autonomous bourgeois subject can define the good life as his mind and conscience dictate.

The transition to modernity does not only privatize the self's relation to the cosmos and to ultimate questions of religion and being. First with western modernity the conception of privacy is so enlarged that an intimate domestic-familial sphere is subsumed under it. Relations of "kinship, friendship, love, and sex," indeed, as Kohlberg takes them to be, come to be viewed as spheres of "personal decision-making." At the beginning of modern moral and political theory, however, the "personal" nature of the spheres does not mean the recognition of equal, female autonomy, but rather the removal of gender relations from the sphere of justice. While the bourgeois male celebrates his transition from conventional to post-conventional morality, from socially accepted rules of justice to their generation in light of the principles of a social contract, the domestic sphere remains at the conventional level. The sphere of justice from Hobbes through Locke and Kant is regarded as the domain where independent, male heads of household transact with one another, while the domestic-intimate sphere is put beyond the pale of justice and restricted to the reproductive and affective needs of the bourgeois paterfamilias. Agnes Heller has named this domain the "household of the emotions."[13] An entire domain of human activity, namely, nurture, reproduction, love and care, which becomes the woman's lot in the course of the development of modern, bourgeois society, is excluded from moral and political considerations, and relegated to the realm of "nature."

Through a brief historical genealogy of social contract theories, I want to examine the distinction between justice and the good life as it is translated into the split between the public and the domestic. This analysis will also allow us to see the implicit ideal of autonomy cherished by this tradition.

At the beginning of modern moral and political philosophy stands a powerful metaphor: the "state of nature." This metaphor is at times said to be fact. Thus, in his *Second Treatise of Civil Government*, John Locke reminds us of "the two men in the desert island, mentioned by Garcilasso de la Vega . . . or a Swiss and an Indian, in the woods of America."[14] At other times it is acknowledges as fiction. Thus, Kant dismisses the colorful reveries of his predecessors and transforms the "state of nature" from an empirical fact into a transcendental concept. The state of nature comes to represent the idea of *Privatrecht*, under which are subsumed the right of property and "thinglike rights of a personal nature" ("auf dingliche Natur persönliche Rechte"), which the male head of a household exercises over his wife, children and servants.[15] Only Thomas Hobbes compounds fact and fiction, and against those who consider it strange "that Nature should thus dissociate, and render men apt to invade, and destroy one another,"[16] he asks each man who does not trust "this Inference, made from the passions," to reflect why "when taking a journey, he arms himself, and seeks to go well accompanied; when going to sleep, he lockes his dores; when even in his house he lockes his chests . . . Does he not there as much accuse mankind by his actions, as I do by my words?" (*Leviathan*, p. 187). The state of nature is the looking glass of these early bourgeois thinkers in which they and their societies are magnified, purified and reflected in their original, naked verity. The state of nature is both nightmare (Hobbes) and utopia (Rousseau). In it the bourgeois male recognizes his flaws, fears and anxieties, as well as dreams.

The varying content of this metaphor is less significant than its simple and profound message: in the beginning man was alone. Again it is Hobbes who gives this thought its clearest formulation. "Let us consider men . . . as if but even now sprung out of the earth, and suddenly, like mushrooms, come to full maturity, without all kind of engagement to each other."[17] This vision of men as mushrooms is an ultimate picture of autonomy. The female, the mother of whom every individual is born, is now replaced by the earth. The denial of being born of woman frees the male ego from the most natural and basic bond of dependence. Nor is the picture very different for Rousseau's noble savage who, wandering wantonly through the woods, occasionally mates with a female and then seeks rest.[18]

The state-of-nature metaphor provides a vision of the autonomous self: this is a narcissist who sees the world in his own image; who has no awareness of the limits of his own desires and passions; and who cannot see himself through the eyes of another. The narcissism of this sovereign self is destroyed by the presence of the other. As Hegel expresses it: "Self-consciousness is faced by another self-consciousness; it has come *out of itself*. This has a twofold significance: first, it has *lost* itself, for it finds itself as an *other* being; secondly, in doing so it has superseded the other, for it does not see the other as an essential being, but in the other sees its own self."[19] The story of the autonomous male ego is the saga of this initial sense of *loss* in confrontation with the other, and the gradual recovery from this original narcissistic wound through the sobering experience of war, fear, domination, anxiety and death. The last installment in this drama is the social contract: the establishment of the law to govern all. Having been thrust out of their narcissistic universe into a world of insecurity by their sibling brothers, these individuals have to reestablish the authority of the father in the image of the law. The early bourgeois individual not only has no mother but no father as well; rather, he strives to reconstitute the father in his own self-image. What is usually celebrated in the annals of modern moral and political theory as the dawn of liberty is precisely this destruction of political patriarchy in bourgeois society.

The constitution of political authority civilizes sibling rivalry by turning their attention from war to property, from vanity to science, from conquest to luxury. The original narcissism is not transformed; only now ego boundaries are clearly defined. The law reduces insecurity, the fear of being engulfed by the other, by defining mine and thine. Jealousy is not eliminated but tamed; as long as each can keep what is his and attain more by fair rules of the game, he is entitled to it. Competition is domesticized and channeled towards acquisition. The law contains anxiety by defining rigidly the boundaries between self and other, but the law does not cure anxiety. The anxiety that the other is always on the lookout to interfere in your space and appropriate what is yours; the anxiety that you will be subordinated to his will; the anxiety that a group of brothers will usurp the law in the name of the "will of all" and destroy "the general will," the will of the absent father, remains. The law teaches how to repress anxiety and to sober narcissism, but the constitution of the self is not altered. The establishment of private rights and duties does not overcome the inner wounds of the self; it only forces them to become less destructive.

This imaginary device of early moral and political theory has had an amazing hold upon the modern consciousness. From Freud to Piaget, the relationship to the brother is viewed as the humanizing experience that teaches us to become social, responsible adults.[20] As a result of the hold of this metaphor upon our imagination, we have also come to inherit a number of philosophical prejudices. For Rawls and Kohlberg, as well, the autonomous self is disembedded and disembodied; moral impartiality is learning to recognize the claims of the other who is just like oneself; fairness is public justice; a public system of rights and duties is the best way to arbitrate conflict, to distribute rewards and to establish claims.

Yet this is a strange world; it is one in which individuals are grown up before they have been born; in which boys are men before they have been children; a world where neither mother, nor sister, nor wife exist. The question is not what Hobbes says about men and women, or what Rousseau sees the role of Sophie to be in Emile's education. The point is that in this universe the experience of the early modern female has no place. Woman is simply what man is not; namely they are not autonomous, independent, but by the same token, nonaggressive but nurturant, not competitive but giving, not public but private. The world of the female is constituted by a series of negations. She is simply what he happens not to be. Her identity becomes defined by a lack – the lack of autonomy, the lack of independence, the lack of the phallus. The narcissistic male takes her to be just like himself, only his opposite.

It is not the misogynist prejudices of early modern moral and political theory alone that lead to women's exclusion. It is the very constitution of a sphere of discourse which bans the female from history to the realm of nature, from the light of the public to the interior of the household, from the civilizing effect of culture to the repetitious burden of nurture and reproduction. The public sphere, the sphere of justice, moves into historicity, whereas the private sphere, the sphere of care and intimacy, is unchanging and timeless.

It pulls us toward the earth even when we, as Hobbesian mushrooms, strive to pull away from it. The dehistoricization of the private realm signifies that, as the male ego celebrates his passage from nature to culture, from conflict to consensus, women remain in a timeless universe, condemned to repeat the cycles of life.

This split between the public sphere of justice, in which history is made, and the atemporal realm of the household, in which life is reproduced, is internalized by the male ego. The dichotomies are not only without but within. He himself is divided into the public person and the private individual. Within his chest clash the law of reason and the inclination of nature, the brilliance of cognition and the obscurity of emotion. Caught between the moral law and the starry heaven above and the earthly body below,[21] the autonomous self strives for unity. But the antagonism – between autonomy and nurturance, independence and bonding, sovereignty of the self and relations to others – remains. In the discourse of modern moral and political theory, these dichotomies are reified as being essential to the constitution of the self. While men humanize outer nature through labor, inner nature remains ahistorical, dark and obscure. I want to suggest that contemporary universalist moral theory has inherited this dichotomy between autonomy and nurturance, independence and bonding, the sphere of justice and the domestic, personal realm. This becomes most visible in its attempt to restrict the moral point of view to the perspective of the "generalized other."

3 The Generalized versus the Concrete Other

Let me describe two conceptions of self–other relations that delineate both moral perspectives and interactional structures. I shall name the first the standpoint of the "generalized"[22] and the second that of the "concrete" other. In contemporary moral theory these conceptions are viewed as incompatible, even as antagonistic. These two perspectives reflect the dichotomies and splits of early modern moral and political theory between autonomy and nurturance, independence and bonding, the public and the domestic, and more broadly, between justice and the good life. The content of the generalized as well as the concrete other is shaped by this dichotomous characterization, which we have inherited from the modern tradition.

The standpoint of the generalized other requires us to view each and every individual as a rational being entitled to the same rights and duties we would want to ascribe to ourselves. In assuming the standpoint, we abstract from the individuality and concrete identity of the other. We assume that the other, like ourselves, is a being who has concrete needs, desires and affects, but that what constitutes his or her moral dignity is not what differentiates us from each other, but rather what we, as speaking and acting rational agents, have in common. Our relation to the other is governed by the norms of *formal equality* and *reciprocity*: each is entitled to expect and to assume from us what we can expect and assume from him or her. The norms of our interactions are primarily public and institutional ones. If I have a right to X, then you have the duty not to hinder me from enjoying X and conversely. In treating you in accordance with these norms, I confirm in your person the rights of humanity and I have a legitimate claim to expect that you will do the same in relation to me. The moral categories that accompany such interactions are those of right, obligation and entitlement, and the corresponding moral feelings are those of respect, duty, worthiness and dignity.

The standpoint of the concrete other, by contrast, requires us to view each and every rational being as an individual with a concrete history, identity and affective-emotional constitution. In assuming this standpoint, we abstract from what constitutes our commonality, and focus on individuality. We seek to comprehend the needs of the other, his or her motivations, what she searches for, and what s/he desires. Our relation to the other is governed by the norms of *equity* and *complementary reciprocity*: each is entitled to expect and to assume from the other forms of behavior through which the other feels recognized and confirmed as a concrete, individual being with specific needs, talents and capacities. Our differences in this case complement rather than exclude one another. The norms of our interaction are usually, although not exclusively private, non-institutional ones. They are norms of friendship, love and care. These norms require in various ways that I exhibit more than the simple assertion of my rights and duties in the face of your needs. In treating you in accordance with the norms of friendship, love and care, I confirm not only your *humanity* but your human *individuality*. The moral categories that accompany such interactions are those of responsibility, bonding and sharing. The corresponding moral feelings are those of love, care and sympathy and solidarity.

In contemporary universalist moral psychology and moral theory, it is the viewpoint of the "generalized other" that predominates. In his article on "Justice as Reversibility: The Claim to Moral Adequacy of a Highest Stage of Moral Development," for example, Kohlberg argues that:

> moral judgments involve role-taking, taking the viewpoint of the others conceived as *subjects* and coordinating these viewpoints . . .

Second, equilibriated moral judgments involve principles of justice of fairness. A moral situation in disequilibrium is one in which there are unresolved, conflicting claims. A resolution of the situation is one in which each is "given his due" according to some principle of justice that can be recognized as fair by all the conflicting parties involved.[23]

Kohlberg regards Rawl's concept of "reflective equilibrium" as a parallel formulation of the basic ideas of reciprocity, equality and fairness intrinsic to all moral judgments. The Rawlsian "veil of ignorance," in Kohlberg's judgment, not only exemplifies the formalist idea of universalizability but that of perfect *reversibility* as well.[24] The idea behind the veil of ignorance is described as follows: "The decider is to initially decide from a point of view *that ignores his identity* (veil of ignorance) under the assumption that decisions are governed by maximizing values from a viewpoint of rational egoism in considering each party's interest" ("Justice as Reversibility," p. 200; my emphasis).

What I would like to question is the assumption that "taking the viewpoint of others" is truly compatible with this notion of fairness as reasoning behind a "veil of ignorance."[25] The problem is that the defensible kernel of the ideas of reciprocity and fairness are thereby identified with the perspective of the disembedded and disembodied generalized other. Now since Kohlberg presents his research subjects with hypothetically constructed moral dilemmas, it may be thought that his conception of "taking the standpoint of the other" is not subject to the epistemic restrictions that apply to the Rawlsian original position. Subjects in Kohlbergian interviews do not stand behind a veil of ignorance. However, the very language in which Kohlbergian dilemmas are presented incorporates these epistemic restrictions. For example, in the famous Heinz dilemma, as in others, the motivations of the druggist as a concrete individual, as well as the history of the individuals involved, are excluded as irrelevant to the definition of the moral problem at hand. In these dilemmas, individuals and their moral positions are represented by abstracting from the narrative history of the self and its motivations. Gilligan also notes that the implicit moral epistemology of Kohlbergian dilemmas frustrates women, who want to phrase these hypothetical dilemmas in a more contextual voice, attuned to the standpoint of the concrete other. The result is that

> though several of the women in the abortion study clearly articulate a postconventional metaethical position, none of them are considered principled in their normative moral judgments of Kohlberg's hypothetical dilemmas. Instead, the women's judgments point toward an identification of the violence inherent in the dilemma itself, which is

seen to compromise the justice of any of its possible resolutions. (Gilligan, *In a Different Voice*, p. 101)

Through an immanent critique of the theories of Kohlberg and Rawls, I want to show that ignoring the standpoint of the concrete other leads to epistemic incoherence in universalistic moral theories. The problem can be stated as follows: according to Kohlberg and Rawls, moral reciprocity involves the capacity to take the standpoint of the other, to put oneself imaginatively in the place of the other, but under conditions of the "veil of ignorance" the *other as different from the self* disappears. Unlike in previous contract theories, in this case the other is not constituted through projection, but as a consequence of total abstraction from his or her identity. Differences are not denied; they become irrelevant. The Rawlsian self does not know

> his place in society, his class position or status; nor does he know his fortune in the distribution of natural assets and abilities, his intelligence and strength, and the like. Nor, again, does anyone know his conception of the good, the particulars of his rational plan of life, or even the special features of his psychology such as his aversion to risk or liability to optimism or pessimism.[26]

Let us ignore for a moment whether such selves who also do not know "the particular circumstances of their own society" can know anything at all that is relevant to the human condition, and ask instead, are these individuals *human selves* at all? In his attempt to do justice to Kant's conception of noumenal agency, Rawls recapitulates a basic problem with the Kantian conception of the self, namely, that noumenal selves cannot be *individuated*. If all that belongs to them as embodied, affective, suffering creatures, their memory and history, their ties and relations to others, are to be subsumed under the phenomenal realm, then what we are left with is an empty mask that is everyone and no one. Michael Sandel points out that the difficulty in Rawls's conception derives from his attempt to be consistent with the Kantian concept of the autonomous self, as a being freely choosing his or her own ends in life.[27] However, this moral and political concept of autonomy slips into a metaphysics according to which it is meaningful to define a self independently of *all* the ends it may choose and all and any conceptions of the good it may hold.[28] At this point we must ask whether the identity of any human self can be defined with reference to its capacity for agency alone. Identity does not refer to my potential for choice alone, but to the actuality of my choices, namely to how I, as a finite, concrete, embodied individual, shape and fashion the circumstances of my birth and family, linguistic, cultural and gender identity into a coherent narrative that stands as my life's story. Indeed, if we recall that every autonomous being is one born of others and not, as Rawls, following Hobbes, assumes, a being "not bound by prior moral ties to another,"[29] the question becomes: how does this finite, embodied creature constitute into a coherent narrative those episodes of choice and limitation, agency and suffering, initiative and dependence? The self is not a thing, a substrate, but the protagonist of a life's tale. The conception of selves who can be individuated prior to their moral ends is incoherent. We could not know if such a being was a human self, an angel, or the Holy Spirit.

If this concept of the self as mushroom, behind a veil of ignorance, is incoherent, then it follows that there is no real plurality of perspectives in the Rawlsian original position, but only a definitional identity. For Rawls, as Sandel observes, "our individuating characteristics are given empirically, by the distinctive concatenation of wants and desires, aims and attributes, purposes and ends that come to characterize human beings in their particularity."[30] But how are we supposed to know what these wants and desires are independently of knowing something about the person who holds these wants, desires, aims and attributes? Is there perhaps an "essence" of anger that is the same for each angry individual; an essence of ambition that is distinct from ambitious selves? I fail to see how individuating characteristics can be ascribed to a transcendental self who can have any and none of these, who can be all or none of them.

If selves who are epistemologically and metaphysically prior to their individuating characteristics, as Rawls takes them to be, cannot be human selves at all; if, therefore, there is no human *plurality* behind the veil of ignorance but only *definitional identity*, then this has consequences for criteria of reversibility and universalizability said to be constituents of the moral point of view. Definitional identity leads to *incomplete reversibility*, for the primary requisite of reversibility, namely, a coherent distinction between me and you, the self and the other, cannot be sustained under these circumstances. Under conditions of the veil of ignorance, the other disappears.

It is no longer plausible to maintain that such a standpoint can universalize adequately. Kohlberg views the veil of ignorance not only as exemplifying reversibility but universalizability as well. This is the idea that "we must be willing to live with our judgment or decision when we trade places with others in the situation being judged."[31] But the question is, *which* situation? Can moral situations be individuated independently of our knowledge of the agents involved in these situations, of their histories, attitudes, characters and desires? Can I describe a situation as one of arrogance or hurt pride without knowing something about you as a concrete other? Can I know how to distinguish between a breach of confidence and a harmless slip of the tongue, without knowing your history and your character? Moral situations, like moral emotions and attitudes, can only be individuated if they are evaluated in light of our knowledge of the history of the agents involved in them.

While every procedure of universalizability presupposes that "like cases ought to be treated alike" or that I should act in such a way that I should also be willing that all others in a like situation act like me, the most difficult aspect of any such procedure is to know what constitutes a "like" situation or what it would mean for another to be exactly in a situation like mine. Such a process of reasoning, to be at all viable, must involve the viewpoint of the concrete other, for situations, to paraphrase Stanley Cavell, do not come like "envelopes and golden finches" ready for definition and description, "nor like apples ripe for grading."[32] When we morally disagree, for example, we do not only disagree about the principles involved; very often we disagree because what I see as a lack of generosity on your part you construe as your legitimate right not to do something; we disagree because what you see as jealousy on my part I view as my desire to have more of your attention. Universalistic moral theory neglects such everyday, interactional morality and assumes that the public standpoint of justice, and our quasi-public personalities as right-bearing individuals, are the center of moral theory.[33]

Kohlberg emphasizes the dimension of ideal role-taking or taking the viewpoint of the other in moral judgment. Because he defines the other as the generalized other, however, he perpetuates one of the fundamental errors of Kantian moral theory. Kant's error was to assume that I, as a pure rational agent reasoning for myself, could reach a conclusion that would be acceptable for all at all times and places.[34] In Kantian moral theory, moral agents are like geometricians in different rooms who, reasoning alone for themselves, all arrive at the same solution to a problem. Following Habermas, I want to name this the "monological" model of moral reasoning. Insofar as he interprets ideal role-taking in the light of Rawls's concept of a "veil of ignorance," Kohlberg as well sees the silent thought process of a single self who imaginatively puts himself in the position of the other as the most adequate form of moral judgment.

I conclude that a definition of the self that is restricted to the standpoint of the generalized other becomes incoherent and cannot individuate among selves. Without assuming the standpoint of the concrete other, no coherent universalizability test can be carried out, for we lack the necessary epistemic information to judge my moral situation to be "like" or "unlike" yours.

4   The "Generalized" versus the "Concrete" Other Reconsidered

In the preceding parts of this chapter I have argued that the distinction between justice and the good life, the restriction of the moral domain to questions of justice, as well as the ideal of moral autonomy in these theories, result in the privatization of women's experience and lead to epistemological blindness toward the concrete other. The consequence of such epistemological blindess is an internal inconsistency in universalistic moral theories, insofar as these define "taking the standpoint of the other" as essential to the moral point of view. My aim has been to take universalistic moral theories at their word and to show through an immanent critique, first of the "state of nature" metaphor and then of the "original position," that the conception of the autonomous self implied by these thought experiments is restricted to the "generalized other."

The distinction between the generalized and the concrete other raises questions in moral and political theory. It may be asked whether, without the standpoint of the generalized other, it would be possible to define a moral point of view at all. Since our identities as concrete others are what distinguish us from each other according to gender, race, class, cultural differentials, as well as psychic and natural abilities, would a moral theory restricted to the standpoint of the concrete other not be a racist, sexist, cultural relativist and discriminatory one? Furthermore, without the standpoint of the generalized other, a political theory of justice suited for modern, complex societies is unthinkable. Certainly rights must be an essential component of any such theory. Finally, the perspective of the "concrete other" defines our relations as private, noninstitutional ones, concerned with love, care, friendship and intimacy. Are these activities so gender specific? Are we not all "concrete others"?

The distinction between the "generalized" and the "concrete" other, as drawn in this chapter so far, is not a *prescriptive* but a *critical* one. My goal is not to prescribe a moral or political theory consonant with the standpoint of the concrete other. As I have argued throughout part I, my purpose is to develop a universalistic moral theory that defines the "moral point of view" in light of the reversibility of perspectives and an "enlarged mentality." Such a moral theory allows us to recognize the dignity of the generalized other through an acknowledgement of the moral identity of the concrete other. Substitutionalist universalism dismisses the concrete other behind the facade of a definitional identity of all as rational beings, while interactive universalism acknowledges that every generalized other is also a concrete other.

To highlight this distinction between "substitutionalist" and "interactive" universalisms further, I would like to explore here a number of responses taking issue with my criticisms of the Rawlsian "original position."[35] In an illuminating article entitled "Reason and Feeling in Thinking about Justice," Susan Moller Okin has argued that the frequent criticisms voiced of John Rawls's *Theory of Justice* by feminist theorists rest on a misunderstanding of the central device of the "original position" in Rawls's theory.[36] Okin proposes an alternative account of this device "which is," she argues," both consistent with much that he says about it and much more compatible with his own account of moral development. It is this alternative account of what goes on in the original position that leads me to suggest that one is not forced to choose between an ethic of justice and an ethic of sympathy or care, nor between an ethic that emphasizes universality and one that takes account of differences."[37] Okin has to spend considerable time disentangling the frequent representations of the "original position" by Rawls himself as a "rational choice" model from the alternative account she proposes. In her view it makes no sense to view the original position as a moral device representing the reasoning of "mutually disinterested" individuals pursuing their interests, when these individuals do not even have knowledge about their interests to the extent that these are "distinct and differentiated"[38] from each other. Okin maintains that in effect it is not the image of mutually disinterested maximizers which captures Rawls's meaning but rather that of empathy, benevolence, and equal concern for others as for the self. She writes:

> The original position requires that, as moral subjects, we consider the identities, aims and attachments of every other person, however different they may be from ourselves, as of equal concern with our own. If we, who *do* know who we are, are to think *as if* we were in the original position, we must develop considerable capacities for empathy and powers of communicating with others about what different human lives are like. But these alone are not enough to maintain in us a sense of justice. Since we know who we are, and what are our particular interests and conceptions of the good, we need as well a great commitment to benevolence; to *caring* about each and every other as much as about ourselves.[39]

In stressing the aspects of benevolence, caring and empathy as being central to the Rawlsian project, Okin undoubtedly has contributed to a richer understanding of Rawls's work. One need only recall the following passage from the section on "The Morality of Principles." "But secondly," writes Rawls,

> it is also the case that the sense of justice is continuous with the love of mankind . . . benevolence is at a loss when the many objects of its love oppose one another. The principles of justice are needed to guide it. The difference between the principles of justice and the love of mankind is that the latter is supererogatory, going beyond the moral requirements and not invoking the exemptions which the principles of natural duty and obligation allow. Yet clearly the objects of these two sentiments are closely related, being defined in large part by the same conception of justice.[40]

Giving the moral sentiments of care, benevolence and love of mankind their due in Rawls's theory of justice surely reduces the stark opposition between reason and feeling, justice and care.

Nonetheless, this uncovering of the emotional or affective bases of Rawlsian theory does not meet the criticism of "epistemic incoherence" I have raised in section 3. My point is not that Rawlsian agents are egotistical, but that they are "disembedded" and "disembodied" selves, who are supposed to be able to reason from the standpoint of everyone else behind a "veil of ignorance." My point is that under the epistemic conditions of the "veil of ignorance" the other as distinct from the self disappears because the relevant criteria for *individuating* among selves are lacking. Okin herself admits as much when, in considering why Rawlsian selves in the original position cannot be rational interest maximizers, she asks: "But what sense does it make to talk of mutually disinterested individuals pursuing their interests when, to the extent that their interests are distinct and differentiated, they have no knowledge of them?"[41] Selves who do not have knowledge of their distinct interests can also not have adequate information about the interests of relevant others. All they really can know under conditions of the "veil of ignorance" is that it is reasonable to assume that each and every one would have certain very general interests, for example in the securing of a certain standard of material well-being with dignity. Rawls then asks us to imagine what distribution of material goods it would be most rational and reasonable to choose under the circumstances if we did not know who we were, what our talents and abilities, class, gender and race, etc., would be. Instead of thinking from the standpoint of all involved, that is instead of reversing perspectives and asking ourselves "what would it really be like to reason from the standpoint of a black welfare mother?" we are simply asked to think what distribution of material goods would be most rational and reasonable to adopt, if we did know in a general way that our society is such that one may be a black welfare mother of three children out of wedlock living in a rapidly decaying urban neighborhood.[42] There is no moral injunction in the original position to face the "otherness of the other," one might even say to face their "alterity," their irreducible distinctness and difference from the self. I do not doubt that respect for the other and their individuality is a central guiding concern of the Rawlsian theory; but the problem is that the Kantian presuppositions also guiding the Rawlsian theory are so weighty that the equivalence of all selves qua rational agents dominates and stifles any serious acknowledgment of difference, alterity and of the standpoint of the "concrete other." Okin writes: "To think as a person in the original position is not to be a disembodied nobody. This, as critics have rightly pointed out, would be impossible. Rather, it is to think from the point of view of everybody, of every 'concrete other' whom one might turn out to be."[43] Let me dwell on this issue one more time: are there really "concrete others" in the Rawlsian construction of the original position behind a "veil of ignorance?"

The issue is both epistemic and political. Let us begin by recalling that certainly we never are and neither will we ever be in an "original position." This device is intended "to make vivid to ourselves the restrictions that it seems reasonable to impose on arguments for principles of justice, and therefore on these principles themselves."[44] The original position is intended to illustrate the conception of justice as fairness. In this sense, Okin is right that "we, who *do* know who we are, are to think *as if* we were in the original position,"[45] and did not know who we were. Now how do we know who the others are? The first answer is that of course we bring with us into the original position all the knowledge, information, as well as assumptions and prejudices, we have about "others" given who we previously were in society. The second answer is that this knowledge and these assumptions are then "deactivated," so to speak, behind the "veil of ignorance" so that what we know about "others" is that "we are all similarly situated," and that there is a "symmetry of everyone's relations to each other."[46] Thus on the one hand selves in the "original position" bring with them into this process of imaginary deliberation all the assumptions and prejudices which guide them in everyday life; on the other hand, these assumptions and prejudices are not really "defused," that is confronted, discussed, worked out and worked through in an open dialogue with concrete others, instead they are simply "deactivated," that is placed behind a "veil of ignorance." There is therefore the very real danger that in not making room to confront the "otherness" of the other, the original position, despite all of Rawls's own intentions to the contrary, can leave all our prejudices, misunderstandings and hostilities in society, just as they are, hidden behind a veil. By contrast, only a moral dialogue that is truly open and reflexive and that does not function with unnecessary epistemic limitations can lead to a mutual understanding of otherness.

Neither the concreteness nor the otherness of the "concrete other" can be known in the absence of the *voice* of the other. The viewpoint of the concrete other emerges as a distinct one only as a result of self-definition. It is the other who makes us aware both of her concreteness and her otherness.[47] Without engagement, confrontation, dialogue and even a "struggle for recognition" in the Hegelian sense, we tend to constitute the otherness of the other by projection and fantasy or ignore it in indifference. I therefore trust much less than Okin (and even Gilligan) the sentiments of empathy and benevolence; for, as Arendt also has noted,[48] the capacity for exercising an "enlarged mentality," the ability to take the standpoint of the other into account is not empathy although it is related to it. Empathy means the capacity to "feel with, to feel together." Yet precisely very empathetic individuals may also be the ones lacking an "enlarged mentality," for their empathetic nature may make it difficult for them to draw the boundaries between self and other such that the standpoint of the "concrete other" can emerge. Ironically, I agree here much more with Rawls than with either Okin or Gilligan that "because the objects of benevolence" – and I would add empathy – oppose one another, one needs principles, institutions and procedures to enable articulation of the voice of "others."

There is a certain point in the argumentation of *A Theory of Justice* when the issue of the "concrete other" returns but is left dangling, without any kind of resolution. Rawls proposes that the second principle should be read such as to imply that "social and economic inequalities are to be arranged so that they are both (a) to the greatest benefit of the least advantaged and (b) attached to offices and positions open to all under considerations of fair equality of opportunity."[49] How do we identify the "least disadvantaged" individual in society? This involves Rawls's theory in extremely complex issues of intersubjective utility comparisons, but even more significantly, the moral and political process by which citizens in a democratic polity could learn to identify "the least disadvantaged" is short-circuited. Rawls falls back upon "substitutionalist" reasoning when in fact he assumes that we can, for purposes of distribution, identify "the expectations of representative men."[50] But who are the "least disadvantaged" in our society: the black welfare mother of three? the white Detroit autoworker, father of four, who loses his position after 20 years of work? the divorced suburban housewife whose household is liquidated and who has no skills to enter the workforce? etc. I see no satisfactory resolution to this question within the scope of *A Theory of Justice*.[51]

In the final analysis then, my critique of Rawls is a procedural one: I am critical of the construction of the "original position" as an implausibly restricted process of individual deliberation rather than as an open-ended process of collective moral argumentation. As I have argued at many points above, the model of discourse or communicative ethics is to be preferred to this for it institutionalizes an actual dialogue among actual selves who are both "generalized others," considered as equal moral agents, and "concrete others," that is individuals with irreducible differences.

Both the Rawlsian "original position" and the Habermasian model of "discourse ethics" are idealizations intended to make vivid to us the ideal of impartiality or of what it means to assume the moral standpoint. Their differences center around the following points. According to discourse ethics, the moral standpoint is not to be construed primarily as a *hypothetical* thought process, carried out singly by the moral agent or by the moral philosopher, but rather as an *actual* dialogue situation in which moral agents communicate with one another. Second, in the discourse model no epistemic restrictions are placed upon moral reasoning and moral disputation, for the more knowledge is availabe to moral agents about each other, their history, the particulars of their society, its structure and future, the more rational will be the outcome of their deliberations. Practical rationality involves epistemic rationality as well, and more knowledge rather than less contributes to a more informed and rational judgment. To judge rationally is not to judge as if one did not know what one could know (the effect of hanging the "veil of ignorance"), but to judge in light of all available and relevant information. Third, if there are no knowledge restrictions to be placed upon such an argumentative situation, then it also follows that there is no privileged subject matter of moral disputation. In the discourse model, moral agents are not only limited to reasoning about primary goods which they are assumed to want whatever else they want. Instead, both the *goods* they desire and their *desires* themselves can become subjects of moral disputation. Finally, in such moral discourses agents can also change levels of reflexivity, that is they can introduce metaconsiderations about the very conditions and constraints under which such dialogue takes place and they can evaluate their fairness. There is no closure of reflexivity in this model as there is in the Rawlsian one.

A consequence of this model of communicative or discourse ethics would be that the language of rights can now be challenged in light of our need interpretations, and that the object domain of moral theory is so enlarged that not only issues of justice but questions of the good life as well are moved to the center of discourse. The discourse or communicative model of ethics subverts the distinction between an ethics of justice and rights and one of care and responsibility, insofar as it moves the limits of moral discourse to the point when visions of the good life underlying conceptions of justice and assumptions about needs and interests sustaining rights claims become visible. We reach here a conclusion already attained at the end of chapter 3, namely the need to reconsider, revise, and perhaps reject the dichotomies between justice versus the good life, interests versus needs, norms versus values upon which the discourse model, upon Habermas's interpretation of it, rests. The following chapter will therefore consider the challenge posed to discourse ethics by Gilligan's work; for certainly what I would like to claim on behalf of this model and the manner in which I want to assimilate Gilligan's insights into it are not the same as what Habermas himself has written in response to Gilligan's work. Ironically, what I claim to be the virtues of the discourse model when compared to the Rawlsian one Habermas diffuses and retracts when, much like Lawrence Kohlberg, he proceeds to distinguish sharply between moral and ego development, justice versus the good life, norms versus values, needs versus interests. However, it is Carol Gilligan's lasting contribution to moral theory and moral psychology that she has made us aware of the implicit models of selfhood, autonomy, impartiality and justice sustained and privileged by such dichotomous reasoning. The ideal of autonomy in universalistic moral theories from the social contract tradition down to Rawls's and Kohlberg's work is based upon an implicit politics which defines the "personal," in the sense of the intimate/domestic sphere, as ahistorical, immutable and unchanging, thereby removing it from discussion and reflexion. Needs, interests, as well as emotions and affects, are then considered properties of individuals which moral philosophy recoils from examining on the grounds that it may interfere with the autonomy of the sovereign self. What Carol Gilligan has heard are those mutterings, protestations and objections voiced by women who were confronted with ways of posing moral dilemmas that seemed alien to them and who were faced with visions of selfhood which left them cold. Only if we can understand why this voice has been so marginalized in moral theory, and how the dominant ideals of moral autonomy in our culture, as well as the privileged definition of the moral sphere, continue to silence women's voices, do we have a hope for moving to a more integrated vision of ourselves and of our fellow humans as generalized as well as "concrete others."

Notes

Earlier versions of this chapter were read at the conference on Women and Morality, State University of New York at Stony Brook. 22–4 March, 1985, and at the Philosophy and Social Science course at the Inter-University Center in Dubrovnik, Yugoslavia, 2–4 April, 1985. I would like to thank participants at both conferences for their criticisms and suggestions. Larry Blum and Eva Feder Kittay have made valuable suggestions for corrections. Nancy Fraser's commentary on this work, "Toward a Discourse Ethic of Solidarity," *Praxis International*, 5.4 (Jan. 1986), pp. 425–30, as well as her "Struggle over Needs," in *Unruly Practices* (Polity, Cambridge, 1989), have been crucial in helping me articulate the political implications of the position developed here. Versions of this chapter have appeared in the proceedings of the Women and Moral Theory conference, edited by E. F. Kittay and Diana T. Meyers, *Women and Moral Theory* (Rowman and Littlefield, Totowa, NJ, 1987), pp. 154–78, and in *Feminism as Critique*, ed. Seyla Benhabib and Drucilla Cornell (University of Minnesota Press, Minneapolis, 1987).

1 Thomas Kuhn, *The Structure of Scientific Revolutions*, 2nd edn (University of Chicago Press, Chicago, 1970), pp. 52ff.
2 John Michael Murphy and Carol Gilligan, "Moral Development in Late Adolescence and Adulthood: A Critique and Reconstruction of Kohlberg's Theory," *Human Development*, 23 (1980), pp. 77–104.
3 Carol Gilligan, *In a Different Voice: Psychological Theory and Women's Development* (Harvard University Press, Cambridge, Mass., 1982), pp. 18–19.
4 Lawrence Kohlberg, "Synopses and Detailed Replies to Critics," with Charles Levine and Alexandra Hewer, in L. Kohlberg, *Essays on Moral Development* (Harper and Row, San Francisco, 1984), vol. 2: *The Psychology of Moral Development* p. 341.
5 There still seems to be some question as to how the data on women's moral development is to be interpreted. Studies which focus on late adolescents and adult males and which show sex differences, include J. Fishkin, K. Keniston and C. MacKinnon, "Moral Reasoning and Political Ideology," *Journal of Personality and Social Psychology*, 27 (1983), pp. 109–19; N. Haan, J. Block and M. B. Smith, "Moral Reasoning of Young Adults: Political–Social Behavior, Family Background, and Personality Correlates," *Journal of Personality and Social Psychology*, 10 (1968), pp. 184–201; C. Holstein, "Irreversible, Stepwise Sequence in the Development of Moral Judgment: A Longitudinal Study of Males and Females," *Child Development*, 47 (1976), pp. 51–61. While it is clear that the available evidence does not throw the model of stage-sequence development as such into question, the prevalent presence of sex differences in moral reasoning does raise questions about *what* exactly this model might be measuring. Norma Haan sums up this objection to the Kohlbergian paradigm as follows: "Thus the moral reasoning of males who live in technical, rationalized societies, who reason at the level of formal operations and who *defensively intellectualize and deny interpersonal and situational detail*, is especially favored in the Kohlbergian scoring

system," in "Two Moralities in Action Contexts: Relationships to Thought, Ego Regulation, and Development," *Journal of Personality and Social Psychology*, 36 (1978), p. 287; emphasis mine. I think Gilligan's studies also support the finding that inappropriate "intellectualization and denial of interpersonal, situational detail" constitutes one of the major differences in male and female approaches to moral problems. This is why, as I argue in the text, the neat separation between ego and moral development, as drawn by Kohlberg and Habermas, is inadequate to deal with this problem, since certain ego attitudes – defensiveness, rigidity, inability to empathize, lack of flexibility – do seem to be favored over others like nonrepressive attitudes toward emotions, flexibility, presence of empathy.

6   L. Kohlberg, "A Reply to Owen Flanagan and Some Comments on the Puka–Goodpaster Exchange," *Ethics*, 92 (April 1982), p. 316. Cf. also Gertrud Nunner-Winkler, "Two Moralities? A Critical Discussion of an Ethic of Care and Responsibility Versus an Ethics of Rights and Justice," in *Morality, Moral Behavior and Moral Development* ed. W. M. Kurtines and J. L. Gewirtz (John Wiley, New York, 1984), p. 355. It is unclear whether the issue is, as Kohlberg and Nunner-Winkler suggest, one of distinguishing between "moral" and "ego" development or whether cognitive-development moral theory does not presuppose a model of ego development which clashes with more psychoanalytically oriented variants. In fact, to combat the charge of "maturationism" or "nativism" in his theory, which would imply that moral stages are a priori givens of the mind unfolding according to their own logic, regardless of the influence of society or environment upon them, Kohlberg argues as follows: "Stages," he writes, "are equilibrations arising from interaction between the organism (with its structuring tendencies) and the structure of the environment (physical or social). Universal moral stages are as much a function of universal features of social structure (such as institutions of law, family, property) and social interactions in various cultures, as they are products of the general structuring tendencies of the knowing organism" ("A Reply to Owen Flanagan," p. 521). If this is so, then cognitive-developmental moral theory must also presuppose that there is a *dynamic* between self and social structure whereby the individual learns, acquires or internalizes the perspectives and sanctions of the social world. But the mechanism of this dynamic may involve learning as well as resistance, internalization as well as projection and fantasy. The issue is less whether moral development and ego development are distinct – they may be distinguished conceptually and yet in the history of the self they are related – but whether the model of ego development presupposed by Kohlberg's theory is not distortingly *cognitivistic* in that it ignores the role of affects, resistance, projection, phantasy-and defense mechanisms in socialization processes.

7   For this formulation, see J. Habermas, "Interpretive Social Science vs. Hermeneuticism," in *Social Science as Moral Inquiry*, ed. N. Haan, R. Bellah, P. Rabinow and W. Sullivan (Columbia University Press, New York, 1983), p. 262.

8   Imre Lakatos, "Falsification and the Methodology of Scientific Research Programs," in *Criticism and the Growth of Knowledge*, ed. Lakatos and A. Musgrave, (Cambridge University Press, Cambridge, 1970), pp. 117ff.

9   Let me explain the status of this premise. I would characterize it as a "second-order research hypothesis" that both guides concrete research in the social sciences and can, in turn, be falsified by them. It is not a statement of faith about the way the world is: the cross-cultural and transhistorical universality of the sex-gender system is an empirical fact. It is also most definitely not a normative proposition about the way the world *ought* to be. To the contrary, feminism radically challenges the validity of the sex-gender system in organizing societies and cultures, and advocates the emancipation of men and women from the unexamined and oppressive grids of this framework.

10   For further clarification of these two aspects of critical theory, see part 2, "The Transformation of Critique," in my *Critique, Norm, and Utopia: A Study of the Foundations of Critical Theory* (Columbia University Press, New York, 1986).

11   Although frequently invoked by Kohlberg, Nunner-Winkler and also Habermas, it is still unclear *how* this distinction is drawn and how it is justified. For example, does the justice/good life distinction correspond to sociological definitions of the public versus the private? If so, what is meant by the "private"? Is women-battering a "private" or a "public" matter? As I have argued in chapter 3 above, the relevant sociological definitions of the private and the public are shilfting in our societies, as they have shifted historically. For further discussion, see below pp. 186ff.

12   Alasdair MacIntyre, *After Virtue* (University of Notre Dame Press, Notre Dame, 1981), pp. 50–1.

13   Agnes Heller, *A Theory of Feelings* (Van Gorcum, Holland, 1979), pp. 184ff.

14   John Locke, "The Second Treatise of Civil Government" in *Two Treatises of Government*, ed. and introd. Thomas I. Cook (Haffner, New York, 1947), p. 128.

15   Immanuel Kant, *The Metaphysical Elements of Justice*, trans. John Ladd (Liberal Arts Press, New York, 1965), p. 55.

16   Thomas Hobbes, *Leviathan* (1651), ed. and introd. C. B. Macpherson (Penguin, Harmondsworth, 1980), p. 186. All future citations in the text are to this edition.

17   Thomas Hobbes, "Philosophical Rudiments Concerning Government and Society," in *The English Works of Thomas Hobbes*, ed. W. Molesworth (Wissenschaftliche Buchgesellschaft, Darmstadt, 1966), vol. 2, p. 109.

18   J. J. Rousseau, "On The Origin and Foundations of Inequality Among Men," in Rousseau, *The First and Second Discourse*, ed. R. D. Masters, trans. Roger D. Masters and Judith R. Masters (St Martin's, New York, 1964), p. 116.

19   G. W. F. Hegel, *Phänomenologie des Geistes*, 6th edn, ed. Johannes Hoffmeister (Felix Meiner, Hamburg, 1952), Philosophische Bibliothek

114, p. 141; translation used here *Phenomenology of Spirit*, trans. A. V. Miller (Clarendon, Oxford, 1977), p. 111.

20 Sigmund Freud, *Moses and Monotheism*, trans. Katharine Jones (Random House, New York, 1967), pp. 103ff.; Jean Piaget, *The Moral Judgment of the Child*, trans. Majorie Gabain (Free Press, New York, 1965), pp. 65ff., cf. the following comment on boys' and girls' games: "The most superficial observation is sufficient to show that in the main the legal sense is far less developed in little girls than in boys. We did not succeed in finding a single collective game played by girls in which there were as many rules and, above all, as fine and consistent an organization and codification of these rules as in the game of marbles examined above" (p. 77).

21 Kant, "Critique of Practical Reason" in *Critique of Practical Reason and Other Writings in Moral Philosophy*, trans., ed. and introd. Louis White Beck (University of Chicago Press, Chicago, 1949), p. 258.

22 Although the term "generalized other" is borrowed from George Herbert Mead, my definition of it differs from his. Mead defines the "generalized other" as follows: "The organized community or social group which gives the individual his unity of self may be called the 'generalized other.' The attitude of the generalized other is the attitude of the whole community." George Herbert Mead, *Mind, Self and Society. From the Standpoint of a Social Behaviorist*, ed. and introd. Charles W. Morris (University of Chicago Press, Chicago, 1955), p. 154. Among such communities Mead includes a ball team as well as political clubs, corporations and other more abstract social classes or subgroups such as the class of debtors and the class of creditors (p. 157). Mead himself does not limit the concept of the "generalized other" to what is described in the text. In identifying the "generalized other" with the abstractly defined, legal and juridical subject, contract theorists and Kohlberg depart from Mead. Mead criticizes the social contract tradition precisely for distorting the psychosocial genesis of the individual subject, cf. ibid., p. 233.

23 Kohlberg, "Justice as Reversibility: The Claim to Moral Adequacy of a Highest Stage of Moral Judgment," in *Essays on Moral Development*, (Harper and Row, San Francisco, 1981), vol. 1: *The Philosophy of Moral Development* p. 194.

24 Whereas all forms of reciprocity involve some conceptions of reversibility these vary in degree: reciprocity can be restricted to the reversibility of actions but not of moral perspectives, to behavioral role models but not to the principles which underlie the generation of such behavioral expectations. For Kohlberg, the "veil of ignorance" is a model of perfect reversibility, for it elaborates the procedure of "ideal role-taking" or "moral musical chairs" where the decider "is to successively put himself imaginatively in the place of each other actor and consider the claims each would make from his point of view" (Kohlberg, "Justice as Reversibility," p. 199). My question is: are there any real "others" behind the "veil of ignorance" or are they indistinguishable from the self?

25 I find Kohlberg's general claim that the moral point of view entails

reciprocity, equality and fairness unproblematic. Reciprocity is not only a fundamental *moral* principle, but defines, as Alvin Gouldner has argued, a fundamental *social norm*, perhaps in fact the very concept of a social norm: "The Norm of Reciprocity: A Preliminary Statement," *American Sociological Review*, 25 (April 1960), pp. 161–78. The existence of ongoing social relations in a human community entails some definition of reciprocity in the actions, expectations and claims of the group. The fulfillment of such reciprocity, according to whatever interpretation is given to it, would then be considered fairness by members of the group. Likewise, members of a group bound by relations of reciprocity and fairness are considered equal. What changes through history and culture are not these formal structures implicit in the very logic of social relations (we can even call them social universals), but the criteria of inclusion and exclusion. Who constitutes the relevant human groups: masters versus slaves, men versus women, Gentiles versus Jews? Similarly, which aspects of human behavior and objects of the world are to be regulated by norms of reciprocity: in the societies studied by Levi-Strauss, some tribes exchange sea shells for women. Finally, in terms of what is the equality among members of a group established: would this be gender, race, merit, virtue, or entitlement? Clearly Kohlberg presupposes a *universalist-egalitarian* interpretation of reciprocity, fairness and equality, according to which all humans, in virtue of their mere humanity, are to be considered beings entitled to reciprocal rights and duties.

26 John Rawls, *A Theory of Justice*, 2nd edn. (Harvard University Press, Cambridge, Mass., 1971), p. 137.
27 Michael J. Sandel, *Liberalism and the Limits of Justice* (Harvard University Press, Cambridge, Mass., 1982), p. 9.
28 Ibid., pp. 47ff.
29 Rawls, *A Theory of Justice*, p. 128.
30 Sandel, *Liberalism and the Limits of Justice*, p. 51.
31 Kohlberg: "Justice as Reversibility," p. 197.
32 Stanley Cavell, *The Claims of Reason* (Oxford University Press, Oxford, 1982), p. 265.
33 A most suggestive critique of Kohlberg's neglect of interpersonal morality has been developed by Norma Haan in "Two Moralities in Action Contexts," pp. 286–305. Haan reports that "formulation of formal morality appears to apply best to special kinds of hypothetical, rule-governed dilemmas, the paradigmatic situation in the minds of philosophers over the centuries" (p. 302). Interpersonal reasoning, by contrast, "arises within the context of moral dialogues between agents who strive to achieve balanced agreement, based on compromises they reach or on their joint discovery of interests they hold in common" (p. 303). For a more extensive statement see also Norma Haan, "An Interactional Morality of Everyday Life," in *Social Science as Moral Inquiry*, pp. 218–51.
34 Cf. E. Tugendhat, "Zur Entwicklung von moralischen Begründungsstrukturen im modernen Recht," *Archiv für Recht und Sozialphilosophie*, 68 (1980), pp. 1–20.

35   The following sections of this article are new and were not contained in the original version.

36   Susan Moller Okin, "Reason and Feeling in Thinking about Justice," *Ethics*, 99.2 (Jan. 1989), pp. 229ff.

37   Ibid., p. 238.

38   Ibid., p. 242.

39   Ibid., p. 246.

40   Rawls, *A Theory of Justice*, p. 476.

41   Okin, "Reason and Feeling in Thinking about Justice," p. 242.

42   In "The Methodological Illusions of Modern Political Theory," I explored some of the difficulties linked with Rawls's understanding of social science. Behind the conditions of the "veil of ignorance" individuals are allowed knowledge of "general social facts" (see Rawls, *A Theory of Justice*, pp. 137ff.). I ask whether one can separate the general and the particular so neatly in social-scientific information as Rawls assumes, and how much in effect one would have to know about society and history even to be able to construct the standpoint of the "least disadvantaged" person in the theory. See Benhabib, "The Methodological Illusions," *Neue Hefte für Philosophie*, 21 (Spring 1982), pp. 47–74. I return to the problem of the "least advantaged person" in Rawls's theory below.

43   Okin, "Reason and Feeling in Thinking about Justice," p. 248.

44   Rawls, *A Theory of Justice*, p. 18.

45   Okin, "Reason and Feeling in Thinking about Justice," p. 246.

46   The last two quotes are from Rawls, *A Theory of Justice*, p. 12.

47   Agreeing with Okin's critique of my objections to the Rawlsian position as stated above, Will Kymlicka has recently written that "The fact that people are asked to reason in abstraction from their own social position, natural talents, and personal preferences when thinking about others does not mean that they must ignore the particular preferences, talents and social position of others . . . Benhabib assumes that the original position works by requiring contractors to consider the interests of the other contractors (who all become 'generalized others' behind the veil of ignorance)." Will Kymlicka, *Contemporary Political Philosophy: An Introduction* (Clarendon, Oxford, 1990), p. 274. Kymlicka points out that behind the veil of ignorance it no longer matters who, if anyone, occupies this position or what its occupant's interests are. Citing Jean Hampton, he concludes that "What matters to him are the desires and goals of every *actual* member of his society, because the veil forces him to reason *as if he were any one of them* . . . Both devices, impartial contractors and ideal sympathizers, work by requiring people to consider concrete others" (ibid.). I have two objections to this argument: First, as I have pointed out in the text, there is an epistemic deficit in the construction of the original position such as would not enable individuals to discover the desires and goals "of every actual member of his society." What we would know about the "actual" others we would only know either by the partial informations we had before we entered the thought-experiment of the "original position" or we would know by assuming that the other is so much like us that we can safely attribute

to her the same concatenation of needs and interests we attribute to ourselves. I believe from a moral point of view neither procedure is very satisfactory, since it allows one to avoid a crucial aspect of the moral experience, namely the recognition of the alterity of the other and the necessity to come to a shared standpoint by taking cognizance of this otherness. Second, the standpoint of the "concrete others" are constructed in the Rawlsian original position via a series of idealizations and attributions. As Rawls has made amply clear in his writings subsequent to *A Theory of Justice*, his intention was not to proceed from a conception of self based upon strong metaphysical presuppositions, but rather to construct a conception of the "person" as a public-moral agent who has "a rational plan of life in the light of which they schedule their most important endeavors and allocate their various resources (including those of mind and body) so as to pursue their conceptions of the good over a complete life, if not in the most rational, then at least in a sensible (or satisfactory) way." John Rawls, "The Priority of Right and Ideas of the Good," *Philosophy and Public Affairs*, 19 (1988), p. 254. While these subsequent clarifications have elucidated the "constructivist" rather than metaphysical aspects of Rawls's procedure, I would still maintain that behind the device of the "veil of ignorance" individuals cannot be individuated and thus distinguished from one another and that we are still reasoning from the standpoint of the "generalized" other; the concrete others are in fact only "pseduo-other" and "pseduo-concrete." Kymlicka does not accept this conclusion, for he assumes all too readily that the psychology of the "impartial contractor" and the "ideal observer" are plausible. As my discussion of the standpoint of "the least disadvantaged individual" below will indicate, I see difficulties here.

48 Hannah Arendt, "Crisis in Culture," in *Between Past and Future* (Meridian, Cleveland and New York, 1961) p. 221.

49 Rawls, *A Theory of Justice*, p. 83.

50 Ibid., p. 70.

51 This whole issue touches upon the difficult problem of intersubjective utility comparisons in economic theory, but even before one gets to that set of comparisons, there is another question which one must face: certainly from the standpoint of policies of distribution, which guide the principles according to which institutions allocate scarce resources, it may be necessary to construct some fiction of the "least disadvantaged individual." Moral theory, however, and particularly a theory of justice for a democratic polity must be concerned with the process of public dialogue through which individuals come to an understanding of the sufferings, miseries and humiliations of those fellow citizens who are quite unlike themselves. Reaching a definition of the "least disadvantaged individual" is very much dependent upon furthering the process of moral and political understanding in an inegalitarian society, still very much divided along class, race and gender lines.

6 The Debate over Women and Moral Theory Revisited

The contemporary debate over women and moral theory, which was prompted in 1982 with the publication of Carol Gilligan's *In a Different Voice*, by now has generated an impressive literature of a truly multidisciplinary nature. Reflecting back on the various themes and disagreements of this debate, we can isolate several reasons why Gilligan's work, in addition to its intrinsic merits, insights and elegance, would become the focus of such an intense, and interestingly enough, non-acrimonious controversy.

In a Different Voice reflected a coming of age of women's scholarship within the domain of "normal science," in Thomas Kuhn's sense of the word. Like Nancy Chodorow's *The Reproduction of Mothering* in socialization theory, Evelyn Fox Keller's *A Feeling for the Organism* and *Reflections on Gender and Science* in the social studies of science, and Geneviève Lloyd's *The Man of Reason* in the history of philosophy, Gilligan's work showed the consequences of raising the "women's question" from within the parameters of established scientific discourse. Once women are inserted into the picture, be it as objects of social-scientific research or as subjects conducting such inquiry, established paradigms are unsettled. The definition of the *object domain* of a research paradigm, its units of measurement, its method of verification, the alleged neutrality of its theoretical terminology, and the claims to universality of its models and metaphors are all thrown into question.

Gilligan's work in cognitive and moral development theory recapitulated an experience that women's historians had first encountered in their own field. Joan Kelly Gadol has described this in a 1975 article entitled "The Social Relations of the Sexes: Methodological Implications of Women's History" as follows:

> Once we look at history for an understanding of women's situation, we are, of course, already assuming that women's situation is a social

matter. But history, as we first come to it, did not seem to confirm this awareness . . . The moment this is done – the moment that one assumes that women are a part of humanity in the fullest sense – the period or set of events with which we deal takes on a wholly different character or meaning from the normally accepted one. Indeed, what emerges is a fairly regular pattern of relative loss of status for women in periods of so-called progressive changes . . . Suddenly we see these ages with a new double vision – and each eye sees a different picture.[1]

Kelly Gadol writes of a "doubled vision," each eye seeing something different. Gilligan writes of hearing a different voice. In each case, the experience is the same. The women's question – women as objects of inquiry and as subjects carrying out such inquiry – upsets established paradigms. Women discover difference where previously sameness had prevailed; they sense dissonance and contradiction where formerly uniformity had reigned; they note the double meaning of words where formerly the signification of terms had been taken for granted; and they establish the persistence of injustice, inequality and regression in processes that were formerly characterized as just, egalitarian and progressive.

In the following discussion I shall isolate two broad ranges of issues from among the complex set of problems within and outside the confines of feminist theory which Gilligan's work has given rise to. While the second half of this chapter will look at the methodological status of the category of "gender" and at the question of "difference" in Gilligan's research on women and moral theory, in the first half I shall continue to explore the implications of Gilligan's research for universalist moral philosophy.

Universalist Moral Philosophies and Carol Gilligan's Challenge

Undoubtedly, Carol Gilligan's work invoked the widespread recognition and controversy that it did not only because it reflected the coming of age of women's scholarship within the paradigms of normal science; equally significant was that the kinds of questions which Gilligan was asking of the Kohlbergian paradigm were also being asked of universalist neo-Kantian moral philosophies by a growing and influential number of critics. As I have explored previously, these communitarian, neo-Aristotelian, and even neo-Hegelian critics of Kantianism like Michael Walzer, Michael Sandel, Alasdair MacIntyre and Charles Taylor, like Gilligan herself, questioned the formalism, cognitivism and claims to universality of Kantian theories. Just as Gilligan challenged the separation of form from content in the evaluation of moral judgment, so too MacIntyre argued that out of the pure form of the moral law alone no substantive moral principles could be deduced.[2] Just as Gilligan reported her female subjects' sense of bewilderment in view of a language of morals which would pose even the most personal of all dilemmas like abortion in terms of formal rights, so too Michael Sandel maintained that a polity based on the procedural and juridical model of human relationships alone would lack a certain solidarity and depth of identity.[3] And just as Gilligan doubted that the Kohlbergian model of the development of moral judgment could claim the universality that it did in view of the difficulties this model encountered in accounting for women's judgment and sense of self,[4] others like Taylor and Walzer questioned whether the form of moral judgments of justice could be so neatly isolated from the content of cultural conceptions of the good life.[5] There was a remarkable convergence then between the Gilligan-type feminist critique of Kantian universalism and the objections raised by these other thinkers.[6]

But exactly what implications should one draw from Gilligan's findings, which themselves have been moderated over time, for universalist moral philosophies? Does Gilligan's work suggest and even warrant replacing an ethics of justice with an ethics of care? My own position on this complex issue is that Gilligan's work to date does not provide us with sufficient reasons to want to reject universalist moral philosophies. Gilligan has not explained what "an ethic of care" as opposed to an "ethical orientation to care reasoning" would consist of, nor has she provided the philosophical argumentation necessary to formulate a different conception of the moral point of view or of impartiality than the Kohlbergian one. Many of her formulations rather suggest that she would like to see the ethics of justice complemented by an ethical orientation to care.[7] These approaches are complementary and not antagonistic. Undoubtedly, one can also attempt to formulate a "feminine ethic of care,"[8] but this is not an implication supported by Gilligan's own work. Precisely because I do not think that a moral theory adequate to the way of life of complex modern societies can be formulated without some universalist specification of impartiality and the moral point of view, I find it more fruitful to read Gilligan's work not as a wholesale rejection of universalism – for which there is little evidence in her own texts – but as a contribution to the development of a non-formalist, contextually sensitive and postconventional understanding of ethical life. I shall attempt to specify this claim by taking my cue from a penetrating analysis of the relation between the justice and care perspectives provided by Lawrence Blum.

In a recent article on "Gilligan and Kohlberg: Implications for Moral Theory," Lawrence A. Blum outlines a hypothetical response to Carol Gilligan that could be given by defenders of the "impartialist conception of morality." Impartialism is understood in this context to characterize not only Lawrence Kohlberg's view of morality, but to have been "the dominant conception of morality in contemporary Anglo-American moral philosophy, forming the core of both a Kantian conception of morality and important strands in utilitarian (and, more generally, consequentialist) thinking as well."[9] Impartialism demands that the moral point of view articulate impersonality, justice, formal rationality, and universal principle. Blum then suggests that the relation between impartialist moralities and a morality of care can be conceived of in eight different ways:

1   One can deny that the care orientation constitutes a genuinely distinct moral position from impartialism. "Acting from care is actually acting on perhaps complex but nevertheless fully universalizable principles, generated ultimately from an impartial point of view."[10]

2   While care for others, it may be argued, constitutes a genuinely important set of concerns and relationships in human life, nevertheless such concerns are more personal than moral ones.[11]

3   This position admits that concerns of care and responsibility in relationships are truly moral (as opposed to being merely personal) but it claims that they are secondary to, parasitic upon and/or less important than principles of impartiality, right and universality.[12]

4   Care, it is said, is genuinely moral and is a moral orientation distinct from impartiality, but it is inadequate because it cannot be universalized. An ethics of care, it may be argued, is ultimately inadequate from a moral point of view for the objects of our care and compassion can never encompass all of mankind but must always remain particularistic and personal. An ethics of care can thus revert to a conventional group ethics, for which the well-being of the reference group is the essence of morality. This reference group may be the family, the nation, a particular affinity group, let us say a political or an artistic avant-garde, to whom the individual owes special allegiance. An ethics of care yields a non-universalizable group morality.

5   According to this position, the difference between an ethics of care and one of impartiality is in the "objects of moral assessment" or in the "construal of the domain of the moral." While care is concerned with the evaluation of persons, motives and character, impartiality is concerned with the evaluation of actions, principles, and rules of institutional life.

6   While care and responsibility are appropriate moral responses

in certain situations, it is claimed, considerations of an impartialist conception of right set the constraints within which care is allowed to guide our conduct. "Considerations of impartiality trump considerations stemming from care; if the former conflict with the latter, it is care which must yield."[13]

7 Position 7 can be seen as an elaboration of position 6. While considerations of care are genuinely moral, nevertheless their ultimate justifiability "rests on their being able to be validated or affirmed from an impartial perspective."[14]

8 The last position is one that suggests that in the final, most mature stage of moral reasoning the perspectives of "justice and care" will be integrated to form a single moral principle.[15]

Using this scheme, I shall first look more closely at Habermas's response to the challenge posed by Gilligan's work; in the second place, I shall suggest how on my own understanding of discourse ethics as a conversational model of enlarged mentality, a different response to Gilligan becomes not only possible but also desirable.

(a) In "Moral Consciousness and Communicative Action," Jürgen Habermas suggests that Carol Gilligan, particularly in her article co-authored with J. M. Murphy on "Moral Development in Late Adolescence and Adulthood: A Critique and Reconstruction of Kohlberg's Theory," fails to disentangle the complex set of problems which arise when, in the transition from adolescence to adulthood, the everyday lifeworld of our community loses its prima facie validity for the individual and is judged from a moral point of view. Habermas writes:

> Thus the formation of the moral point of view goes hand in hand with a differentiation within the sphere of the practical: *moral questions*, which can in principle be decided rationally in terms of criteria of *justice* or the universalizability of interests are now distinguished from *evaluative questions*, which fall into the general category of issues of the *good life* and are accessible to rational discussion only *within* the horizon of a concrete historical form of life or an individual life style. The concrete ethical life of a naively habituated lifeworld is characterized by the fusion of moral and evaluative issues. Only in a rationalized lifeworld do moral issues become independent of issues of the good life.[16]

How does this observation bear on Gilligan's and Murphy's argument for the necessity of formulating a "postconventional contextualist" position which will take into account the dilemmas of applying ethical principles in complex life-situations? On Habermas's reading of her, "Carol Gilligan fails to make an adequate distinction

between the *cognitive problem* of application and the *motivational problem* of the anchoring of moral insights."[17] For both the cognitive
problem of how to make contextually sensitive moral judgments and
the motivational problem of how to act in concrete life-situations
according to principles the validity of which one hypothetically
acknowledges, only arise when the moral point of view has been
abstracted from the certainties of a shared way of life and this way
of life has been submitted to the hypothetical test of impartiality. In
other words, although Gilligan and Murphy put their finger on an
important problem – namely how moral agents who have attained a
postconventional stage of moral reasoning behave and judge in
concrete life-situations – their insights bear on the "application" of a
universalist and postconventional morality to life-situations; the
program of a "postconventional contextualism" has no relevance
then for the justification or delineation of the moral domain.
Habermas agrees with one of Kohlberg's early objections to Gilligan
that her work confuses "issues of justice" with those of the "good
life," thus blurring the boundaries of the moral domain.[18] "In terms
of the conduct of an individual life, this corresponds to the distinction between self-determination and self-realization," writes
Habermas. "Typically questions of preferences as to forms of life or
life goals (ego ideals) and questions of the evaluation of personality
types and modes of action only arise after moral issues, narrowly
understood, have been resolved."[19]

With this response, Habermas maintains that the kinds of issues
raised by Gilligan belong not to the center but to the margins of
ethical theory, and that they are "anomalies" or residual problems
of an otherwise adequate scientific paradigm. Using Lawrence
Blum's scheme, we can say that for Habermas the relations between
the justice and care orientations follow positions 1 and 2. That is,
issues of care and responsibility toward others which arise out of the
special relations in which we stand to them are "evaluative questions of the good life," concerned with forms of life or with life goals
and with the "evaluation of personality types and modes of action."
In modern societies, in which moral questions of justice have been
distinguished from evaluative questions of the good life, relations
and obligations of care and responsibility are "personal" matters of
self-realization. Since much of this discussion of Gilligan is couched
in the language of Habermas's own terminology deriving from
his social theory, an example may help us understand Habermas's
position better.

Take the by now fairly generally accepted principle that younger
members of a family should not continue the family business or the
father's profession but should pursue the career and way of life
most compatible with their abilities and talents. Historically, this

principle originates with the eventual development of a universal market economy and with the continuing decline of the family household as an economic unit of production in the modern world. Whereas in most precapitalist economic formations and even in some forms of merchant and industrial capitalism, generations within a single household acted as an economic unit, in the form of the family business or the family firm, with the spread of capitalism and the continuing decline of the feudal estates system sons no longer followed in father's footsteps and did not assume the family vocation or business. Eventually, it became accepted that children, and primarily male children, could and should follow the vocation most suitable to their talents. The moral expectations which governed family life in most western countries up until the late 1920s or 1930s have been subject to a differentiation. The choice of a career by the younger generation is no longer a "moral" issue of obligation owed to other family members, and in particular to the *pater familias*, but an "evaluative" matter of the good life. Now for the modern liberal family the question whether the less talented first-born son should get to attend an expensive private college as opposed to sending the more talented younger daughter to medical school may continue to be a moral problem, for this involves a question of justice, of conflicting interests over scarce resources. But neither the one child's decision to study business administration nor the other's decision to study medicine are moral issues; they have become evaluative matters of the good life.

Yet this conclusion is profoundly counter-intuitive and remote from everyday moral reality. If my example captures Habermas's meaning correctly, then there is something profoundly odd in his insistence that these issues are "personal" as opposed to "moral;" in fact, this claim runs just as contrary to our moral intuitions as Kohlberg's assertion that "the spheres of kinship, love, friendship, and sex that elicit considerations of care are usually understood to be spheres of personal decision-making, as are, for instance the problems of marriage and divorce."[20] These issues are obviously both personal and highly moral. Even in highly rationalized modern societies where most of us are wage-earners and political citizens, the moral issues which preoccupy us most and which touch us most deeply derive not from problems of justice in the economy and the polity, but precisely from the quality of our relations with others in the "spheres of kinship, love, friendship, and sex." We may lament the sterility of our political lives as citizens and long for a more vibrant and compelling civic life; certainly I have argued for this position at various points above. We may strongly oppose the fact that our economic arrangements are so unjust and so immoral from the point of view of satisfying the basic needs of millions upon this

earth, but none of this detracts from the fact that for the democratic citizen and economic agent, the moral issues that touch her
most deeply arise in the personal domain. How can Habermas and
Kohlberg defend such a counter-intuitive position, counter that is, to
the phenomenology of our moral experience? Let us look more
closely at the argument distinguishing moral issues of justice from
evaluative matters of the good life.

(b)   My thesis is that Habermas as well as Kohlberg conflate the
standpoint of a universalist morality with a narrow definition of the
moral domain as being centered around "issues of justice." These,
however, are different matters. How we define the *domain of the
moral* is a separate matter than the kinds of *justificatory constraints*
which we think moral judgments, principles and maxims should be
subject to.[21] Universalism in moral theory operates at the level of
specifying acceptable forms of the justification of moral principles,
judgments and maxims. "Universalism" in morality implies first of
all a commitment to the equal worth and dignity of every human
being in virtue of her or his humanity; secondly, the dignity of the
other as a moral individual is acknowledged through the respect we
show for their needs, interests and points of view in our concrete
moral deliberations. Moral respect is manifested in moral deliberations by taking the standpoint of the other, as a generalized and
concrete other, into account. Third, universalism implies a commitment to accept as valid intersubjective norms and rules of action as
generated by practical discourses, taking place under the constraints
specified above (see pp. 29ff.). The universalizability procedure in
ethics specifies a model of individual and collective deliberation and
imposes constraints upon the kinds of justification leading to certain
conclusions rather than specifying the moral domain itself. An
example may help explain matters.

   Suppose in a family of three brothers one of them is struggling
financially and is unable to make ends meet. The moral standpoint
of care, which Gilligan, Lawrence Blum and myself acknowledge,
would say that there is a prima facie moral claim here, namely the
claim whether we, if we were the more successful brothers of the
family, would have a moral obligation to help this brother. This
moral obligation would arise out of the special nature of the relationships in which we stood to this particular individual. The obligation may or may not be construable as one of justice. If we, as the
older brothers, got to where we did in life by helping ourselves to a
family inheritance and leaving the younger brother destitute, then
the moral situation is also one of justice and of what is morally owed
to the youngest sibling. But if we owe our position in life to nothing
but our own hard work and good fortune, then the obligation owed

to the other sibling is not a matter of justice. From a Kantian point of view, this obligation would be construed as one of "benevolence." Indeed, it has been frequently maintained with respect to Gilligan's work that the ethic of care and responsibility covers the same domain that Kant himself had classified as "positive duties" of benevolence or altruism. The domain of the moral, it is maintained, is distinct from supererogation or altruism although such acts may crown a virtuous character.[22]

As opposed to this classification of issues of care as issues of supererogation and altruism, I would like to argue, again with Gilligan and Blum, and against Habermas and Kohlberg, that obligations and relations of care are genuinely moral ones, belonging to the center and not at the margins of morality. If in the situation described above, the involved family members do not see or even acknowledge that there is a moral situation, in other words if they cannot recognize this situation as being "morally relevant," then they lack moral sense. Nonetheless, the morally relevant situation is not a situation of justice. There would be nothing "unjust" in the decision of the two elder brothers not to help the younger one, but there would be something morally "callous," lacking in generosity and concern in their actions. Unlike Habermas and Kohlberg, I am not ready to say that "callousness, lack of generosity and concern," are evaluative but not moral categories; that they pertain to the quality of our lives together rather than to the general procedures for regulating intersubjective conflicts of interests. Such a claim is an unnecessary and unwarranted narrowing of the domain of the moral, and does not follow from a universalist moral position. A universalist moral position of enlarged mentality provides us with a procedure for judging the validity of our judgments in this context as well.

What a commitment to universalism in ethics requires from us in this context is to act in such a way as is consistent with respecting the dignity and worth of all the individuals involved and a willingness to settle controversial matters through the open and unconstrained discussion of all. What does this mean concretely? The successful siblings and the younger brother should be willing to engage in a discourse about the needs of the one and the responsibilities and expectations of the others. Respect for the worth and need of the youngest brother as a generalized and concrete other would require no less. The outcome of such a discourse, however, is not dictated by the procedure of the discourse itself. It is indeed possible for all involved to see that the financial help of the elder brothers is undesirable at this point because it may reinforce patterns of dependency, create resentment, etc. It is also possible to decide that with some help at this crucial juncture the youngest brother may be on his way toward a more self-sufficient existence. Procedures do not dictate specific outcomes; they constrain the kinds of justification we can use for our actions, judgments and principles. As I have outlined in chapter 1 above, discourse ethics is a deontological and universalist moral theory where conceptions of the right do constrain the good. Here is where I depart from a care perspective and rejoin the universalists.

So far, I have argued that the definition or specification of the domain of the moral and the level of justification or argumentation required by a commitment to universalism must be distinguished from each other. If universalism is interpreted procedurally, as it must be, then such a procedure can be applied to test the validity of moral judgments, principles and maxims even in situations which, according to Habermas's and Kohlberg's definitions of them, appear to be concerned with "evaluative questions of the good life" rather than with "moral matters of justice." Questions of care are moral issues and can also be dealt with from within a universalist standpoint. Such a universalism supplies the constraints within which the morality of care must operate.

(c) If we return to Lawrence Blum's scheme discussed above then my position would be captured by theses 4, 6 and 7. Care issues are genuinely moral, yet the care perspective does not amount to a moral theory with a distinct account of a moral point of view (thesis 4 above). Considerations of a universalist morality do set the constraints within which concerns of care should be allowed to operate and they "trump" over them if necessary (thesis 6 above); and considerations of care should be "validated or affirmed from an impartialist perspective" (thesis 7). Let me return to the example given above to spell out these more clearly. Now suppose the members of this family are part of the clan of Don Corleone (the Godfather) and belong to the Mafia. The Mafia is an organization based on care and mutual responsibility toward members of one's own clan or extended family, yet this morality of care is accompanied by a morality of injustice and contempt toward the lives, dignity and property of non-group members. Theorists of care must specify the criteria according to which such clans as the Mafia are to be considered "immoral" from the standpoint of a morality of care. I consider Kantian universalism to be indispensable at this point. A morality of care can revert simply to the position that what is morally good is what is best for those who are like me. Such a claim is no different than arguing that what is best morally is what pleases me most.

Thesis 6 says that a universalist morality should set the constraints within which concerns of care can operate. In the case of our example this would mean that the elder brothers cannot recommend to the younger one, from a moral point of view, that the murder of X would be an appropriate way to put his financial life in order; nor would any other recommendation which violated the dignity and worth of another person be consistent with the moral point of view. The right limits the precepts of virtuous conduct and good judgment. It would not be moral to recommend to the younger brother for example that he marry a rich woman and thus put his life in order since this would be treating the woman involved as a means to an end and would be incompatible with her human dignity.

As thesis 7 states, considerations of care "must be validated or affirmed from an impartialist perspective." The principle that "Family members should show support, concern and care for one another" is, in my view, justifiable for all and not only for some, because if we could enter into a practical discourse and consider whether a world in which families exercised no solidarity would be more acceptable for all involved than a world in which families did show such support and solidarity, we could all agree that the latter alternative would be in the interests of all involved. There is a distinction between saying that "Jewish, Irish or Italian family members should show support, concern and care for one another" and the claim that whoever we are and whatever our background, a world in which families or family-like household arrangements showed support, concern and care for one another would be preferable to a world in which this were not the case. The latter is a universalizable moral claim whereas the former remains an ethnocentric articulation of a group morality which can cut both ways: group solidarity may often be achieved at the expense of moral disregard and contempt for individuals who are not group members.

Suppose, however, a more strictly Kantian theorist questioned us about the status of the claim "a world that would be preferable to": is this a utilitarian or a consequentialist claim? Am I arguing that the sum of all happinesses and well-being in such a universe would be greater than in another? At some level, of course, these considerations about morally intact families derive from a concern for human well-being and flourishing. Metatheoretically I am committed to the position that the discursive procedure alone and not some additional moral principles of utility or human well-being define the validity of general moral norms. Yet as a discourse theorist who is also a feminist, the needs and well-being of the concrete other are as much of a concern to me as the dignity and worth of the generalized other.

In this respect as well, Habermas and Kohlberg have dismissed all too quickly a central insight of Gilligan and of other feminists: namely that we are children before we are adults, and that the nurture, care and reponsibility of others is essential for us to develop into morally competent, self-sufficient individuals. Ontogenetically, neither justice nor care are primary; they are each essential for the development of the autonomous, adult individual out of the fragile and dependent human child. Not only as children, but also as concrete embodied beings with needs and vulnerabilities, emotions and desires we spend our lives caught in the "web of human affairs," in Hannah Arendt's words, or in networks of "care and dependence" in Carol Gilligan's words. Modern moral philosophy, and particularly universalist moralities of justice, have emphasized our dignity and worth as moral subjects at the cost of forgetting and repressing our vulnerability and dependency as bodily selves. Such networks of dependence and the web of human affairs in which we are immersed are not simply like clothes which we outgrow or like shoes which we leave behind. They are ties that bind; ties that shape our moral identities, our needs, and our visions of the good life. The autonomous self is not the disembodied self; universalist moral theory must acknowledge the deep experiences in the formation of the human being to which care and justice correspond. Gilligan formulates the interdependence of justice and care thus:

> Theoretically, the distinction between justice and care cuts across the familiar divisions between thinking and feeling, egoism and altruism, theoretical and practical reasoning. It calls attention to the fact that all human relationships, both public and private, can be characterized *both* in terms of equality and in terms of attachment, and that both inequality and detachment constitute grounds for moral concern. Since everyone is vulnerable both to oppression and to abandonment, two moral visions – one of justice, and one of care – recur in human experience. The moral injunctions, not to act unfairly toward others, and not to turn away from someone in need, captures these different concerns.[23]

The continuing challenge posed by Gilligan's findings to universalist moral philosophies is how to acknowledge the centrality of justice as well as care in human lives and how to expand the moral domain to include consideration of care without giving up the justificatory constraints imposed upon the articulation of the moral by universalism.

There is a belated acknowledgment of some of the issues raised by the Gilligan debate in Habermas's article "Justice and Solidarity: On the Discussion Concerning 'Stage 6'." Commenting on Kohlberg's last efforts to integrate justice and benevolence into a unified moral perspective, Habermas writes:

> Thus, the perspective complementing that of equal treatment of individuals is not benevolence but solidarity. This principle is rooted

in the realization that each person must take responsibility for the other because as consociates all must have an interest in the integrity of their shared life context in the same way. Justice conceived deontologically requires solidarity as its reverse side . . . Every autonomous morality has to serve two purposes at once: it brings to bear the inviolability of socialized individuals by requiring equal treatment and thereby equal respect for the dignity of each one; and it protects intersubjective relations of mutual recognition requiring solidarity of individual members of a community, in which they have been socialized. *Justice* concerns the equal freedom of unique and self-determining individuals, while *solidarity* concerns the welfare of consociates who are ultimately linked in an intersubjectively shared form of life . . .[24]

The similarities in these two formulations are striking. Gilligan writes of "equality and attachment," of the need "not to act unfairly toward others" and not "to turn away from someone in need." Habermas writes of "solidarity," of the interest each has in protecting "intersubjective relations of mutual recognition."[25] Certainly, there are differences of emphases as well. For Habermas, justice is tempered by "mutual recognition" (*Anerkennung*) among individuals of each others' welfare; for Gilligan justice must be tempered by care and a mutual acknowledgment of dependence and vulnerability. Yet in both formulations, the ideals of moral autonomy and justice are traced back to their foundations in fragile human relations and thus "reduced to size." The generalized other of the justice perspective is always also a concrete other, and we can acknowledge this concreteness of the other by recalling those human relations of dependence, care, sharing and mutuality within which each human child is socialized. If feminist theory has reminded universalist moralities in the Kantian tradition of the need to compensate "for the vulnerability of living creatures who through socialization are individuated in such a way that they can never assert their identity for themselves alone . . ."[26] then a significant paradigm shift is occurring in such theories – a paradigm shift which I described in the introduction to this work as the move away from "legislative and substitutionalist toward interactive universalism."

Gender and Difference in the Gilligan Debate

Carol Gilligan's work challenges universalist moral theories in the Kantian tradition to expand their definition of the moral domain, to question their ideals of the autonomous self in the light of the experiences of women and children, and to acknowledge that a universalist moral theory must also heed the voice of the "excluded others." In recent years the debate over women and moral theory has also been at the center of the general concern within feminist theory with the question of "difference." Some of the most vehement criticisms of Gilligan's work have been voiced by feminists who have taken her to hypostatize illegitimately the "voice" of professional, heterosexual, white women to be the voice of all women.[27] Whereas for established academic disciplines the very fact of "difference" is a subversive issue, for feminist theory the existence of difference, the unravelling of its ideological construction and the explication of its social and historical constitution is the central task.

Is a "different" voice really the women's voice? Can there be a "woman's voice" independently of race and class differences, and abstracted from social and historical context? What is the origin of the difference in moral reasoning among men and women which Gilligan has identified? Does not Gilligan's analysis of women's tendency to reason from the "care and responsibility" approach merely repeat established stereotypes of femininity? To untangle the many issues involved, I shall distinguish between the methodological, the reductionist and the postmodernist approaches to the question of women's difference in moral theory.

Methodological aspects

In subsequent reflections on her work, Gilligan noted that she had deliberately called her work "in a different voice" and not a "women's voice."[28] She was not concerned to identify "sex difference in moral reasoning," as some of her critics maintained. Rather, she compared women's experience with psychological theory – the subtitle of her book – in order to show that the exclusion of women and their experiences from mainstream developmental theories in psychology generated a number of models and hypotheses which were neither "universal" nor "neutral."

"Gender" was not an analytical and methodological category guiding Gilligan's early work. For her the empirical identification of gender difference appears to have preceded the use of gender as an explicit research category. By "gender" I mean the differential construction of human beings into male and female types. Gender is a relational category. It is one that seeks to explain the construction of a certain kind of difference among human beings. Feminist theorists, whether psychoanalytical, postmodern, liberal or critical, are united around the assumption that the constitution of gender differences is a social and historical process, and that gender is not a natural fact. Furthermore, and although there is some disagreement on this issue, I would agree with the recent work of Londa Schiebinger, Judith Butler and Jane Flax[29] that the opposition of sex and gender itself must be questioned. It is not as if sexual difference were merely an anatomical fact. The construction and interpretation of anatomical difference is itself a social and historical process. That the male and the female of the species are different is a fact, but this fact itself is always also socially constructed. Sexual identity is an aspect of gender identity. Sex and gender are not related to each other as nature to culture. Sexuality itself is a culturally constructed difference.

It is the absence of gender as a research category in Gilligan's work that has created some of the most serious misgivings about her conclusions. Linda Kerber comments on this issue in her remarks entitled "Some Cautionary Words for Historians."[30]

> *In a Different Voice* is part of a major feminist redefinition of social vocabulary. What was once dismissed as gossip can now be appreciated as the maintenance of oral tradition; what was once devalued as mere housewifery can be understood as social reproduction and a major contribution to the gross national product. Gilligan is invigorating in her insistence that behavior once denigrated as waffling, indecisive and demeaningly "effeminate" ought rather to be valued as complex, constructive and humane. Yet, this historian, at least, is haunted by the argument that we have heard this argument before, vested in different language. Some variants of it are as old as western civilization itself; central to the traditions of our culture has been the ascription of reason to men and of feeling to women . . . Ancient tradition has long been reinforced by explicit socialization that arrogated public power to men and relegated women to domestic concerns, a socialization sometimes defended by arguments from expediency, sometimes by argument from biology. Although now Gilligan appears to be adding arguments from psychology, her study infers at times that gendered behavior is biologically determined and at others that it, too, is learned, albeit at an earlier stage of socialization than previous analysts had assumed.

Kerber's point is well taken. However, it is hardly convincing that Gilligan thought that the styles of moral reasoning she identified in her research and the preferences of women to reason more frequently in one style rather than in another reflected some ontological and universal essence called "femaleness." The problem of gender difference is much more complicated in her work, and ultimately rests with the ahistoricity of the cognitive-developmental framework within which Gilligan – at least initially – set out her research. This theory, as developed by Piaget and Kohlberg, is concerned with ontogeny, that is individual development, and not with phylogeny, that is species development. This theory generates a model for explaining how the development of the moral judgment of the child and of the adolescent is a maturation process, involving an interaction between the potentials of the human mind to structure experience and the environment. This interaction between self and world creates certain incongruities and crises as the child grows. These cannot be resolved within an earlier pattern of moral resoning but require the movement unto "higher" stages of moral reasoning. The "higher" stages of moral reasoning, Kohlberg maintains, are not simply developmentally later; they are also more "adequate" to the resolution of moral dilemmas from a cognitive and philosophical point of view.

The subject of this theory is by definition gender neutral; for these abilities are said to be species specific. Of course, this theory has a gender subtext. Since moral learning results from certain kinds of activities, we might well ask what these are for young boys and girls. Are children's games gender neutral? Remember Piaget's remark that in their game of marbles, boys show a degree of precision and complex attention to rules and a propensity for rule-governed negotiations which he finds lacking in girls' games.[31] Furthermore, since this theory claims that the development of "higher" levels of moral reasoning is tied to the opportunities of the self to assume different roles in social life, we might well expect that in a gendered universe the kinds of roles men and women will assume will be different.

Carol Gilligan rejected the gender neutrality of the Kohlbergian model at a different level. Instead of focussing on the gender subtext of activities and social roles, she focussed on personality patterns. Gilligan relied on Nancy Chodorow's work in *The Reproduction of Mothering*. Briefly, Chodorow maintains that processes of separation and individuation which each human child must go through proceed differently for males and females. In the case of the male child, separation and individuation involve the establishment of a gender identity which is the opposite of the primary nurturant figure, the woman, although not necessarily of the biological mother. To become a boy means to become not only other than mama but different than her; it involves repressing those aspects his person most closely identified with the mother. For girls, to become a girl means to become different than mama but also like her. Gender identity is established by the age of two-and-a-half to three years. In a patriarchal society, based on the denigration and oppression of women, gender identity goes hand in hand with the internalization of those attitudes that also devalue and denigrate women.

Gilligan and Chodorow agree that the consequences of this psychosexual development of the young child are certain personality patterns among the adults of the species. The male has a more firmly established sense of ego boundaries; the distinction between self and other is more rigid. For females the boundaries between self and other are more fluid. Women are more predisposed to show feelings of empathy and sympathy for the other. Each of these personality patterns brings with it certain deformations as well. Males experience closeness and bonding as a threat to their person, whereas females have a hard time establishing a firm sense of identity and individuality over and against the claims of others.

This psychosexual model, as we know by now, is not a theory which explains the emergence of gender difference; it simply gives us a scheme for its "reproduction." In this model the mothering figure is already a female; the father is absent during the first three years of the child. It is also assumed that mothering is socially denigrated by the larger societal context so that the young male child learns to associate this activity with negative characteristics and values or at least with highly ambivalent ones. Chodorow's model presupposes gender difference in its characteristically modern form; it does not explain its historical and social constitution. This model presupposes the patriarchal denigration of female gender attributes; it explains their reproduction but not their historical origin. To the extent to which Gilligan relied on this model, she also did not explain the social construction of gender: on the one hand she identified its neglect by mainstream psychological theory, and on the other hand called attention to its persistence within these theories as a continuing but inexplicit subtext.

Linda Kerber is right then that gender difference is left unexplained in Gilligan's work. For this task we have to move from moral theory to a social theory of gender relations; we have to leave behind psychological theory for a historical sociology of the development and constitution of gender. Gender as an analytical category thus subverts established disciplinary boundaries.

Reductionist objections

While feminists and women's historians like Linda Kerber criticized Carol Gilligan's work methodologically for neglecting the historicity of her results and for ignoring the historical determinants of women's difference which she had identified in moral theory, others argued that the kind of "difference" which Gilligan had described as being primarily, even if not exclusively, female was *oppressive*. Claudia Card and Catharine MacKinnon have voiced the view that the morality of "care and responsibility" is a version of Nietzschean slave morality.[32] Card writes: "Study of women's values could profit from Nietzsche, whose writings on ethics speak directly to the consequences of domination and subordination for the development of character and ideals. Although his target was Christian ethics, his ideas are applicable to recently identified women's values."[33] Following Nietzsche, Card pleads for a consideration "of the underside of women's ethics."[34] For Nietzsche, morality is a sublimation of the life drive of the stronger to dominate the weaker; the origins of morality are the internalized controls imposed upon the strong by the weak such that the weak will not be damaged.[35]

MacKinnon does not go back to Nietzsche but to the Marxian theory of class struggle. Just as the "ruling ideas" are the ideas of the "ruling classes," so too, dominant moral conceptions are the result of a system of gender and class oppression of compulsory heterosexuality. Gilligan, in MacKinnon's view, ultimately has done little else but raise to scientific status the "good girl" image which heterosexual culture has of women and whose purpose is to "domesticate" women by portraying them as "gentle, caring and responsible." She writes:

> On the other hand, what is infuriating about it (which is a very heavy thing to say about a book [that is, *In A Different Voice* – S.B.] which is so cool and graceful and gentle in its emotional touch), and this is a political infuriation, is that it neglects the explanatory level. She also has found the voice of the victim – yes, women are a victimized group. The articulation of the voice of the victim is crucial because laws about victimization are typically made by people with power, and come from the perspective with power . . . But I am troubled by the possibility of women identifying with what is a positively valued feminine stereotype. It is the "feminine."[36]

These feminist appropriations of Nietzschean and Marxian views reduce normative problems of justice and morality in complex societies to simple patterns of interest and power camouflaging. Both views are ultimately profoundly anti-political: for Nietzsche the ultimate vision is that of an aesthetic utopia of wisdom, in which a wise old sage, Zarathustra, reaches a state of autonomy beyond community. But if instead of parroting the master thinkers of the past, one would apply feminist methodology to Nietzsche's final moral utopia, one would discover here once more a version of the autonomous, male ego – certainly now presented not as the stern Kantian legislator but as the artistic, poetic, multifaceted, but all-too-masculine hero – Zarathustra "who is lamb and lion" at once.[37] This archaic ideal of the beautiful and wise male hero is hardly what the contemporary debate on women and moral theory should lead to.

Nietzsche's reductionist treatment of morality in his early writings is coupled by the aesthetic utopia of a beautiful male in his later work who lives "beyond good and evil." The reductionist Marxian theory of morality which views it as being a mere expression of the interests of the ruling classes is, in turn, inseparable from the utopia of a society of total reconciliation. Just as with the elimination of class conflict, all interpersonal conflict and conflict over scarce resources will also come to an end, and so too, with the elimination of the current regime of gender, or in MacKinnon's language, with the end of the regime of "compulsory heterosexuality," "gender difference" will cease to exist.[38] The "rule of men over women" will be replaced by the "administration over things." In the case of MacKinnon then the utopia is not that of an archaic beautiful male but the image of a totally rationally ruled, self-transparent society of perfect power. If, however, one accepts, as I do, that neither interpersonal conflict nor economic scarcity nor the sources of human vulnerability and need are likely to be wholly eliminated, even in a more just society, moral theory cannot be rejected as simply representing the ruling idea's of compulsory heterosexuality. There will always be a need to regulate the sources of human conflict and dispute, and to protect the commitments of a shared human existence. A statement like the following which proceeds from a series of dogmatic oppositions, as between morality and politics, liberalism and radicalism, indicates very clearly that MacKinnon's understanding of politics, as well as of morality, has more in common with the authoritarian utopias of Leninist politics than it does with the tradition of critical Marxist theory:

> In my opinion, to take the differences approach is to take a moral approach, whereas to criticize hierarchy is to take a political approach. To take a difference view is also to take a liberal view (although that view, of course, includes conservatism as well), and to take the view that we are dealing with a hierarchy is to take a radical approach. I also think that to make issues of gender turn on the so-called gender difference is, ultimately, to take a male perspective. I therefore call the differences approach masculinist. The position that gender is first a political hierarchy of power, is in my opinion, a feminist position.[39]

The flip side of the denial of politics is an authoritarian politics which will put an end to all difference, controversy, conflict and violence among humans.[40]

Postmodernist reservations

Claudia Card and Catharine MacKinnon would dispense with the ideal of autonomy and maybe even of morality altogether. Postmodernist feminists, by contrast, strive to develop a "decentered" and "fractured" concept of the self in place of the "connected" or "relational" self which they find to be privileged in Gilligan's work.

Jane Flax and Iris Young, inspired by postmodernist critiques of the "identitary self," have challenged the "relational" self. The western philosophical tradition, they argue, has always prized identity over difference, unity over multiplicity, permanence over change. The subject of western philosophical discourse is constituted at the price of repressing difference, excluding otherness and denigrating heterogeneity. From Plato over Descartes to Kant the self is the unitary, identical substratum; reason reigns over the passions, the I reigns over the will, otherness must be suppressed.

Young argues that the view of the empathetic, connected self presupposes a state "in which persons will cease to be opaque, other, not understood, and instead become fused, mutually sympathetic, understanding one another as they understand themselves. Such an ideal of shared subjectivity, or the transparence of subjects to one another, denies difference in the sense of the basic asymmetry of subjects."[41] Not only is intersubjective transparency presupposed, but equally objectionable is the fiction of the subject as the unified center of desire: but "because the subject is not a unity, it cannot be present to itself, know itself. I do not always know what I mean, need, want, desire because these do not arise from some ego origin . . . Consequently, any individual subject is a play of differences that cannot be comprehended . . . the subject is (a) heterogeneous presence."[42] Young concludes that the Cartesian/Kantian concept of the unitary self, as well as the feminist theory of the relational self, perpetrate a "metaphysics of presence" and a "logic of identity."

Young's position is that Gilligan's view of the self, far from challenging traditional views of autonomy and selfhood in the western philosophical tradition, continues their fundamental assumptions in presupposing that subjects can truly understand one another and that the individual is a coherent subject of desire. But Young's claim that mutual care and responsibility must presuppose a "transparency" of understanding is exaggerated. Such a perfect understanding or meeting of minds would perhaps be a fair criticism of the Kantian view of noumenal selves, but neither my concept of the "concrete other", which Young also criticizes, nor Arendt's view of the "enlarged mentality" must presuppose that there is ever a state of perfect understanding. Young is not heeding the distinction between "consensus" and "reaching understanding" introduced above. Admittedly, rationalistic theories of the Enlightenment and, in particular, Rousseau's theory of democracy were based on the illusion that a perfect consensus was possible; but the dialogic model of ethics defended in this book envisages a continuous process of conversation in which understanding and misunderstanding, agreement as well as disagreement are intertwined and always at work. The very commitment to conversation as the means through which the enlarged mentality is to be attained suggests the infinite revisability and indeterminacy of meaning.

The objection that the self, viewed as a unified center of desire, is a fiction again overstates the issue. Young seems to celebrate heterogeneity, opacity and difference at the cost of belittling the importance of a coherent core of individual identity. Not all difference is empowering, not all heterogeneity can be celebrated; not all opacity leads to a sense of self-flourishing. We do not have to think of "coherent identities" along the lines of the sameness of physical objects. We can think of coherence as a narrative unity. What makes a story unitary can be the point of view of the one who tells it, the point of view of the one who listens to it, or some interaction between the meaning conveyed and the meaning received. Personal identity is no different. As Hannah Arendt has emphasized, from the time of our birth we are immersed in "a web of narratives," of which we are both the author and the object. The self is both the teller of tales and that about whom tales are told. The individual with a coherent sense of self-identity is the one who succeeds in integrating these tales and perspectives into a meaningful life history. When the story of a life can only be told from the perspective of the others, then the self is a victim and sufferer who has lost control over her existence. When the story of a life can only be told from the standpoint of the individual, then such a self is a narcissist and a loner who may have attained autonomy without solidarity. A coherent sense of self is attained with the successful integration of autonomy and solidarity, or with the right mix of justice and care. Justice and autonomy alone cannot sustain and nourish that web of narratives in which human beings' sense of selfhood unfolds; but solidarity and care alone cannot raise the self to the level not only of being the subject but also the author of a coherent life-story.

With these considerations we reach some fundamental issues about the normative core of contemporary feminism, namely whether feminism must engage in a reconstruction or deconstruction of the western philosophical tradition. What do postmodernism and a deconstruction of tradition promise to feminism? Are feminism and postmodernism allies? What are the commonalities and tensions among them? The next chapter will look at the contemporary alliance between feminism and postmodernism.

Notes

A much shorter early version of this article appeared as "The Debate over Women and Moral Theory Revisited," in *Feministische Philosophie*, ed. Herta Nagl-Docekal (Oldenbourg, Vienna/Munich, 1990), pp. 191–201.

1 Joan Kelly Gadol, "The Social Relations of the Sexes: Methodological Implications of Women's History," in *Women, History and Theory* (University of Chicago Press, Chicago, 1984), pp. 1–14, here pp. 2–3.
2 Alasdair MacIntyre, *After Virtue* (University of Notre Dame Press, Notre Dame, 1981), pp. 44ff.
3 Michael Sandel, "The Procedural Republic and the Unencumbered Self," *Political Theory*, 12.1 (1984).
4 Gilligan has been remarkably silent on the issue of the cultural and ethnic relativity of the Kohlbergian paradigm.
5 Charles Taylor, "Die Motive einer Verfahrensethik," in *Moralität und Sittlichkeit*, ed. Wolfgang Kuhlmanm (Suhrkamp, Frankfurt, 1986), pp. 194–217; Michael Walzer, *Interpretation and Social Criticism* (Harvard University Press, Cambridge, Mass., 1987).
6 We have explored the commonalities and the tensions in these approaches in the introduction to *Feminism as Critique*, ed. S. Benhabib and Drucilla Cornell (University of Minnesota Press, Minneapolis, 1987).
7 Owen Flanagan and Kathryn Jackson give a very clear and helpful overview of the problems involved in Gilligan's various formulations to date concerning the two perspectives. They write: "her recent work still shifts between the ideas that the two ethics are incompatible alternatives to each other but are both adequate from a normative point of view; that they are complements of one another involved in some sort of tense interplay; and that each is deficient without the other and ought to be integrated." See "Justice, Care, and Gender: The Kohlberg–Gilligan Debate Revisited," *Ethics*, 97 (April 1987), pp. 622–37, here p. 628.
8 See Nel Noddings, *Caring: A Feminine Approach to Ethics and Moral Education* (University of California Press, Berkeley, 1984). Noddings's dichotomous reasoning which sharply distinguishes between "law and justice" as male and "receptivity, relatedness, and responsiveness" as female is deeply at odds with Gilligan's and my attempts to overcome these sharp dichotomies in a more integrated approach to moral reasoning and moral judgment. See Noddings, pp. 2ff. for a particularly sharp statement.
9 Lawrence A. Blum, "Gilligan and Kohlberg: Implications for Moral Theory," *Ethics*, 98 (April 1988), pp. 472–91; here p. 472.
10 Ibid., p. 477.
11 Lawrence Kohlberg himself has at different points in the debate subscribed to a version of most of the positions to be presented in this enumeration. Some of the ambivalences in his responses to Gilligan have been outlined above, cf. pp. 150–1, 153.
12 Blum, "Gilligan and Kohlberg: Implications for Moral Theory," p. 478.

13   Ibid., p. 479.

14   Ibid., p. 481.

15   Ibid., p. 482. Blum here refers to Kohlberg's position in "Synopses and Detailed Replies to Critics," see Kohlberg, with Charles Levine and Alexandra Hewer, in *Essays on Moral Development* (Harper and Row, San Francisco, 1984), vol. 2: *The Psychology of Moral Development*, p. 343.

16   J. Habermas, "Moral Consciousness and Communicative Action," in *Moral Consciousness and Communicative Action*, trans. Christian Lenhardt and Shierry Weber Nicholsen (MIT Press, Boston, 1990), p. 178.

17   Ibid., p. 179.

18   Ibid., p. 180.

19   Ibid.

20   Kohlberg, "Synopses and Detailed Replies to Critics," pp. 229–30.

21   There is a brief acknowledgment of this point in Habermas's article, "Justice and Solidarity: On the Discussion Concerning 'Stage 6'": "But justifications through procedural ethics apply just as naturally to principles of distributive justice . . . or to principles of care and aid to those in need of help; to conventions of self-restraint, consideration, truthfulness, the duty to enlighten others, and so on." In *Philosophical Forum*, 21.1–2 (Fall–Winter 1989–90), p. 43. This point though remains undeveloped and its import unclear, for, if procedural ethics applies to issues of distributive justice as well as to principles of care and various forms of self-regarding virtues, then the moral domain is not only concerned with issues of justice but with evaluative matters pertaining to the good life as well. Or does Habermas mean that procedural ethics applies to such phenomena as "consideration, truthfulness," and the like *insofar as*, and only insofar as, these can be reconceptualized as matters of justice? While it is not difficult to imagine how care and aid toward others as well as truthfulness can be moral phenomena of justice *and* matters of the good life for the individual and for the collectivity, it is more difficult to see how "considerateness" and "self-restraint" can be classified as phenomena of justice. Habermas cannot have it both ways: on the one hand, he insists that there is a clear distinction between matters of justice and issues of the good life, and that discourse ethics concerns the former alone; on the other hand, he wants to define the discourse principle, not as delimiting the moral domain, but as specifying levels and forms of justifiable moral argument. As I argue in the text, it is the latter position that is most defensible, while the former claim must be dropped. The issue is not the definition of the moral domain, of what are and are not moral questions; obviously both matters of justice and questions of the good life are moral matters. Rather the question is how to circumscribe the domain of individual autonomy (legally and politically) in which choices concerning different forms of the good life are exercised in such manner as would be compatible with universalistic principles of justice. See my discussion of "neutrality" in chapter 1 above.

22   See G. Nunner-Winkler, "Two Moralities? A Critical Discussion of an Ethic of Care and Responsibility versus an Ethic of Rights and Justice," in *Morality, Moral Behavior, and Moral Development* ed. W. M. Kurtines and J. L. Gewirtz (Wiley, New York, 1984), pp. 348–61.

23 Carol Gilligan, "Moral Orientation and Moral Development," in *Women and Moral Theory*, ed. E. F. Kittay and Diane T. Meyers (Rowman and Littlefield, Totowa, NJ, 1987), p. 20.

24 Habermas, "Justice and Solidarity," p. 47.

25 The theme of "mutual recognition" and the significance of these relations of recognition for moral theory are at the center of Axel Honneth's *Habilitationsschrift*, "Kampf um Anerkennung. Ein Theorieprogram im Anschluss an Hegel und Mead," submitted to the University of Frankfurt, 1990.

26 Habermas, "Justice and Solidarity," p. 46.

27 See Linda Nicholson for an early statement of this criticism, "Women, Morality and History," *Social Research*, special issue on Women and Morality, 50.3 (Autumn 1983), pp. 514–37.

28 Carol Gilligan, Ellen C. Dubois, Mary C. Dunlop, Catharine A. MacKinnon, Carrie J. Menkel-Neadow, "Feminist Discourse, Moral Values and the Law – A Conversation," The 1984 James McCormick Mitchell Lecture, *Buffalo Law Review*, 34.1 (Winter 1985), here at p. 39.

29 See Londa Schiebinger, "Skeletons in the Closet: The First Illustrations of the Female Skeleton in Eighteenth-Century Anatomy," in *The Making of the Modern Body: Sexuality and Society in the Nineteenth Century*, ed. Catherine Gallagher and Thomas Laquer (University of California Press, Berkeley, 1987), pp. 42–83; Judith Butler, "Variations on Sex and Gender: De Beauvoir, Wittig and Foucault," in *Feminism as Critique*, ed. Benhabib and Cornell, pp. 128–43; Jane Flax, "Postmodernism and Gender Relations in Feminist Theory," *Signs*, 12.4 (1987), pp. 621–43. I discuss certain disagreements with Butler and Flax in the following chapter.

30 L. Kerber, "Some Cautionary Words for Historians," in "On 'In a Different Voice': An Interdisciplinary Forum," *Signs*, 11.2 (Winter 1986), pp. 304–10, here p. 306; see also Linda Nicholson "Women, Morality and History," pp. 514–37, for similar concerns about Gilligan's work.

31 Jean Piaget, *The Moral Judgment of the Child*, trans. Marjorie Gabain (Free Press, New York, 1965), p. 77.

32 See Claudia Card, "Women's Voices and Ethical Ideals: Must We Mean What We Say,?" *Ethics*, 99.1 (Oct. 1988), pp. 125–36. Card's concern with the way in which an ethics of care may hide or silence feelings of aggression and manipulation among the cared-for parties, and the way in which a too sacrificial ethics of care may be profoundly distortive of personality – think of extreme forms of motherly love and maternal solicitude – is welcome. Nonetheless, she is unfair to Gilligan in maintaining that she idealizes the "care approach." Carol Gilligan herself calls attention at various points to the dangers of self-effacement and self-denial which particularly women are prone to, cf. *In a Different Voice: Psychological Theory and Women's Development* (Harvard University Press, Cambridge, Mass., 1982), pp. 64ff., 123ff. See also Catharine A. MacKinnon's contribution to "Feminist Discourse, Moral Values and the Law – A Conversation," pp. 25ff.

33 Card, "Women's Voices and Ethical Ideals," p. 130.

34 Ibid., p. 135.

35 F. Nietzsche, *The Genealogy of Morals*, trans. Francis Golffing (Doubleday,

New York, 1956), pp. 170ff. It is astonishing that more caution is not exercised by feminists in appropriating Nietzschean categories, since Nietzsche's "naturalistic" categories of human difference as between the "weak" and the "strong" – not to mention his actual and profound dislike of women – are quite incompatible with the fundamental premise of feminist theorizing that "difference" – not only between men and women, but between the "weak" and the "strong", the "Jew" and the "Aryan" – is not a natural but a social-cultural construction.

36　Gilligan et al., "Feminist Discourse, Moral Values and the Law – A Conversation," pp. 73–4.

37　Mark Warren uses the apt phrase of "neoaristocratic conservatism" to characterize Nietzsche's political ideology but distinguishes between Nietzsche's insights into power relations and his political views, see *Nietzsche and Political Thought* (MIT Press, Cambridge, Mass., 1988), p. 3. Despite elegant and cogent treatments of Nietzsche's political thought, as that of Warren, I remain skeptical about his usefulness for feminist theory and believe that appropriations of Nietzsche by feminists, as I will also argue against Judith Butler in the next chapter, cause more trouble than insight.

38　See her statement, "Dominance and submission made into sex, made into the gender difference, constitute the suppressed social content of the gender definitions of men and women." In "Feminist Discourse, Moral Values and the Law – A Conversation," p. 27.

39　In "Feminist Discourse, Moral Values and the Law – A Conversation," pp. 21–2.

40　For an analysis of the often contradictory visions of the political in Marx's work and in the Marxist tradition, see Jean Cohen, *Class and Civil Society: The Limits of Marxian Critical Theory*, (University of Massachusetts Press, Amherst, 1982); Dick Howard, *The Marxian Legacy* (University of Minnesota Press, Minneapolis, 1988); S. Benhabib, *Critique, Norm and Utopia: A Study of the Foundations of Critical Theory*, (Columbia University Press, New York, 1986), part 1.

41　Iris Young, "The Ideal of Community and the Politics of Difference," *Social Theory and Practice*, 12.1 (Spring 1986), p. 10.

42　Ibid., p. 11.

7   Feminism and the Question of Postmodernism

Perhaps no other text has marked the contemporary discussion concerning the complex cultural, intellectual, artistic, social and political phenomena which we have come to designate as "post-modernism" as much as Jean-François Lyotard's short treatise on *The Postmodern Condition: A Report on Knowledge*.[1] Written at the request of the president of the Conseil des Universités of the government of Quebec as a report on knowledge "in the most highly developed societies," or as a sociology of knowledge under late capitalism, Lyotard's treatise soon became the central text for the philosophical and literary discussions of postmodernism.[2] For feminist debates on postmodernism as well, Lyotard's presentation and conceptualization of the "postmodern problematic" has been crucial.[3]

This chapter will consider the contemporary alliance between feminism and postmodernism. Viewed from within the intellectual and academic culture of western capitalist democracies, feminism and postmodernism have emerged as two leading currents of our time, and each is in its own way profoundly critical of the principles and meta-narratives of western Enlightenment and modernity. Although exactly what constitutes such Enlightenment and modernity, and what those principles and meta-narratives are to which we should bid farewell is by no means clear. Feminism and post-modernism are often mentioned as if they were allies; yet certain other characterizations of postmodernism should make us rather ask "feminism or postmodernism?" At issue, of course, are not merely terminological quibbles. Both feminism and postmodernism are not merely descriptive categories: they are constitutive and evaluative terms, informing and helping define the very practices which they attempt to describe. As categories of the present, they project modes of thinking about the future and evaluating the past. Here

I will consider the complex relationship between feminism and postmodernism with an eye to one issue in particular: are the meta-philosophical premises of the positions referred to as "post-modernism" compatible with the normative content of feminism, not just as a theoretical position but as a theory of women's struggle for emancipation?

The "Postmodern Condition" according to Lyotard

Let us begin by recalling the central features of Lyotard's definition of the "postmodern condition."[4] "I will use the term modern to designate any science that legitimates itself with reference to a metadiscourse of this kind making an explicit appeal to some grand narrative," writes Lyotard, "such as the dialectics of Spirit, the hermeneutics of meaning, the emancipation of the rational or work-ing subject, or the creation of wealth" (p. xxiii). In the current context Lyotard sees the emergence of new cognitive and social options which had been obscured by the "modernist imperatives." He defines the new cognitive option variously as "paralogy" (pp. 60ff.), "agonistics" (p. 16), and "recognition of the heteromorphous nature of language games" (p. 66). The new social option is descri-bed as a "temporary contract," supplanting permanent institutions in the professional, emotional, sexual, cultural, family and inter-national domains, as well as in political affairs (p. 66).

Lyotard offers these cognitive and social options as alternatives that are authentic to the experience of postindustrial societies and to the role of knowledge within them. The hold of the modernist episteme upon contemporary consciousness, however, tends to channel our cognitive as well as our practical imagination in two directions. In the first place, society is conceived of as a functional whole (p. 11), and the condition of knowledge appropriate to it is judged as "performativity." Performativity is the view that knowl-edge is power, that modern science is to be legitimated through the increase in technological capacity, efficiency, control and output it enables (p. 47). The ideal of the theorists of performativity, from Hobbes to Luhmann, is to reduce the fragility intrinsic to the legitimation of power by minimizing risk, unpredictablility and complexity. Not only is knowledge power, but power generates access to knowledge, thus preparing for itself a self-perpetuating basis of legitimacy. "Power . . . legitimates science and the law on the basis of their efficiency, and legitimates this efficiency on the basis of science and law . . . Thus the growth of power, and its self-legitimation, are now taking the route of data storage and accessibility, and the operativity of information" (p. 47).

The second alternative is to view society as divided into two, as an alienated, bifurcated totality, in need of reunification. The corresponding epistemic vision is "critical" as opposed to "functional" knowledge. Critical knowledge is in the service of the subject; its goal is not the legitimation of power but the enabling of empowerment (p. 12ff.). It seeks not to enhance the efficiency of the apparatus but to further the self-formation of humanity; not to reduce complexity but to create a world in which a reconciled humanity recognizes itself. For Lyotard the contemporary representative of this nineteenth-century ideal, born out of the imagination of a German thinker, Wilhelm von Humboldt, is Jürgen Habermas (p. 32). Where it was von Humboldt's ideal to have philosophy restore unity to learning via the development of a language game linking all the sciences together as moments in the becoming of Spirit (p. 33), it is Habermas's purpose to formulate a metadiscourse which is "universally valid for language games" (p. 65). The goal of such discourse is not so much the *Bildung* of the German nation, as it had been for von Humboldt, but the attainment of consensus, transparency and reconciliation. Lyotard comments: "The cause is good, but the argument is not. Consensus has become an outmoded and suspect value . . . We must . . . arrive at an idea and practice of justice that is not linked to that of consensus" (p. 66).

Can Lyotard convince? Is his project of formulating the outlines of a postmodern episteme, beyond the dualism of functional and critical knowledge, beyond instrumental reason and critical theory, viable? What are the epistemological options opened by the demise of the modernist episteme of representation? To mark the epistemological moment which Lyotard himself characterizes as "postmodern," and to situate feminist theory within the broader horizon of transformations which have taken place in the project of modernist philosophy, I would like first to consider the "demise of the episteme of representation." Both feminism and postmodernism are theoretical movements growing out of the demise of this modernist episteme. Depending though on how we conceptualize the intellectual movements and currents leading to this transformation, different epistemic options and normative visions become available to us.

The End of the Episteme of Representation

Modern philosophy began with the loss of the world.[5] The decision of the autonomous bourgeois subject to take nothing and no authority for granted whose content and strictures had not been subjected to rigorous examination, and that had not withstood the test of "clarity and distinctness," began with the withdrawal from the world. It was still possible for Descartes in the seventeenth century to describe this withdrawal in the language of Stoicism and Spanish Jesuit philosophy as an ethical and religious gesture, either as a "suspension" of the involvement of the self with the world (Stoicism) or as the withdrawal of the soul to a communion with itself (Jesuit teaching of meditation). These were stages on the road to an equilibrium with the cosmos and necessary for the purging of the soul in preparation for the truth of God. The future development of modern epistemology succeeded in repressing this ethical and cultural moment to the point where the typical reductions on which the classical episteme of representation rested could emerge. The corporeal, ethico-moral self was reduced to a pure subject of knowledge, to consciousness or to mind. The object of knowledge was reduced to "matters of fact" and "relations of ideas," or to "sensations" and "concepts." The question of classical epistemology from Descartes to Hume, from Locke to Kant was how to make congruous the order of representations in consciousness with the order of representations outside the self. Caught in the prisonhouse of its own consciousness, the modern epistemological subject tried to recover the world it had well lost.[6] The options were not many: either one reassured oneself that the world would be gained by the direct and immediate evidence of the senses (empiricism) or one insisted that the rationality of the creator or the harmony of mind and nature would guarantee the correspondence between the two orders of representations (rationalism).

Whether empiricist or rationalist, modern epistemologists agreed that the task of knowledge, whatever its origins, was to build an adequate representation of things. In knowledge, mind had to "mirror" nature.[7] As Charles Taylor points out, "When we hold that having X is having a (correct) representation of X, one of the things we establish is the neat separation of ideas, thoughts, descriptions and the like, on the one hand, and what these ideas, etc. are about on the other."[8] Actually, modern epistemology operated with a threefold distinction: the order of representations in our consciousness (ideas and sensations); the signs through which these "private" orders were made public, namely words, and that of which our representations were representations, and to which they referred.[9] In this tradition, meaning was defined as "designation;" the meaning of a word was what it designates, while the primary function of language was denotative, namely to inform us about objectively existing states of affairs. The classical episteme of representation presupposed a spectator conception of the knowing self, a designative theory of meaning, and a denotative theory of language.

Already in the nineteenth century three directions of critique of the classical episteme, leading to its eventual rejection, developed. Stylizing somewhat, the first can be described as the critique of the modern epistemic subject, the second as the critique of the modern epistemic object, and the third as the critique of the modern concept of the sign. The critique of the Cartesian, spectator conception of the subject begins with German Idealism, and continues with Marx and Freud to Horkheimer in 1937, and to Habermas in *Knowledge and Human Interests*.[10] This tradition substitutes for the spectator model of the self the view of an active, producing, fabricating humanity, creating the conditions of objectivity by forming nature through its own historical activity. The Hegelian and Marxist tradition also shows that the Cartesian ego is not a self-transparent entity and that the epistemic self cannot reach full autonomy as long as the historical origin and social constitution of the "clear and distinct" ideas it contemplates remain a mystery. At this point this critique joins hands with the Freudian one which likewise shows that the self is not "transparent" to itself, for it is not "master in its own house" (*Herr im eigenen Haus*). It is controled by desires, needs and forces whose effects upon it shape both the contents of its clear and distinct ideas, as well as its capacity to organize them. The historical and psychoanalytic critique of the Cartesian ego sees the task of reflection neither as the withdrawal from the world nor as access to clarity and distinctness, but as the rendering conscious of those unconscious forces of history and society which have shaped the human psyche. Although generated by the subject, these forces necessarily escape its memory, control and conduct. The goal of reflection is emancipation from self-incurred bondage.

The second line of criticism can be most closely associated with the names of Nietzsche, Heidegger, and Adorno and Horkheimer in *Dialectic of Enlightenment*. The modern episteme is viewed as an episteme of domination. For Nietzsche modern science universalizes Cartesian doubt. Modern knowledge divides the world into the realm of appearance on the one hand, and that of essence or things-in-themselves on the other.[11] This dualistic vision is internalized by the subject of knowledge who in turn is split into body and mind, the senses and the conceptual faculty. Nietzsche has no difficulty in showing that in this sense modern science signifies the triumph of Platonism. Heidegger drives the error underlying the modern episteme of representation further back than its Platonic origins, to a conception of being as presence, as what is available and present to the consciousness of the subject.[12] This conception of being as "presence-to" reduces the manyness of the appearances by presenting them as "things" available to and disposable by a sovereign consciousness. By reducing appearances to what is present to the sovereign self, consciousness attains the option of controlling them. In a spirit that is quite akin to Heidegger's, in the *Dialectic of Enlightenment* Adorno and Horkheimer argue that it is the "concept," the very unit of thought in the western tradition that imposes homogeneity and identity upon the heterogeneity of material. This drive for identity of conceptual thought culminates in the technical triumph of western *ratio*, which can only know things in that it comes to dominate them. "The Enlightenment relates to things as the dictator to humans."[13]

The third tradition of criticism is initiated by Ferdinand de Saussure and Charles Sanders Peirce, and given sharper contours by Frege and Wittgenstein in our century. They argue that it is impossible to make sense of meaning, reference and language in general when the view of linguistic signs as "private marks"[14] prevails. Instead, the public and shared character of language is a beginning point. Both de Saussure and Peirce point out that there is no natural relation between a sound, the word it represents in a language, and the content it refers to. For Peirce, the relation of the sign, of which words are but one species, to the signified is mediated by the interpretant.[15] For de Saussure, it is within a system of differential relations that certain sounds get arbitrarily frozen to stand for words.[16] Language is that sedimented set of relations which stands ideally behind the set of enunciations, called "parole." This move in the analysis of language from the private to the public, from consciousness to sign, from the individual word to a system of relations among linguistic signs, is followed by Frege and Wittgenstein, insofar as they too argue that the unit of reference is not the word but the sentence (Frege), and that meaning can only be understood by analyzing the multiple contexts of use (Wittgenstein).

The epistemological juncture at which Lyotard operates is characterized by the triumph of this third tradition. Whether in analytic philosophy, or in contemporary hermeneutics, or in French post-structuralism, *the paradigm of language has replaced the paradigm of consciousness.* This shift has meant that the focus is no longer on the epistemic subject or on the private contents of its consciousness but on the public, signifying activities of a collection of subjects. Not only has there been a shift in the size of the interrogated epistemic unit from idea, sensation and concept to the threefold character of the sign as signifier, signified and interpretant (Peirce), to language and parole (Saussure) or to language games as "forms of life" (Wittgenstein). The identity of the epistemic subject has changed as well: the bearer of the sign cannot be an isolated self – there is no private language, as Wittgenstein has observed; the epistemic subject is either the community of selves whose identity extends as far as their horizon of interpretations (Gadamer) or it is a social community of actual language users (Wittgenstein). This enlargement of the relevant epistemic subject is one option. A second option, followed by French structuralism and poststructuralism, is to deny that in order to make sense of the epistemic object one need appeal to an epistemic subject at all. The subject is replaced by a system of structures, oppositions and différances which, to be intelligible, need not be viewed as products of a living subjectivity at all.[17]

Lyotard wants to convince that the destruction of the episteme of representation allows only one option, namely a recognition of the irreconcilability and incommensurability of language games, and the acceptance that only local and context-specific criteria of validity can be formulated. One must accept, in other words, an "agonistics" of language: "to speak is to fight, in the sense of playing, and speech-acts fall within the domain of a general agonistics" (p. 10). This cognitive option yields a "polytheism of values," and a politics of justice beyond consensus, characterized by Lyotard vaguely as the "temporary contract."

The shift in contemporary philosophy from consciousness to language, from the order of representations to that of speech-acts, from denotation to performance need not lead to a "polytheism of values" and to an "agonistics" of language. In the introduction to this book and throughout the previous chapters I have investigated the *alternative normative and epistemic options* made possible by the demise of the episteme of representation and the transition from a "substantivist" to a "proceduralist" and "interactive" concept of rationality. Whereas the demise of the modernist episteme for Lyotard suggests an "agonistics of language" and a "polytheism of values," I have pleaded for a social pragmatic conception of language, viewed as a form of speech in action between two human beings;[18] to the "polytheism of values," I have juxtaposed not a "monotheism," but the possibility of reasonable and open-ended ethical conversation about matters of justice as well as those of the good life. To bring this complex epistemological dispute to a simple formula one can say: like Dostoevsky and Nietzsche before them, postmodernists seem to say that "God is dead; everything is allowed." In their case the phrase would be "Transcendental guarantees of truth are dead; in the agonal struggle of language games there is no commensurability; there are no criteria of truth transcending local discourses, but only the endless struggle of local narratives vying with one another for legitimation."[19] But just as the "death of God" does not destroy all bases of normative human coexistence – societies based on religious agnosticism and tolerance are not less stable, perhaps to the contrary they are more stable than premodern societies full of interfaith disputes and theological wars –

so too the demise of rationalistic and transcendental philosophies from Descartes to Kant and Husserl does not signify the end of but yet another "transformation" of the philosophical project.[20] One way to understand this transformation has been outlined in this book: it is the emergence of a fallibilistic and procedural concept of rationality and the normative options allowed by this in ethics and politics.[21]

Faced with these debates about the "end" or "transformation" of philosophy and the emergence of a postmodernist agonistics of language, feminists feel ambivalent:[22] on the one hand, they want to extract from the postmodernism debate only those intellectual conclusions which will aid us in the task of thinking and rethinking the western intellectual tradition and creating a new one of our own in the light of the question of gender; on the other hand, in allying themselves with postmodernist positions, feminists, willy-nilly, are getting embroiled in this dispute and entangled in a set of assumptions which go well beyond research interest centering on gender as a "useful category"[23] to the heart of contemporary philosophical thought. Many feminists share an impulse on this issue which is quite like the "constructivist" vein of John Rawls's later writings on justice in democratic societies. Inasmuch as Rawls wants to articulate principles of justice on the basis of presuppositions "common to the democratic culture" of advanced capitalist democracies, thus avoiding philosophically controversial concepts of self and society, so too many contemporary feminists want to adopt postmodernist premises without getting embroiled in the philosophical argumentation necessary to establish the cogency of these premises. But is their position tenable? Can feminists become postmodernists and claim to develop a theory in the interests of women's emancipation?

Let us begin by considering one of the more comprehensive characterizations of the "postmodern moment" provided by a feminist theorist. In the following discussion, I shall attempt to show that just as Lyotard is right in marking the end of the episteme of representation and in searching for alternative cognitive and normative options to this no longer convincing intellectual paradigm, so too, feminists friends of postmodernism are correct in noting the profound alliances between the postmodernist critique of western thought and their own positions. Where Lyotard as well as the feminist friends of postmodernism go wrong is in their assumption that the end of meta-narratives, or the death of Man, History and Metaphysics (Jane Flax), allow only one set of conceptual and normative options. By sorting out from one another the strong and weak versions of these theses, I shall argue that the strong postmodernist position is incompatible with and in fact renders incoherent feminism as a theoretical articulation of a struggling social movement.

Feminist Friends of Postmodernism

In her recently published book, *Thinking Fragments: Psychoanalysis, Feminism and Postmodernism in the Contemporary West*, Jane Flax characterizes the postmodern position as subscription to the theses of the death of Man, of History and of Metaphysics.[24]

The Death of Man. "Postmodernists wish to destroy," she writes, "all essentialist conceptions of human being or nature . . . In fact Man is a social, historical or linguistic artifact, not a noumenal or transcendental Being . . . Man is forever caught in the web of fictive meaning, in chains of signification, in which the subject is merely another position in language."[25]

The Death of History. "The idea that History exists for or is his Being is more than just another precondition and justification for the fiction of Man. This idea also supports and underlies the concept of Progress, which is itself such an important part of Man's story . . . Such an idea of Man and History privileges and presupposes the value of unity, homogeneity, totality, closure and identity."[26]

The Death of Metaphysics. According to postmodernists, "Western metaphysics has been under the spell of the 'metaphysics of presence' at least since Plato . . . For postmodernists this quest for the Real conceals most Western philosophers' desire, which is to master the world once and for all by enclosing it within an illusory but absolute system they believe represents or corresponds to a unitary Being beyond history, particularity and change . . . Just as the Real is the ground of Truth, so too philosophy as the privileged representative of the Real and interrogator of truth claims must play a 'foundational' role in all 'positive knowledge'."[27]

Flax's clear and cogent characterization of the postmodernist position will enable us to see why feminists find in this critique of the ideals of western rationalism and the Enlightenment more than a congenial ally. But let me also note certain important discrepancies between my formulation of the conceptual options made possible by the end of the classical episteme of representation and Flax's version of postmodernism. First, whereas in the course of the transition from "nineteenth century idealism to twentieth century contextualism" (R. Rorty),[28] I see a move toward the radical situatedness and contextualization of the subject, Flax follows the French tradition in stipulating the "death of the subject." Second, whereas I see a transformation in the object as well the medium of epistemological representation from consciousness to language, from claims about truth and reality to a more limited investigation of the conditions under which a community of inquirers can make warranted assertions about truth and the real, Flax maintains that "philosophy as the privileged representative of the Real" has not been transformed but has died off. So far, I have not dealt with the thesis of the Death of History, but as I shall argue below, of all the claims associated with postmodernist positions this one is the least problematical. Critical theorists as well as postmodernists, liberals as well as communitarians, could agree upon some version of the thesis of the "death of history," in the sense of a teleologically determined progression of historical transformations; but the controversial questions concern the relation of historical narrative to the interests of present actors in their historical past. These discrepancies between Flax's formulations and my own as to how to characterize the epistemic options of the present will play a larger role as the argument progresses.

Consider for the time being how, like postmodernism, feminist theory as well has created its own versions of the three theses concerning the death of Man, History and Metaphysics.

The feminist counterpoint to the postmodernist theme of the *Death of Man* can be named the "Demystification of the Male Subject of Reason." Whereas postmodernists substitute for Man, or the sovereign subject of the theoretical and practical reason of the tradition, the study of contingent, historically changing and culturally variable social, linguistic and discursive practices, feminists claim that "gender" and the various practices contributing to its constitution are one of the most crucial contexts in which to situate the purportedly neutral and universal subject of reason.[29] The western philosophical tradition articulates the deep structures of the experiences and consciousness of a self which it claims to be representative for humans as such. The deepest categories of western philosophy obliterate differences of gender as these shape and structure the experience and subjectivity of the self. Western reason posits itself as the discourse of the one self-identical subject, thereby blinding us to and in fact delegitimizing the presence of otherness and difference which do not fit into its categories. From Plato over Descartes to Kant and Hegel western philosophy thematizes the story of the male subject of reason.

The feminist counterpoint to the *Death of History* would be the "Engendering of Historical Narrative." If the subject of the western intellectual tradition has usually been the white, propertied, Christian, male head of household, then History as hitherto recorded and narrated has been "his story." Furthermore, the various philosophies of history which have dominated since the Enlightenment have forced historical narrative into unity, homegeneity and linearity with the consequence that fragmentation, heterogeneity and above all the varying pace of different temporalities as experienced by different groups have been obliterated.[30] We need only remember Hegel's belief that Africa has no history.[31] Until very recently neither did women have their own history, their own narrative with different categories of periodization and with different structural regularities.

The feminist counterpoint to the *Death of Metaphysics* would be "Feminist Skepticism Toward the Claims of Transcendent Reason." If the subject of reason is not a suprahistorical and context-transcendent being, but the theoretical and practical creations and activities of this subject bear in every instance the marks of the context out of which they emerge, then the subject of philosophy is inevitably embroiled with knowledge-governing interests which mark and direct its activities. For feminist theory, the most important "knowledge-guiding interest" in Habermas's terms, or disciplinary matrix of truth and power in Foucault's terms, are gender relations and the social, economic, political and symbolic constitution of gender differences among human beings.[32]

Despite this "elective affinity" between feminism and postmodernism, each of the three theses enumerated above can be interpreted to permit if not contradictory then at least radically divergent theoretical strategies. And for feminists which set of theretical claims they adopt as their own cannot be a matter of indifference. As Linda Alcoff has recently observed, feminist theory is undergoing a profound identity crisis at the moment.[33] The postmodernist position(s) thought through to their conclusions may eliminate not only the specificity of feminist theory but place in question the very emancipatory ideals of the women's movements altogether.

Feminist Skepticism toward Postmodernism

The following discussion will formulate two versions of the three theses enumerated above with the goal of clarifying once more the various conceptual options made available with the demise of the episteme of representations. Put in a nutshell, my argument is that strong and weak versions of the theses of the death of Man, of History and of Metaphysics are possible. Whereas the weak versions of these theses entail premises around which critical theorists as well as postmodernists and possibly even liberals and communitarians can unite, their strong versions undermine the possibility of normative criticism at large. Feminist theory can ally itself with this strong version of postmodernism only at the risk of incoherence and self-contradictoriness.

(a)   Let us begin by considering the thesis of the Death of Man for a closer understanding of the conceptual option(s) allowed by the end of the episteme of representation. The weak version of this thesis would *situate* the subject in the context of various social, linguistic and discursive practices. This view would by no means question the desirability and theoretical necessity of articulating a more adequate, less deluded and less mystified vision of subjectivity than those provided by the concepts of the Cartesian cogito, the "transcendental unity of apperception," "Geist and consciousness," or "das Man" (the they). The traditional attributes of the philosophical subject of the West, like self-reflexivity, the capacity for acting on principles, rational accountability for one's actions and the ability to project a life-plan into the future, in short, some form of autonomy and rationality, could then be reformulated by taking account of the radical situatedness of the subject.

The strong version of the thesis of the Death of the Man is perhaps best captured in Flax's own phrase that "Man is forever caught in the web of fictive meaning, in chains of signification, *in which the subject is merely another position in language*." The subject thus dissolves into the chain of significations of which it was supposed to be the initiator. Along with this dissolution of the subject into yet "another position in language" disappear of course concepts of intentionality, accountability, self-reflexivity and autonomy. The subject that is but another position in language can no longer master and create that distance between itself and the chain of significations in which it is immersed such that it can reflect upon them and creatively alter them.

The strong version of the Death of the Subject thesis is not compatible with the goals of feminism.[34] Surely, a subjectivity that would not be structured by language, by narrative and by the symbolic codes of narrative available in a culture is unthinkable. We tell of who we are, of the "I" that we are, by means of a narrative. "I was born on such and such a date, as the daughter of such and such ..." etc. These narratives are deeply colored and structured by the codes of expectable and understandable biographies and identities in our cultures.[35] We can concede all that, but nevertheless we must still argue that we are not merely extensions of our histories, that vis-à-vis our own stories we are in the position of author and character at once. The situated and gendered subject is heteronomously determined but still strives toward autonomy. I want to ask how in fact the very project of female emancipation would be thinkable without such a regulative ideal of enhancing the agency, autonomy and selfhood of women.

Feminist appropriations of Nietzsche on this question can only be incoherent. In her recent book, *Gender Trouble: Feminism and the*

Subversion of Identity, Judith Butler wants to extend the limits of reflexivity in thinking about the self beyond the dichotomy of "sex" and "gender." Her convincing and original arguments rejecting this dichotomous reasoning within which feminist theory has operated until recently get clouded, however, by the claim that to reject this dichotomy would mean subscribing to the view that the "gendered self" does not exist; all that the self is, is a series of performamces. "Gender," writes Butler, "is not to culture as sex is to nature; gender is also the discursive/cultural means by which 'sexed nature' or a 'natural sex' is produced and established as 'prediscursive,' prior to culture, a politically neutral surface *on which* culture acts."[36] For Butler the myth of the already sexed body is the epistemological equivalent of the myth of the given: just as the given can only be identified within a discursive framework, so too it is the culturally available codes of gender that "sexualize" a body and that construct the directionality of that body's sexual desire.[37]

But Butler also maintains that to think beyond the univocality and dualisms of gender categories, we must bid farewell to the "doer behind the deed," to the self as the subject of a life-narrative. "In an application that Nietzsche himself would not have anticipated or condoned, we might state as a corollary: There is no gender identity behind the expressions of gender; that identity is performatively constituted by the very 'expressions' that are said to be its results."[38] Yet if this view of the self is adopted, is there any possibility of transforming those "expressions" which constitute us? If we are no more than the sum total of the gendered expressions we perform, is there ever any chance to stop the performance for a while, to pull the curtain down, and only let it rise if one can have a say in the production of the play itself? Isn't this what the struggle over gender is all about? Surely we can criticize the "metaphysical pre-suppositions of identity politics" and challenge the supremacy of heterosexist positions in the women's movement. Yet is such a challenge only thinkable via a complete debunking of any concepts of selfhood, agency and autonomy? What follows from this Nietzschean position is a vision of the self as a masquerading performer, except of course we are now asked to believe that there is no self behind the mask. Given how fragile and tenuous women's sense of selfhood is in many cases, how much of a hit-and-miss affair their struggles for autonomy are, this reduction of female agency to a "doing without the doer" at best appears to me to be making a virtue out of necessity.[39]

The view that gendered identity is constituted by "deeds without the doer," or by performances without a subject, not only undermines the normative vision of feminist politics and theory. It is also impossible to get rid of the subject altogether and claim to be a fully accountable participant in the community of discourse and inquiry: the strong thesis of the death of the subject undermines the discourse of the theorist herself. If the subject who produces discourse is but a product of the discourse it has created, or better still is but "another position in language," then the responsibility for this discourse cannot be attributed to the author but must be attributable to some fictive "authorial position," constituted by the intersection of "discursive planes." (I am tempted to add that in geometry the intersection of planes produces a line!) Butler entertains this possibility in the introduction to her work: "Philosophy is the predominant disciplinary mechanism that currently mobilizes this author-subject."[40] The "subject" here means also the "object of the discourse;" not the one who utilizes the discourse but the one who is utilized by the discourse itself. Presumably that is why Butler uses the language of "a discourse mobilizing an author/subject." The center of motility is not the thinking, acting and feeling self but "discourses," "systems of signification," "chains of signs," etc. But how then should we read *Gender Trouble*?

The kind of reading I am engaging here presupposes that there is a thinking author who has produced this text, who has intentions, purposes and goals in communicating with me; that the task of theoretical reflection begins with the attempt to understand what the author meant. Certainly, language always says much more than what the author means; there will always be a discrepancy between what we mean and what we say; but we engage in communication, theoretical no less than everyday communication, to gain some basis of mutual understanding and reasoning. The view that the subject is not reducible to "yet another position in language," but that no matter how constituted by language the subject retains a certain autonomy and ability to rearrange the significations of language, is a regulative principle of all communication and social action. Not only feminist politics, but also coherent theorizing becomes impossible if the speaking and thinking self is replaced by "authorial positions," and if the self becomes a ventriloquist for discourses operating through her or "mobilizing" her.[41]

Perhaps I have overstated the case against Butler.[42] Perhaps Butler does not want, any more than Flax herself, to dispense with women's sense of selfhood, agency and autonomy. In the concluding reflections to *Gender Trouble* Butler returns to questions of agency, identity and politics. She writes:

> The question of locating "agency" is usually associated with the viability of the "subject," where the subject is understood to have some stable existence prior to the cultural field that it negotiated. Or, if the subject is culturally constructed, it is nevertheless vested with an

agency, usually figured as the capacity for reflexive mediation, that remains intact regardless of its cultural embeddedness. On such a model, "culture" and "discourse" *mire* the subject, but do not constitute that subject. This move to qualify and to enmire the preexisting subject has appeared necessary to establish a point of agency that is not fully *determined* by that culture and discourse. And yet, this kind of reasoning falsely presumes (a) agency can only be established through recourse to a prediscursive "I," even if that "I" is found in the midst of a discursive convergence, and (b) that to be *constituted* by discourse is to be *determined* by discourse, where determination forecloses the possibility of agency."[43]

Butler rejects that identity can only be established through recourse to an "'I' that preexists signification."[44] She points out that "the enabling conditions for an assertion of 'I' are provided by the structure of signification, the rules that regulate the legitimate and illegitimate invocation of that pronoun, the practices that establish the terms of intelligibility by which that pronoun can circulate." The narrative codes of a culture then define the content with which this pronoun will be invested, the appropriate instances when it can be invoked, by whom and how. Yet one can agree with all that and still maintain that no individual is merely a blank slate upon whom are inscribed the codes of a culture, a kind of Lockean tabula rasa in latter-day Foucaultian garb![45] The historical and cultural study of diverse codes of the constitution of subjectivity, or the historical study of the formation of the individual, does not answer the question: what mechanisms and dynamics are involved in the developmental process through which the human infant, a vulnerable and dependent body, becomes a distinct self with the ability to speak its language and the ability to participate in the complex social processes which define its world? Such dynamics and mechanisms enabled the children of the ancient Egyptians to become members of that cultural community no less than they enabled Hopi children to become social individuals. The study of culturally diverse codes which define individuality is not the same as an answer to the question as to *how* the human infant becomes the social self, regardless of the cultural and normative content which defines selfhood. In the latter case we are studying *structural processes and dynamics of socialization and individuation*; in the former, historical processes of signification and meaning constitution. Indeed, as Butler observes, "to be constituted by discourse is not to be determined by discourse." We have to explain how a human infant can become the speaker of an infinitely meaningful number of sentences in a given natural language, how it acquires, that is, the competence to become a linguistic being; furthermore, we have to explain how every human infant can become the initiator of a unique life-story, of a meaningful tale – which certainly is only meaningful if we know the cultural codes under which it is constructed – but which we cannot predict even if we knew these cultural codes.

Butler writes "that 'agency' then is to be located within the possibility of a variation on that repetition" (the repetition of gender performances).[46] But where are the resources for that variation derived from? What is it that enables the self to "vary" the gender codes? to resist hegemonic discourses? What psychic, intellectual or other sources of creativity and resistance must we attribute to subjects for such variation to be possible?

The answers to these questions, even if they were fully available to me at this point, which they are not, would go beyond the boundaries of this essay. Yet we have reached an important conclusion: the issues generated by the complex interaction between feminism and postmodernism around concepts of the self and subjectivity cannot be captured by bombastic proclamations of the "Death of the Subject." The central question is how we must understand the phrase: "the I although constituted by discourse is not determined by it." To embark upon a meaningful answer to this query from where we stand today involves not yet another decoding of metaphors and tropes about the self, but a serious interchange between philosophy and the social sciences like sociolinguistics, social interactionist psychology, socialization theory, psychoanalysis and cultural history among others. To put it bluntly: the thesis of the Death of the Subject presupposes a remarkably crude version of individuation and socialization processes when compared with currently available social-scientific reflections on the subject.[47] But neither the fundamentalist models of inquiry of the tradition, which privilege the reflective I reflecting upon the conditions of its reflexive or non-reflexive existence, nor the postmodernist decoding of the subject into bodily surfaces "that are enacted *as* the natural, so [that] these surfaces can become the site of a dissonant and denaturalized performance" (Butler) will suffice in the task of explaining how the individual can be "constituted by discourse and yet not be determined by it." The analysis of gender once more forces the boundaries of disciplinary discourses toward a new integration of theoretical paradigms.

(b) Consider now the thesis of the Death of History. Of all positions normally associated with postmodernism this particular one appears to me to be the least problematical. Disillusionment with the ideals of progress, awareness of the atrocities committed in this century in the name of technological and economic progress, the political and moral bankruptcy of the natural sciences which put themselves in the service of the forces of human and planetary destruction – these are the shared sentiments of our century. Intellectuals and philosophers in the twentieth century are to be distinguished from one another less as being friends and opponents of the belief in progress but more in terms of the following: whether the farewell from the "meta-narratives of the Enlightenment" can be exercised in terms of a continuing belief in the power of rational reflection or whether this farewell is but a prelude to a departure from such reflection.

Interpreted as a *weak* thesis, the Death of History could mean two things: theoretically, this could be understood as a call to end the practice of "grand narratives" which are essentialist and monocausal. It is futile, let us say, to search for an essence of "motherhood," as a cross-cultural universal; just as it is futile to seek to produce a single grand theory of female oppression and male dominance across cultures and societies – be such a theory psychoanalytic, anthropological or biological. Politically, the end of such grand narratives would mean rejecting the hegemonial claims of any group or organization to "represent" the forces of history, to be moving with such forces, or to be acting in their name. The critique of the various totalitarian and totalizing movements of our century from National Socialism and Fascism to Stalinism and other forms of authoritarianism is certainly one of the most formative political experiences of postmodernist intellectuals like Lyotard, Foucault and Derrida.[48] This is also what makes the Death of History thesis interpreted as the end of "grand narratives" so attractive to feminist theorists. Nancy Fraser and Linda Nicholson write for example:

> the practice of feminist politics in the 1980s has generated a new set of pressures which have worked against metanarratives. In recent years, poor and working-classs women, women of color, and lesbians have finally won a wider hearing for their objections to feminist theories which fail to illuminate their lives and address their problems. They have exposed the earlier quasi-metanarratives, with their assumptions of universal female dependence and confinement to the domestic sphere, as false extrapolations from the experience of the white, middle-class, heterosexual women who dominated the beginnings of the second wave ... Thus, as the class, sexual, racial and ethnic awareness of the movement has altered, so has the preferred conception of theory. It has become clear that quasi-metanarratives hamper rather than promote sisterhood, since they elide differences among women and among the forms of sexism to which different women are differentially subject.[49]

The *strong* version of the thesis of the Death of History would imply, however, a prima facie rejection of any historical narrative that concerns itself with the long durée and that focusses on macro-rather than on micro-social practices. Nicholson and Fraser also warn against this "nominalist" tendency in Lyotard's work.[50] I agree with them that it would be a mistake to interpret the death of "grand narratives" as sanctioning in the future local stories as opposed to global history. The decision as to how local or global a historical narrative or piece of social-scientific research need be cannot be determined by epistemological arguments extraneous to the task at hand. It is the empirical researcher who should answer this question; the philosopher has no business legislating the scope of research to the empirical scientist. To the extent that Lyotard's version of postmodernism seems to sanctify the "small" or "local narrative" over the grand one, he engages in unnecessary a priorism with regard to open-ended questions of scientific inquiry.

The more difficult question suggested by the strong thesis of the "death of history" appears to me to be different: even while we dispense with grand narratives, how can we rethink the relationship between politics, historiography and historical memory? Is it possible for struggling groups not to interpret history in light of a moral-political imperative, namely, the imperative of the future interest in emancipation? Think for a moment not only of the way in which feminist historians in the last two decades have discovered women and their hitherto invisible lives and work, but of the manner in which they have also revalorized and taught us to see with different eyes such traditionally female and previously denigrated activities like gossip, quilt-making, and even forms of typically female sickness like headaches, hysteria and taking to bed during menstruation.[51] In this process of the "feminist transvaluation of values" our *present* interest in women's strategies of survival and historical resistance has led us to imbue these *past* activities, which were wholly uninteresting from the standpoint of the traditional historian, with new meaning and significance.

While it is no longer possible or desirable to produce "grand narratives" of history, the "death of history" thesis occludes the epistemological interest in history and in historical narrative which accompany the aspirations of all struggling historical actors. Once this "interest" in recovering the lives and struggles of those "losers" and "victims" of history are lost, can we produce engaged feminist theory?

Defenders of "postmodern historiography" like Fraser and Nicholson who issue calls for a "postmodern-feminist theory" look away from these difficulties in part because what they mean by this kind of theorizing is less "postmodernist" but more "neopragmatist." By "postmodern feminist theory" they mean a theory that would be pragmatic and fallibilistic, that "would tailor its method and categories to the specific task at hand, using multiple categories when appropriate and forswearing the metaphysical comfort of a single feminist method or feminist epistemology".[52] Yet this even-handed and commonsensical approach to tailoring theory to the tasks at hand is not postmodernist. Fraser and Nicholson can reconcile their political commitments with their theoretical sympathies for postmodernism, only because they have substituted theoretical pragmatism for, in effect, the "hyper-theoretical" claims of postmodern historiography. Let me illustrate with an example from recent feminist debates.

The Summer 1990 issues of the journal *Signs* carried an exchange between Linda Gordon and Joan Scott which involved reviews by each of the other's recent books and the authors' responses.[53] This exchange contains a very succinct statement of the kinds of political cum theoretical issues currently facing feminist theorists who may or may not want to adopt postmodernist methodologies in their own work. Central to postmodernist methodology in historiography no less than in philosophy and cultural analysis is the status of the subject and of subjectivity. After reviewing Linda Gordon's presentation of the history of family violence as it was treated and defined by professional social workers in three child-saving agencies in Boston from the 1880s to the 1960s, Scott observes that Gordon's book "is aimed at refuting simple theories of social control and rejecting interpretations that stress the top-down nature of welfare policies and the passivity of their recipients."[54] Instead Gordon proposes an interactive model of relationships, according to which power is negotiated among family members and among the victims and state agencies. Joan Scott sees little evidence for women as "active agents" in Gordon's book; the title of Gordon's book – *Heroes of their Own Lives: The Politics and History of Family Violence* – Scott observes "is more a wish than a historical reality, more a politically correct formulation than anything that can be substantiated by the sources."[55] And the methodological difficulty is stated succinctly, in terms which immediately remind us of Butler's claims examined in the previous section concerning the "social and cultural construction of agency." Scott writes:

> A different conceptualization of agency might have avoided the contradictions Gordon runs into and articulated better the complex relationship between welfare workers and their clients evident in the book. *This conceptualization would see agency not as an attribute or trait inhering in the will of autonomous individual subjects, but as a discursive effect, in this case the effect of social workers' constructions of families, gender, and family violence. It would take the idea of "construction" seriously, as something that has positive social effects.* (For the most part Gordon uses "construction" as if it were synonymous with "definition," but definition

lacks the materiality connoted by "construction.") It was, after all, the existence of welfare societies that not only made family violence a problem to be dealt with but also gave family members a place to turn to, a sense of responsibility, a reason for acting, and a way of thinking about resistance.[56] (Emphasis added.)

What one sees in Scott's critique of Gordon's book is a clash of paradigms within women's historiography – a clash between the social history from below paradigm used by Gordon, the task of which is to illuminate the gender, class and race struggles through which power is negotiated, subverted as well as resisted by the so-called "victims" of history, and the paradigm of postmodernist historiography, influenced by Foucault's work, in which the emphasis is on the "construction" of the agency of the victims through mechanisms of social and discursive control. Just as for Michel Foucault there is no history of the victims but only a history of the construction of victimization, a history of the agencies of victim control, so too for Scott as well, it is the "social construction of family violence," rather than the actual lives of the victims of family violence which is methodologically central. Just as for Foucault every act of resistance is but another manifestation of an omni-present discourse-power complex, for Scott too, women who nego-tiate and resist power do not exist; the only struggles in history are between competing paradigms of discourses, power-knowledge complexes.

Let me tread lightly here: not being a professional historian, it is beyond my competency to arbitrate the dispute between Joan Scott and Linda Gordon. What I am calling attention to here are some of the conceptual issues involved, and which have their source in a version of the "death of the subject" thesis considered above. We see in Scott's critique of Gordon how Foucaultian premises about the social "construction of agency" are juxtaposed to the history-from-below approach espoused by Gordon. If we go along with Joan Scott, one approach to feminist historiography follows; and another, if we are with Gordon. Of course, it could also be that there is no either/or here, that each method and approach should learn from and benefit from the other. Yet before we can issue a Polyanna call to all parties of the debate,[57] we should get clear on what the conceptual constraints of postmodernist historiography are for feminists. Linda Gordon I think puts the matter very succinctly:

In fact Scott's and my differences go to the heart of contemporary controversies about the meanings of gender. Scott's determinist perspective emphasizes gender as "difference," marked by the other-ness and absolute silencing of women. I use gender to describe a power system in which women are subordinated through relations that are contradictory, ambiguous, and conflictual – a subordination maintained against resistance, in which women have by no means always defined themselves as other, in which women face and take choices and action despite constriction. These are only two of many versions of gender, and they are by no means opposite, but they may illuminate the relevant issues here.[58]

We see once more that the "death of history" thesis as well allows conceptual alternatives: agreement on the end of historical meta-narratives either of the Marxian sort which center around class struggle or of the liberal sort which center around a notion of progress is not sufficient. Beyond such agreement begin difficult questions on the relationship between historiography, politics and memory. Should we approach history to retrieve from it the victims' memories, lost struggles and unsuccessful resistances,[59] or should we approach history to retrieve from it the monotonous succession of infinite "power/knowledge" complexes that materially constitute selves? As Gordon points out, these methodological approaches also have implications for how we should think of "gender." Post-modernist historiography too, then, poses difficult alternatives for feminists which challenge any hasty or enthusiastic alliance between their positions.

(c)   Finally, let me articulate strong and weak versions of the "death of metaphysics" thesis. In considering this point it would be import-ant to note right at the outset that much of the postmodernist critique of western metaphysics itself proceeds under the spell of a meta-narrative, namely, the narrative first articulated by Heidegger and then developed by Derrida that "Western metaphysics has been under the spell of the 'metaphysics of presence' at least since Plato . . ." This characterization of the philosophical tradition allows postmodernists the rhetorical advantage of presenting what they are arguing against in its least defensible versions: listen again to Flax's words: "For postmodernists this quest for the Real conceals the philosophers' desire, which is to master the world" or "Just as the Real is the ground of Truth, so too philosophy as the privileged representative of the Real . . ." etc. But is the philosophical tradition so monolithic and so essentialist as postmodernists would like to claim? Would not even Thomas Hobbes shudder at the suggestion that the "Real is the ground of Truth"? What would Kant say when confronted with the claim that "philosophy is the privileged rep-resentative of the Real"? Would not Hegel consider the view that concepts and language are one sphere and the "real" yet another merely a version of a naive correspondence theory of truth which the chapter on "Sense Certainty" in the *Phenomenology of Spirit* so eloquently dispensed with? In its strong version, the "death of metaphysics" thesis suffers not only from a subscription to a grandiose meta-narrative, but more significantly, this grandiose meta-narrative flattens out the history of modern philosophy and the competing conceptual schemes it contains to the point of unrecognizability. Once this history is rendered unrecognizable then the conceptual and philosophical problems involved in this bravado proclamation of the "death of metaphysics" can be neglected.

The weak version of the "death of metaphysics" thesis which is today more influential than the strong Heidegger-Derrida thesis about the "metaphysics of presence" is Richard Rorty's account. In *Philosophy and the Mirror of Nature* Rorty has shown in subtle and convincing manner that empiricist as well as rationalist projects in the modern period presupposed that philosophy, in contradistinction from the developing natural sciences in this period, could articulate the basis of validity of right knowledge and correct action. Rorty names this the project of "epistemology;"[60] this is the view that philosophy is a metadiscourse of legitimation, articulating the criteria of validity presupposed by all other discourses. Once it ceases to be a discourse of justification, philosophy loses its raison d'être. This is indeed the crux of the matter. Once we have detranscendentalized, contextualized, historicized, genderized the subject of knowledge, the context of inquiry, and even the methods of justification, what remains of philosophy?[61] Does not philosophy become a form of genealogical critique of regimes of discourse and power as they succeed each other in their endless historical monotony? Or maybe philosophy becomes a form of thick cultural narration of the sort that hitherto only poets had provided us with? Or maybe all that remains of philosophy is a form of sociology of knowledge, which instead of investigating the conditions of the validity of knowledge and action, investigates the empirical conditions under which communities of interpretation generate such validity claims?

Why is this question concerning the identity and future and maybe the possibility of philosophy of interest of feminists? Can feminist theory not flourish without getting embroiled in the arcane debates about the end or transformation of philosophy? The inclination of the majority of feminist theorists at the present is to argue that we can side-step this question; even if we do not want to ignore it, we must not be committed to answer it one way or another. Fraser and Nicholson ask: "How can we conceive a version of criticism without philosophy which is robust enough to handle the tough job of analyzing sexism in all its endless variety and monotonous similarity?"[62] My answer is that we cannot, and it is this which makes me doubt that as feminists we can adopt postmodernism as a theoretical ally. Social criticism without some form of philosophy is not possible, and without social criticism the project of a feminist theory which is at once committed to knowledge and to the emancipatory interests of women is inconceivable. Sabina Lovibond has articulated the dilemma of postmodernists quite well:

> I think we have reason to be wary, not only of the unqualified Nietzschean vision of an end of legitimation, but also of the suggestion that it would somehow be "better" if legitimation exercises were carried out in a self-consciously parochial spirit. For if feminism aspires to be something more than a reformist movement, then it is bound sooner or later to find itself calling the parish boundaries into question.
>
> . . .
>
> So postmodernism seems to face a dilemma: either it can concede the necessity, in terms of the aims of feminism, of "turning the world upside down" in the way just outlined – thereby opening a door once again to the Enlightenment idea of a total reconstruction of society on rational lines; or it can dogmatically reaffirm the arguments already marshalled against that idea – thereby licensing the cynical thought that, here as elsewhere, "who will do what to whom under the new pluralism is depressingly predictable."[63]

Faced with this objection, the answer of postmodernists committed both to the project of social criticism and to the thesis of the death of philosophy as a meta-narrative of legitimation will be that the "local narratives," "les petits récits," which constitute our everyday social practices or language games, are themselves reflexive and self-critical enough to pass judgments on themselves. The Enlightenment fiction of philosophical reflection, of *episteme* juxtaposed to the non-critical practice of everyday *doxa*, is precisely that, a fiction of legitimation which ignores that everyday practices and traditions also have their own criteria of legitimation and criticism. The question then would be if among the criteria made available to us by various practices, language games and cultural traditions we could not find some which would serve feminists in their task of social criticism and radical political transformation.[64] Following Michael Walzer, such postmodernists might wish to maintain that the view of the social critic is never "the view from nowhere," but always the view of the one situated somewhere, in some culture, society and tradition.[65]

Feminism as Situated Criticism

The initial answer to any defender of the view of "situated criticism" is that cultures, societies and traditions are not monolithic, univocal and homogeneous fields of meaning. However one wishes to characterize the relevant context to which one is appealing for example as "the Anglo-American liberal tradition of thought," "the tradition of progressive and interventionist jurisprudence," "the Judeo-Christian tradition," "the culture of the West," "the legacy of the Suffragates," "the tradition of courtly love," "Old Testament views of justice," "the political culture of democratic welfare states," etc., all these characterizations are themselves "ideal types" in some Weberian sense. They are constructed out of the tapestry of meaning and interpretation which constitutes the horizon of our social lifeworld. The social critic does not find criteria of legitimation and self-criticism to be given in the culture as one might find, say, apples on a tree and goldfish in an aquarium; she no less than social actors is in the position of constantly interpreting, appropriating, reconstructing and constituting the norms, principles and values which are an aspect of the lifeworld. There is never a single set of constitutive criteria to appeal to in characterizing complex social practices. Complex social practices, like constitutional traditions, ethical and political views, religious beliefs, scientific institutions are not like games of chess. The social critic cannot assume that when she turns to an immanent analysis and characterization of these practices that she will find a single set of criteria on which there is such universal consensus that one can simply assume that by juxta-posing these criteria to the actual carrying out of the practice one has accomplished the task of immanent social criticism. So the first defect of situated criticism is a kind of "hermeneutic monism of meaning," the assumption namely that the narratives of our culture are so univocal and uncontroversial that in appealing to them one could simply be exempt from the task of evaluative, ideal-typical reconstruction.[66] Social criticism needs philosophy precisely because the narratives of our cultures are so conflictual and irreconcilable that, even when one appeals to them, a certain ordering of one's normative priorities, a statement of the methodological assumptions guiding one's choice of narratives, and a clarification of those principles in the name of which one speaks is unavoidable.

The second defect of "situated criticism" is to assume that the constitutive norms of a given culture, society and tradition will be sufficient to enable one to exercise criticism in the name of a desirable future. There certainly may be times when one's own culture, society and tradition are so reified, dominated by such brutal forces, when debate and conversation are so dried up or simply made impossible that the social critic becomes the social exile. Not only social critics in modernity from Thoreau to the Frankfurt School, from Albert Camus to the dissidents of Eastern Europe have exemplified this gesture. Antiquity as well as the Middle Ages have had philosophers in exile, chiliastic sects, mystical brotherhoods and sisterhoods, and Prophets who have abandoned their cities. Certainly the social critic need not be the social exile; however, insofar as criticism presupposes a necessary distantiation of oneself from one's everyday certitudes, maybe eventually to return to them and to reaffirm them at a higher level of analysis and justification, to this extent the vocation of the social critic is more like the vocation of the social exile and the expatriate than the vocation of the one who never left home, who never had to challenge the certitude of her own way of life. And to leave home is not to end up nowhere; it is to occupy a space outside the walls of the city, in a host country, in a different social reality. Is this not in effect the quintessential post-modern condition in the twentieth century? Maybe the nostalgia for situated criticism is itself a nostalgia for home, for the certitudes of one's own culture and society in a world in which no tradition, no culture and no society can exist any more without interaction and collaboration, confrontation and exchange. When cultures and societies clash, where do we stand as feminists, as social critics and political activists?

Finally, let me remark upon an ambiguity which may surround the term "situated criticism" itself. Very often in recent discussions this concept has come to signify the practice of "local narratives" or "les petits récits" as opposed to grand theories or narratives of legitimation. Certainly, theorists as divergent as Michael Walzer and Jean-François Lyotard as well as Richard Rorty have this usage in mind. There is also a second tradition of "situated criticism" deriving from the work of the early Marx (the practice of immanent critique of capitalism) and transformed in this century into an extremely powerful tool of social and cultural reflection by Theodor Anorno through his method of practicing "determinate negation." I have explored the strengths and difficulties of this latter tradition elsewhere.[67] In the present context, it is not this second tradition which has concerned me but rather the first. My objections to the practice of situated criticism, as understood by this group of contemporary authors (Walzer, Lyotard, Rorty), does not assume however that there can be "transcendent criticism" or an "Archimedean point of view."[68] The standpoint of "interactive universalism" defended in this book is itself very much situated within the hermeneutic horizon of modernity. *Au fond*, all criticism is situated, but differences arise regarding the construction of the context within which the thinker considers her own thought to be situated. As opposed to the retreat to small narratives and local knowledge, I see even this postmodern moment as being situated within the larger processes of modernization and rationalization which have been proceeding on a world scale since the seventeenth century, and which have truly become global realities in our own.[69] In this sense, interactive universalism is the practice of situated criticism for a global community that does not shy away from knocking down the "parish walls."

Are we closer to resolving the question posed at the end of the previous section as to whether feminist social criticism without philosophy was possible? In considering the postmodernists' thesis of the "death of metaphysics" I suggested that the weak version of this thesis would identify the end of metaphysics with the end of philosophy as a metadiscourse of legitimation, transcending local narratives, while the strong version of the thesis would eliminate, I argued, not only meta-narratives of legitimation but the practice of context-transcending legitimation and criticism altogether. Post-modernists could then respond that this need not be the case, and that there were internal criteria of legitimation and criticism in our culture which the social critic could turn to such that social criticism without philosophy would be possible. I am now arguing that the practice of situated social criticism has two defects: first, the turn to internal criteria of legitimation appears to exempt one from the task of philosophical justification only because the postmodernists assume, inter alia, that there is one obvious set of such criteria to appeal to. But if cultures and traditions are more like competing sets of narratives and incoherent tapestries of meaning, then the social critic must herself construct out of these conflictual and incoherent accounts the set of criteria in the name of which she speaks. The "hermeneutic monism of meaning" brings no exemption from the responsibility of normative justification.

In the second place I have argued that the vocation of social criticism might require social exile, for there might be times when the immanent norms and values of a culture are so reified, dead or petrified that one can no longer speak in their name. The social critic who is in exile does not adopt the "view from nowhere" but the "view from outside the walls of the city," wherever those walls and those boundaries might be. It may indeed be no coincidence that from Hypatia to Diotima to Olympe de Gouges and to Rosa Luxemburg, the vocation of the feminist thinker and critic has led her to leave home and the city walls.

Feminism and the Postmodernist Retreat from Utopia

In the previous sections of this chapter I have disagreed with the view of some feminist theorists that feminism and postmodernism are conceptual and political allies. A certain version of postmodernism is not only incompatible with but would undermine the very possibility of feminism as the theoretical articulation of the emancipatory aspirations of women. This undermining occurs because in its strong version postmodernism is committed to three theses: the death of man understood as the death of the auto-nomous, self-reflective subject, capable of acting on principle; the death of history, understood as the severance of the epistemic interest in history of struggling groups in constructing their past narratives; the death of metaphysics, understood as the imposs-ibility of criticizing or legitimizing institutions, practices and tradi-tions other than through the immanent appeal to the self-legitimation of "small narratives." Interpreted thus, postmodernism undermines the feminist commitment to women's agency and sense of selfhood, to the reappropriation of women's own history in the name of an emancipated future, and to the exercise of radical social criticism which uncovers gender "in all its endless variety and monotonous similarity."

I dare suggest in these concluding considerations that post-modernism has produced a "retreat from utopia" within feminism. By "utopia" I do not mean the modernist vision of a wholesale restructuring of our social and political universe according to some rationally worked-out plan. These utopias of the Enlightenment have not only ceased to convince but with the self-initiated exit of previously existing "socialist utopias" from their state of grace, one of the greatest rationalist utopias of mankind, the utopia of a rationally planned economy leading to human emancipation, has come to an end. The end of these rationalistic visions of social engineering cannot dry up the sources of utopia in humanity. As the longing for the "wholly other" (*das ganz Andere*), for that which is not yet, such utopian thinking is a practical-moral imperative. Without such a regulative principle of hope, not only morality but also radical transformation is unthinkable. What scares the opponents of utopia, like Lyotard for example, is that in the name of such future utopia the present in its multiple ambiguity, plurality and contradiction will be reduced to a flat grand narrative. I share some of Lyotard's concerns insofar as utopian thinking becomes an excuse either for the crassest instrumentalism in the present – the end justifies the means – or to the extent that the coming utopia exempts the undemocratic and authoritarian practices of the present from critique. Yet we cannot deal with these political concerns by rejecting the ethical impulse of utopia but only by articulating the normative principles of democratic action and organization in the present. Will the postmodernists join us in this task or will they be content with singing the swan-song of normative thinking in general?

The retreat from utopia within feminist theory in the last decade has taken the form of debunking as "essentialist" any attempt to formulate a feminist ethic, a feminist politics, a feminist concept of autonomy and even a feminist aesthetic. The fact that the views of Gilligan or Chodorow or Sarah Ruddick (or for that matter Julia Kristeva) only articulate the sensitivities of white, middle-class, affluent, first world, heterosexual women may be true (although I even have empirical doubts about this). Yet what are we ready to offer in their place: as a project of an ethics which should guide us in the future are we able to offer a better vision than the synthesis of autonomous justice thinking and empathetic care? As a vision of the autonomous personality to aspire to in the future are we able to articulate a sense of self better than the model of autonomous individuality with fluid ego-boundaries and not threatened by otherness?[70] As a vision of feminist politics are we able to articulate a better model for the future than a radically democratic polity which also furthers the values of ecology, non-militarism, and solidarity of peoples? Postmodernism can teach us the theoretical and political traps of why utopias and foundational thinking can go wrong, but it should not lead to a retreat from utopia altogether. For we, as women, have much to lose by giving up the utopian hope in the wholly other.[71]

Notes

This paper was first delivered in October 1991 at the Greater Philadelphia Philosophy Consortium. A shorter version has appeared in *Praxis International* 11.3 (July 1991) together with the contributions of Judith Butler and Nancy Fraser. I would like to thank Wolf Schäfer, Lorenzo Simpson and in particular Nancy Fraser for their criticisms of an earlier draft.

1 J.-F. Lyotard, *The Postmodern Condition: A Report on Knowledge*, trans. Geoff Bennington and Brian Massumi, foreword by Fredric Jameson (University of Minnesota Press, Minneapolis, 1984). The page references in parentheses in this chapter are to this text.
2 See Fredric Jameson's foreword to *The Postmodern Condition*, pp. vii–xxiv; Richard Rorty, "Habermas and Lyotard on Postmodernity," *Praxis International*, 4.1 (1984), pp. 32–44; Andreas Huyssen and Klaus Scherpe, eds, *Postmoderne: Zeichen eines kulturellen Wandels* (Reinbeck, Hamburg, 1986); Albrecht Wellmer, *Zur Dialektik von Moderne und Postmoderne: Vernunftkritik Nach Adorno* (Suhrkamp, Frankfurt, 1985); Manfred Frank, *Die Grenzen der Verständigung* (Suhrkamp, Frankfurt, 1988).
3 See the excellent introduction by Linda Nicholson in *Feminism/Postmodernism*, ed. Linda Nicholson (Routledge, New York, 1990), pp. 1–16.

4 Parts of this section, "The 'Postmodern Condition' according to Lyotard" have previously appeared in my essay, "Epistemologies of Postmodernism: A Rejoinder to Jean-François Lyotard," in *New German Critique*, no. 22 (1984), pp. 103–26; reprinted in *Feminism/Postmodernism*, ed. Nicholson, pp. 107–33.

5 Cf. H. Arendt's statement: "Descartes' philosophy is haunted by two nightmares which in a sense became the nightmares of the whole modern age, not because this age was so deeply influenced by Cartesian philosophy, but because their emergence was almost inescapable once the true implications of the modern world view were understood. These nightmares are very simple and very well known. In the one, reality, the reality of the world as well as of human life, is doubted . . . The other concerned . . . the impossibility for man to trust his senses and his reason." *The Human Condition* (University of Chicago Press, Chicago, 1973), p. 277.

6 I borrow the phrase from R. Rorty's well-known article, "The World Well Lost," which argues that the conclusion to be drawn from contemporary epistemological disputes about conceptual frameworks is that "The notion of the 'world' that is correlative with the notion of a 'conceptual framework' is simply the Kantian notion of a thing-in-itself . . ." Originally in *Journal of Philosophy* (1972), reprinted in *Consequences of Pragmatism* (University of Minnesota Press, Minneapolis, 1982), p. 16.

7 Richard Rorty, *Philosophy and the Mirror of Nature* (Princeton, University Press, Princeton, 1979), pp. 131ff.

8 Charles Taylor, "Theories of Meaning," Daves Hickes Lecture, *Proceedings of the British Academy* (Oxford University Press, Oxford, 1982), p. 284.

9 Thomas Hobbes, *Leviathan* (1651), ed. C. B. McPherson (Penguin, Baltimore, 1968), pp. 101ff. Cf. M. Foucault, *The Order of Things: An Archaeology of the Human Sciences* (Random House, New York, 1973), first Vintage Books edition: "In its simple state as an idea, or an image, or a perception associated with or substituted for another, the simplifying element is not a sign. It can become a sign only on condition that it manifests, in addition, the relation that links it to what it signifies. It must represent, but that representation, in turn, must also be represented within it" (p. 64).

10 The transition from "consciousness" to "self-consciousness," from representation to desire in chapter 3 of Hegel's *Phenomenology of Spirit* contains also a critique of the spectator conception of the knowing subject. Hegel's point it that an epistemological standpoint confined to the spectator conception of the self cannot solve the questions it raises; most notably, it cannot explain the genesis and becoming of an object of knowledge. It is only insofar as the knowing self is also an acting one that it can destroy the myth of the given in knowledge. Hegel, *Phenomenology of Spirit*, trans. with an analysis and foreword by J. N. Findlay (Clarendon, Oxford, 1977), pp. 104–10. Cf. "He does not see how the sensuous world around him is not given direct from all eternity, ever the same, but is the product of industry and of the state

of society, and indeed in the sense that it is an historical product, the result of the activity of a whole succession of generations," in K. Marx and F. Engels, *The German Ideology*, ed. and introd. R. Pascal (International, New York, 1969), p. 35. M. Horkheimer, "Traditional and Critical Theory," in *Critical Theory*, trans. M. J. O'Connell et al. (Herder and Herder, New York, 1972), pp. 188–244. J. Habermas, *Knowledge and Human Interests*, trans. J. Shapiro (Beacon, Boston, 1972), pp. 1–65. S. Freud, "A Difficulty in the Path of Psychoanalysis," in the *Standard Edition* (Hogarth, London, 1953), vol. 17, pp. 137–44. For this reading of Freud, I am much indebted to Paul Ricoeur, *Freud and Philosophy: An Essay on Interpretation*, trans. Denis Savage (Yale University Press, New Haven, 1977), pp. 419–59.

11 Friedrich Nietzsche, "The Genealogy of Morals," In *The Birth of Tragedy and the Genealogy of Morals*, trans. F. Golffing (Doubleday, New York, 1958), pp. 289ff.

12 Martin Heidegger, *Being and Time*, trans. John Macquarrie and Edward Robinson (Harper and Row, New York, 1962), pp. 47ff.; "Die Frage nach der Technik?" *Vorträge und Aufsätze*, 4th edn (Gunther Neske, Stuttgart, 1974), pp. 27ff.

13 Max Horkheimer and Theodor Adorno, *Dialektik der Aufklärung* originally published in Amsterdam 1947 (Fischer Verlag, Franufurt, 1980), p. 12; trans. by John Cumming as *Dialectic of Enlightenment* (Seabury, New York, 1973).

14 Cf. Wittgenstein's critique of the "naming" theory of meaning and of the impossibility of viewing language as a private game in *Philosophical Investigations*, trans. G. E. M. Anscombe (Macmillan, New York, 1965), pp. 27–32, 38, 39; 180 and 199ff.

15 Charles Sanders Peirce, "Some Consequences of Four Incapacities," in *Selected Writings*, ed. and with an introd. and notes by Philip Wiener (Dover, New York, 1966), pp. 53–4; K.-O. Apel, "From Kant to Peirce: The Semiotical Transformation of Transcendental Logic," in *Toward a Transformation of Philosophy*, trans. G. Adey and D. Frisby (Roultedge and Kegan Paul, London, 1980), pp. 77–93.

16 Ferdinand de Saussure, *Course in General Linguistics*, ed. C. Bally and A. Sechehaye, trans. and introd. Wade Baskin (McGraw Hill, New York, 1959), pp. 67ff.

17 See Manfred Frank, *Was ist Neostrukturalismus?* (Suhrkamp, Frankfurt, 1984), p. 71ff., 83ff., 259; Pierre Bourdieu and J. C. Passeron, "Sociology and Philosophy in France since 1945: Death and Resurrection of a Philosophy without the Subject," *Social Research*, 34.1 (Spring 1983), pp. 162–212.

18 In the longer version of my article on "Epistemologies of Postmodernism," I have tried to show that one of the crucial differences between an "agonistics" and a "social pragmatics" of language is the following: the agonistic approach conflates all validity claims with "power effects" – or the capacity of the speaker to get the hearer to do something regardless of the hearer's orientation toward the meaning of what s/he is asked to do – whereas for social pragmatics, language can function to coordinate the action of social actors only because these

actors can also meaningfully orient themselves to the claims expressed in speech-acts. Lyotard's conflation of the distinction between "illocutionary" and "perlocutionary" acts in Austin's theory is indicative of this problem. See 'Epistemologies of Postmodernism," pp. 113–16 and footnote 25. See also K.-O. Apel, "Sprechakttheorie und transzendentale Sprachpragmatik zur Frage ethischer Normen," in *Sprechpragmatik und Philosophie,* ed. K.-O. Apel (Suhrkamp, Fraukfurt, 1976), pp. 10–81; J. Habermas, "Was heisst Universalpragmatik?" in ibid., pp. 184–273, trans. by T. McCarthy as "What is Universal Pragmatics?" in *Communication and the Evolution of Society* (Beacon, Boston, 1979), pp. 1–69.

19 Lyotard's construction of narrative knowledge creates more epistemological puzzles than it solves. Narrative knowledge, far from being an alternative to the modern scientific one, is sometimes described as if it were "premodern" knowledge, a historically lost mode of thought (p. 19). Yet narrative knowledge is also viewed as the "other" of discursive knowledge – not its past historical but its contemporaneous other. Narrative knowledge, to use a phrase of Ernst Bloch's, is the "non-contemporaneous contemporary" of discursive knowledge. The scientist "classifies them as belonging to a different mentality: savage, primitive, underdeveloped, backward, alienated, composed of opinions, customs, authority, prejudice, ignorance, ideology. Narratives are fables, myths, legends, fit only for women and children" (p. 27). Is the meaning of Lyotard's postmodernist epistemology then a gesture of solidarity with the oppressed? A gesture toward the recognition of the otherness of the other? This may seem so, but Lyotard constructs the epistemology of narrative knowledge in such a way that the only appropriate attitude to adopt toward it is the standpoint of the curator of an ethnological museum of the past, who gazes "in wonderment at the variety of discursive species" (p. 26). Narrative knowledge belongs to the ethnological museum of the past. "Narrative knowledge," writes Lyotard, "does not give priority to the question of its own legitimation in that it certifies itself in the pragmatics of its own transmission without having recourse to argumentation and proof" (p. 27). This global characterization of narrative knowledge as prereflexive, as a self-sustaining whole, flattens the internal contradictions and tensions which affect narrative no less than discursive practices. (See for example discussions of this issue by E. Gellner, "Concepts and Society," in *Rationality,* ed. B. R. Wilson (Harper and Row, New York, 1970), pp. 18–50; P. Bourdieu, *Outline of a Theory of Practice,* trans. Richard Nice (Cambridge University Press, Cambridge, 1979), pp. 22–30.) It also implies that all change in this episteme must come from without, through violence. Such an episteme has no self-propelling or self-correcting mechanism. But, in fact, this is to condemn the subjects of this episteme to ahistoricity, to deny that they inhabit the same place with us. We do not interact with them as equals, we inhabit a space in which we observe them as ethnologists and anthropologists, we treat them with distance and indifference. But if this is not so, if indeed narrative knowledge is the "other" of our mode of knowledge, then Lyotard must admit that narrative and scientific knowledge are not

merely incommensurable, but that they can and do clash, and that sometimes the outcome is less than certain. To admit this possibility would mean that "narrative" and "discursive" practices occupy the same epistemic space, and that both raise claims to validity, and that an argumentative exchange between them is not only possible but desirable. You cannot respect the "otherness" of the other if you deny the other the right to enter into a conversation with you, if you do not discard the objective indifference of an ethnologist, and engage with the other as an equal. For a recent statement concerning the difficult questions of epistemic rationality and relativism, see Steven Lukes and Martin Hollis, eds, *Rationality and Relativism* (MIT Press, Cambridge, Mass., 1984).

20   See Kenneth Baynes, James Bohman and Thomas McCarthy, eds, *After Philosophy: End or Transformation* (MIT Press, Cambridge, Mass., 1987), pp. 67–71.

21   In his interesting study, *Unsere postmoderne Moderne* (2nd edn, Acta humaniora, Weinheim, 1988), Wolfgang Welsch accuses me of wanting to maintain an "archimedean standpoint of criticism" (p. 155) in the debate with Lyotard. He further argues that I fail to identify criteria of criticism in Lyotard's work because I have not taken *Le Differend* into account (published in French in 1983). Taking Welsch's critique to heart, I have since then familiarized myself with the argument in *The Differend: Phrases in Dispute*, trans. Georges van den Abbeele (University of Minnesota Press, Minneapolis, 1988). Nonetheless, I still fail to see how this text resolves the question concerning criteria of criticism. The difficulty is that Lyotard carries out epistemology only in the "descriptive" mode, retaining the standpoint of the observer who establishes the presence of the "differend," and who distinguishes between "scientific," "narrative," and "deliberative" genres or "phrase regimens" (pp. 13, 149ff.). The standpoint of the participant, of the social agent for whom language is by no means just an instrument of communication alone, but also a mode of coordinating social action, is unheeded by Lyotard's analysis. The conflict between "agonistic" and "social pragmatic" approaches to language is not only unresolved, but I don't even think that the terms of the debate are set out very clearly. This is evidenced from Lyotard's discussion of Plato/Socrates as a "partisan of dialogue" as opposed to Thrasymachus as a partisan of "agonistics" (*The Differend*, p. 26). But to choose the Platonic view of language as the example or paradigm of the "dialogic" model already stacks the cards: for it can then be shown that such a rationalistic, transparency- and consensus-oriented model of dialogue cannot be true; that the dispute between agonistics and dialogue cannot be resolved without begging the question. But the social pragmatic view of language, which views language as a medium through which social action is coordinated, identities framed and culture reproduced, is not based upon a narrow rationalism. Here as well Lyotard identifies "consensus," or "agreement generated through reasons," with a narrowly defined rationalistic model of the meeting of minds. Lyotard's claim that "In the deliberative politics of modern democracies, the

differend is exposed, even though the transcendental appearance of a single finality that would bring it to a resolution persists in helping forget the differend, in making it bearable" (p. 147) is fascinating and would warrant a careful comparison with the Arendtian model of the "enlarged mentality" examined above.

22 Sandra Harding gives an illuminating account of this ambivalence in "Feminism, Science and the Anti-Enlightenment Critiques," in *Feminism and Postmodernism*, ed. Nicholson, pp. 83–106.

23 Joan Scott, "Gender: A Useful Category of Historical Analysis," in *Gender and the Politics of History* (Columbia University Press, New York, 1986), pp. 28–53.

24 Jane Flax, *Psychoanalysis, Feminism and Postmodernism in the Contemporary West* (University of California Press, Berkeley, 1990), pp. 32ff.

25 Ibid., p. 32.

26 Ibid., p. 33.

27 Ibid., p. 34.

28 See R. Rorty, "Nineteenth-Century Idealism and Twentieth-Century Contextualism," in *Consequences of Pragmatism*, pp. 139–60.

29 Luce Irigaray, *Speculum of the Other Woman*, trans. Gillian C. Gill (Cornell University Press, Ithaca, 1985), pp. 133ff.; Genevieve Lloyd, *The Man of Reason: Male and Female in Western Philosophy* (University of Minnesota Press, Minneapolis, 1984); Sandra Harding and M. Hintikka, eds, *Discovering Reality: Feminist Perspectives on Epistemology, Metaphysics, Methodology and Philosophy of Science* (Reidel, Dordrecht, 1983).

30 Joan Kelly Gadol, "The Social Relations of the Sexes: Methodological Implications of Women's History," and "Did Women Have a Renaissance?" in *Women, History and Theory* (University of Chicago Press, Chicago, 1984), pp. 1–19, 19–51.

31 G. W. F. Hegel: "At this point we leave Africa not to mention it again. For it is no historical part of the world: it has no movement or development to exhibit. Historical movements in it – that is in the northern part – belong to the Asiatic or European World . . . What we properly understand by Africa, is the Unhistorical, Undeveloped Spirit, still involved in the conditions of mere nature . . ." in *The Philosophy of History*, trans. J. Sibree, introd. C. J. Friedrich (Dover, New York, 1956), p. 99.

32 For a provocative utilization of a Foucaultian framework for gender analysis, cf. Judith Butler, *Gender Trouble: Feminism and the Subversion of Identity* (Routledge, New York and London, 1990).

33 Linda Alcoff, "Poststructuralism and Cultural Feminism," *Signs*, 13.3 (1988), pp. 4–36. See also Christine di Stefano, "Dilemmas of Difference: Feminism, Modernity, and Postmodernism," in *Feminism/Postmodernism*, ed. Nicholson, pp. 63–83; Susan Bordo, "Feminism, Postmodernism, and Gender Skepticism," in ibid., pp. 133–57; and more recently, Nancy Hartsock, "Postmodernism and Political Change: Issues for Feminist Theory," (*Cultural Critique*, no. 14 (Winter 1989–90), pp. 15–35, for misgivings about the political and theoretical implications of postmodernism for feminism.

34 Similar concerns are raised by Daryl McGowan Tress in her comment

on Jane Flax's "Postmodernism and Gender Relations in Feminist
Theory" (a briefer version of arguments subsequently presented in
Flax's book, in *Signs*, 12.4 (1987), pp. 621–43); cf. Tress and Flax's reply
in *Signs*, 14.1 (Autumn 1988), pp. 196–203. See also Rosi Braidotti,
"Patterns of Dissonance: Women and/in Philosophy," in *Feministische
Philosophie*, ed. Herta Nagl-Docekal (Oldenburg, Vienna and Munich,
1990), pp. 108–23; Herta Nagl-Docekal, "Antigones Trauer und der Tod
des Subjekts," lecture held at the Philosophinnen-Ringvorlesung at the
Institute of Philosophy, Freie Universität Berlin, on 25 May, 1990.

35   Patricia J. Williams's "On Being the Object of Property," is a fascinating
example of discursive transgressions which in turn forces us to rethink
the various narrative codes sanctifying some forms of speech, authority
and identity in our cultures. In *Signs*, 14.1 (Autumn 1988), pp. 5–25.

36   Butler, *Gender Trouble*, p. 7. While I applaud Butler's trenchant analysis
of the dichotomous reasoning which has operated with a simple juxta-
position of sex and gender, my disagreement with her is whether
the directionality of the desire of the body is one that is merely "constructed" through the "order of compulsory heterosexuality." A great
deal hinges upon how we want to understand "construct" here. See
next footnote for a further elaboration.

37   I would want to distinguish here as well between the "social and
cultural construction of sexuality" on the one hand, and the "shaping
of the directionality of the body's desire" on the other. Given all the
information we have today about the sheer multiplicity and variety of
human erotic and sexual rituals, games, fantasies, myths and ideals –
from the homoeroticism of ancient Greek culture to the quasi-magical
and bountiful eroticism of the ancient Indian art of love-making
(kamasutran), from the elaborate courting and seduction rituals of
ancient Islamic cultures to the flaunting of an obvious and flat sexuality
in western mass democracies as a commodity to be obtained like any
other at a certain price – given all this, to dispute the social and cultural
construction of sexuality would be foolhardy. Yet the shaping of
the directionality of desire for the human individual is an extremely
complex process, in which the "memory of the body," of the "soma,"
of the "flesh" plays a crucial role. Culture does not "construct" everything – the human body is not a tabula rasa on which all is inscribed by
mechanisms of agency and socialization. The body is an active medium
with its own dispositions and "habits," which process, channel and
deflect the influences which come to it from the outside, in accordance
with its own accumulated modality of being toward the world. On this
issue as well, the disagreement between myself and Butler concerns the
role of "agency," intentionality and ultimately the sources of human
individual resistance to culture and society.

38   Butler, *Gender Trouble*, p. 25.

39   Rosi Braidotti remarks very appropriately: "It seems to me that contemporary philosophical discussions on the death of the knowing
subject, dispersion, multiplicity, etc. etc. have the immediate effect of
concealing and undermining the attempts of women to find a theoretical voice of their own. Dismissing the notion of the subject at the
very historical moment when women are beginning to have access to it,

while at the same time advocating the 'devenir femme' [as Guattari does – S. B.] of philosophical discourse itself, can at least be described as a paradox. . . . The truth of the matter is: one cannot de-sexualize a sexuality one has never had; in order to deconstruct the subject one must first have gained the right to speak as one; before they can subvert the signs, women must learn to use them; in order to de-mystify meta-discourse one must first have access to a place of enunciation. 'Il faut, au moins, un sujet.'" "Patterns of Dissonance: Women and/in Philosophy", in *Feministische Philosophie*, ed, Nagl-Docekal, pp. 119–20.

40 Butter, *Gender Trouble*, p. xiii. Note also Butler's uneasiness with the category "I": "I have argued ('I' deploy the grammar that governs the genre of the philosophical conclusion, but note that it is the grammar itself that deploys and enables this 'I,' even as the 'I' that insists itself here repeats, redeploys, and – as the critics will determine – contests the philosophical grammar by which it is both enabled and restricted) that . . ." (p. 146).

41 The difficulties in this position derive from the views of the subject and subjectivity of Foucault, upon whom Butler relies. Although Butler critiques Foucault's own understanding of sexuality and particularly his concept of "pleasure" (*Gender Trouble*, pp. 96 ff.), she relies upon his methodological framework in viewing the "subject" as a self constituted or constructed by the impact of various regimes of "power/knowledge." The social-scientific deficit of Foucault's work – his inadequate conceptions of social action and social movements, his inability to explain social change except as the discontinuous displacement of one "power/ knowledge" regime by another – and his thin concepts of self and identity-formation are ultimately related. These problems have been at the center of the critical reception of Foucault's work in Germany in particular, whereas in the USA Foucault has been read less as a social and cultural historian and social theorist but more as a philosopher and literary critic. The result has been an uncritical reception of Foucault's explanatory framework. In her article "Foucault on Modern Power: Empirical Insights and Normative Confusions," first published in *Praxis International* 1.3 (Oct. 1981), pp. 272–87, reproduced in *Unruly Practices* (University of Minnesota Press, Minneapolis, 1989), pp. 17–34) Nancy Fraser very early on drew attention to these difficulties in Foucault's work. An excellent analysis of Foucault's sociological assumptions, and particularly of his theory of modernity, can also be found in Axel Honneth, *Kritik der Macht: Reflexionsstufen einer kritischen Gesellschafts-theorie* (Suhrkamp, Frankfurt, 1985), pp. 169–225 (in English as *The Critique of Power*, trans. Kenneth Baynes (MIT Press, Cambridge, Mass., 1991)).

42 I would like to thank Nancy Fraser for helping me see this point.

43 Butter, *Gender Trouble*, p. 143. Emphasis in the text.

44 Ibid.

45 Alan Wolfe gives an illuminating account of the implications that denying concepts of selfhood as being essentialist have for social theory and normative thinking. In postmodernism as well as in systems-theoretic social science, Wolfe sees a "lack of appreciation for the rule-making, rule-applying, rule-interpreting capacities of human beings

and an emphasis instead on the rule-following character. The price postmodernism pays for its flirtation with algorithmic conceptions of justice is a very high one: the denial of liberation, play and spontaneity that inspired radical epistemologies in the first place." In "Algorithmic Justice," *Benjamin Cardozo Law Review*, special issue on Deconstruction and the Possibility of Justice, 11.5–6 (July-Aug. 1990), p. 1415.

46 Butter, *Gender Trouble*, p. 145.

47 See T. C. Heller, M. Sosna and D. Wellbery eds, *Reconstructing Individualism: Autonomy, Individuality and the Self in Western Thought* (Stanford University Press, Stanford, 1986); Thomas McCarthy gives a very sensitive account of the development and transformations of Foucault's views of selfhood and agency in "The Critique of Impure Reason: Foucault and the Frankfurt School," in *Ideals and Illusions: On Reconstruction and Deconstruction in Contemporary Critical Theory* (MIT Press, Cambridge, 1991), pp. 67ff.

48 Cf. Vincent Descombes, *Modern French Philosophy* (Cambridge University Press, New York, 1980). See the excellent analysis by Peter Dews of the political experiences of the 1968 generation in France, as it has formed contemporary French philosophy, in *Logics of Disintegration: Post-Structuralist Thought and the Claims of Critical Theory* (New Left Books, New York, 1987).

49 Nancy Fraser and Linda J. Nicholson, "Social Criticism Without Philosophy: An Encounter Between Feminism and Postmodernism," in *Feminism/Postmodernism*, ed. Nicholson, p. 33. Iris Young makes the same point in her "The Ideal of Community and the Politics of Difference," in the same volume, pp. 300–01.

50 Ibid., p. 34.

51 See the pioneering anthology, R. Bridenthal, C. Koonz and S. Stuard, eds, *Becoming Visible: Women in European History* (Houghton Mifflin, Boston, 1987).

52 Fraser and Nicholson, "Social Criticism without Philosophy," p. 35. As opposed to this pragmatic pluralism of methodologies guided by research interests, what we have in the case of postmodernist historiography is an "aesthetic" proliferation of styles which increasingly blur the distinctions between history and literature, factual narrative and imaginary creation. F. R. Ankersmit writes: ". . . because of the incommensurability of historiographical views – that is to say, the fact that the nature of historical differences of opinion cannot be satisfactorily defined in terms of research subjects – there remains nothing for us to do but to concentrate on the style embodied in every historical view or way of looking at the past, if we are to guarantee the meaningful progress of historical debate. Style, not content, is the issue in such debates. Content is a derivative of style." F. R. Ankersmit, "Historiography and Postmodernism," *History and Theory* 28.2 (1989), pp. 137–53, here p. 144.

53 See Joan W. Scott's review of *Heroes of their Own Lives: The Politics and History of Family Violence* by Linda Gordon, Linda Gordon's review of *Gender and the Politics of History* by Joan Scott, and their responses, in *Signs*, 15.4 (Summer 1990), pp. 848–60.

54 Ibid., p. 849.
55 Ibid., p. 850.
56 Ibid., p. 851. Emphasis added.
57 This would be my major criticism of Nancy Fraser's thoughtful response to the disagreement between Butler and myself. As Fraser argues, it may be that the antithesis between "Critical Theory and poststructuralism" is arid and boring and we should go beyond it, although let us also note that a serious exchange has hardly started in the United States and that such an antithesis certainly is not "false". I fail to see that there is some third "neopragmatist" position, which in true Hegelian fashion does an *Aufhebung* on our partial truths while avoiding our mistakes. See Nancy Fraser, "False Antitheses: A Response to Seyla Benhabib and Judith Butler," *Praxis International*, 11.2 (July 1991).
58 Linda Gordon, "Response to Scott," p. 852.
59 In the next chapter, "On Hegel, Women and Irony," I try to illustrate the consequences of applying this Walter Benjamin approach to the history of philosophy. See Walter Benjamin, "Theses on the Philosophy of History," in *Illuminations*, ed. Hannah Arendt (New York, 1969).
60 Richard Rorty, *Philosophy and the Mirror of Nature*, pp. 131ff.
61 For trenchant accounts of the various problems and issues involved in this "sublation" and "transformation" of philosophy, see Kenneth Baynes, James Bohman and Thomas McCarthy, eds, *After Philosophy: End or Transformation?*
62 Fraser and Nicholson, "Social Criticism Without Philosophy," p. 34.
63 Sabina Lovibond, "Feminism and Postmodernism," *New Left Review*, no. 178 (Nov.–Dec. 1989), pp. 5–28, here, p. 22.
64 See Lyotard's remark, "narratives . . . thus define what has the right to be said and done in the culture in question, and since they are themselves a part of that culture, they are legitimated by the simple fact that they do what they do." In *The Postmodern Condition: A Report on Knowledge*, p. 23. In his intervention in this debate, Rorty has sided with Lyotard and against Habermas, maintaining that the latter "scratches where it does not itch." Cf. R. Rorty, "Habermas and Lyotard on Postmodernity," *Praxis International* 4.1 (April 1984), p. 34. I have analyzed the difficulties of this turn to immanent social criticism in "Epistemologies of Postmodernism: A Rejoinder to Jean-François Lyotard," in *Feminism and Postmodernism*, ed. Nicholson, pp. 107–30.
65 See Michael Walzer, *Interpretation and Social Criticism* (Harvard University Press, Cambridge, Mass., 1987), esp. pp. 8–18.
66 See Georgia Warnke's discussion of Michael Walzer's position for an alternative account more sympathetic to the possibility of immanent, social criticism than my own, "Social Interpretation and Political Theory: Walzer and his Critics," *Philosophical Forum*, 21.1–2 (Fall–Winter 1989–90), pp. 204ff. An interesting instance of this "hermeneutic monism of meaning" is M. Foucault's statement, "Each society has its regime of truth." Why not many regimes, many competing and contradictory ones? See M. Foucault, "Truth and Power," *Truth and Power* (New York, 1980), pp. 109–33, here p. 131.

67 See my *Critique, Norm and Utopia: A Study of the Foundations of Critical Theory* (Columbia University Press, New York, 1986).

68 Cf. Fraser who writes: 'I remain convinced, therefore, that social criticism without philosophy is possible, if we mean by 'philosophy' what Linda Nicholson and I meant, namely, ahistorical, transcendental discourse claiming to articulate the criteria of validity for all other discourses." Fraser, "False Antitheses: A Response to Seyla Benhabib and Judith Butler," p. 170. But why should this be what we mean by philosophy, when much of modernist philosophy since the nineteenth century and since Hegel has been both critical of ahistoricity and transcendentalism and has *also* claimed that philosophy is a discourse of legitimation, engaged in the critical self-reflection often lacking in other discourses? It is simply implausible as well as poor intellectual history to reduce the term philosophy and its history to a caricature and then to proceed to debunk it. Hegel is not Husserl; Martin Heidegger was not ahistorical – whether or not his philosophy is to be understood as a version of transcendental thought is still an open question; it can even be suggested that the later Wittgenstein, despite all historicist moves in the analysis of language games as life-forms, revived a form of transcendental inquiry into the conditions of the possibility of social and linguistic communities. Contrary to what Fraser claims, not all philosophy that is criteriologically or normatively oriented, or oriented to the question of validity, need be transcendental or ahistorical. The only philosophical response to postmodernism is not a form of foundationalism, but a discourse which accepts the legitimacy of questions of validity while seeking to answer these in the context of the insights of the empirical human and social sciences. The critical social theory of the Frankfurt School was always situated between "philosophy and social science." Fraser wants to hold on to this tradition but only by dispensing with the one partner, namely philosophy.

69 One of the unfortunate aspects of the postmodernism debate has been the lack of synthetic reflection upon the social reality referred to as "postindustrialism," "post-Fordism," post-Keynesianism" on the one hand and the cultural-intellectual phenomena referred to as "postmodernism" on the other. Although I shy from following Jameson's Marxian logic in assuming that postmodernism "corresponds" or "reflects" a certain stage in the development of international capitalism, his contributions to this debate are refreshing and illuminating in their attempt to take the larger view of the matter, and to see postmodernism as a reflection and indication of some kind of global social reality in whose net we are all caught. This line of reflection needs to be pursued by feminists as well. Yet ironically the kind of social theory which would enable us to understand the "truth" of postmodernism as a lived social reality is itself made impossible by the theoretical presuppositions of postmodernism which deny all distinction between culture and society, signification and structure, social meaning and social action. But surely contemporary social theory can move beyond the false antitheses of "Althusser versus Derrida" to a more fruitful integration of structure and signification, action and meaning, society and culture.

See Fredric Jameson, *Postmodernism, or, The Cultural Logic of Capitalism* (Duke University Press, Durham, N. C., 1991). For an illuminating analysis of the emergence of "global" social realities and of a global history in this century, see Wolf Schaefer, "Global History," paper delivered at the meeting of the Global History Association, Lugano, Italy, July, 1992. Postmodernism has indeed forced us to focus on the local rather than the international, thus obscuring the extent to which today the local itself is but an extension of the international. My sense is that as the social reality which we face gets increasingly more global, complicated and intricate, our units of analysis get increasingly smaller, fragmented and marginal.

70 For a powerful statement of these themes, already contained in Adorno's philosophy, see the masterful reflection by Jessica Benjamin on psychoanalysis, feminism and domination. J. Benjamin, *The Bonds of Love: Psychoanalysis, Feminism, and the Problem of Domination* (Pantheon, New York, 1988).

71 For a feminist position which seeks to retain this utopian element even while affirming postmodernist philosophy, see Drucilla Cornell. "Poststructuralism, the Ethical Relation, and the Law," *Cardozo Law Review*, 9.6, pp. 1587–628, and 'From the Lighthouse: The Promise of Redemption and the Possibility of Legal Interpretation," *Cardozo Law Review*, 11.5–6 (July–Aug. 1990), pp. 1687–714.

8   On Hegel, Women and Irony

Das Bekannte überhaupt ist darum, weil es bekannt ist, nicht.erkannt.

(The well-known is unknown, precisely because it is well known.)

G. W. F. *Hegel*, Phaenomenologie des Geistes

Some Methodological Puzzles of a Feminist Approach

The 1980s were named "the decade of the humanities" in the USA. In many institutions of higher learning a debate is still underway as to what constitutes the "tradition" and the "canon" in literary, artistic and philosophical works worth transmitting to future generations in the last quarter of the twentieth century. At the center of this debate is the question: if what had hitherto been considered the major works of the western tradition are, almost uniformly, the product of a specific group of individuals, namely propertied, white, European and North American males, how universal and representative is their message, how inclusive is their scope, and how unbiased their vision?

Feminist theory has been at the forefront of this questioning, and under the impact of feminist scholarship the surface of the canon of western "great works" has been forever fractured, its unity dispersed and its legitimacy challenged. Once the woman's question is raised, once we ask how a thinker conceptualizes the distinction between male and female, we experience a *Gestalt* shift: we begin to see the great thinkers of the past with a new eye, and in the words of Joan Kelly Gadol "each eye sees a different picture."[1] The vision of feminist theory is a "doubled" one: one eye sees what the tradition has trained it to see, the other searches for what the tradition has told her was not even worth looking for. How is a "feminist reading" of the tradition in fact possible? At the present, I see two dominant approaches, each with certain shortcomings.

I describe the first approach as "the teaching of the good father." Mainstream liberal feminist theory treats the tradition's views of women as a series of unfortunate, sometimes embarrassing, but essentially corrigible, misconceptions. Taking their inspiration from the example of a progressive thinker like John Stuart Mill, these theorists seek in the classical texts for those moments of insight into the equality and dignity of women. They are disappointed when their favorite philosopher utters inanities on the subject, but essentially hold that there is no incompatibility between the Enlightenment ideals of freedom, equality and self-realization and women's aspirations.

The second view I would characterize as "the cry of the rebellious daughter." Agreeing with Lacan that language is the symbolic universe which represents the "law of the father," and accepting that all language has been a codification of the power of the father, these rebellious daughters seek for female speech at the margins of the western logocentric tradition. If it is impossible to think in the western logocentric tradition without binary oppositions, then the task of feminist reading becomes the articulation not of a new set of categories but of the transcendence of categorical discourse altogether. One searches not for a new language but for a discourse at the margins of language.

Juxtaposed to these approaches, in this essay I would like to outline a "feminist discourse of empowerment." With the second view, I agree that the feminist challenge to the tradition cannot leave its fundamental categories unchanged. Revealing the gender subtext of the ideals of reason and the Enlightenment compromises the assumed universality of these ideals. Nonetheless, they should not be thrown aside altogether. Instead we can ask what these categories have meant for the actual lives of women in certain historical periods, and how, if women are to be thought of as subjects and not just as fulfillers of certain functions, the semantic horizon of these categories is transformed. Once we approach the tradition to recover from it women's subjectivity and their lives and activities, we hear contradictory voices, competing claims, and see that so-called "descriptive" discourses about the sexes are but "legitimizations" of male power. The traditional view of gender differences is the discourse of those who have won out and who have codified history as we know it. But what would the history of ideas look like from the standpoint of the victims? What ideals, aspirations and utopias of the past ran into a dead-end? Can we recapture their memory from the battleground of history? This essay attempts to apply such a "discourse of empowerment" to G. W. F. Hegel's views of women.

Hegel's treatment of women has received increased attention in recent years under the impact of the feminist questioning of the tradition.[2] This feminist challenge has led us to ask, is Hegel's treatment of women merely a consequence of his conservative predilections? Was Hegel unable to see that he made the "dialectic" stop at women and condemned them to an ahistorical mode of existence, outside the realms of struggle, work and diremption which in his eyes are characteristic of human consciousness as such?[3] Is the "woman question" in Hegel's thought one more instance of Hegel's uncritical endorsement of the institutions of his time, or is this issue an indication of a flaw in the very structure of the dialectic itself? Benjamin Barber, for example, siding with the second option has recently written:

> What this paradox reveals is that Hegel's position on women is neither a product of contingency nor an effect of ad hoc prejudice. Rather, it is the necessary consequence of his belief that the "Prejudices" of his age are in fact *the* actuality yielded by history in the epoch of liberation. Hegel does not have to rationalize them: because they *are*, they are already rational. They need only be encompassed and explained by philosophy. Spirit may guide and direct history, but ultimately, history alone can tell us where spirit means it to go.[4]

Judging, however, where "history alone can tell . . . spirit" it means it to go, requires a more complicated and contradictory account of the family and women's position at the end of the eighteenth and the beginning of the nineteenth century in the German states than either Barber or other commentators who have looked at this issue so far have provided us with. I suggest that to judge whether or not the Hegelian dialectic has stopped at women, we must first attempt to define the "discursive horizon" of competing claims and visions within which Hegel articulated his position. To evaluate the historical options concerning gender relations in Hegel's time, we have to move beyond the methodology of traditional text analysis to the "doubled vision" of feminist theory. In practicing this doubled vision we do not remain satisfied with analyzing textual discourses about women, but we ask where the women themselves were at any given period in which a thinker lived. With one eye we see what stands in the text, and with the other, what the text conceals in footnotes and in the margins. What then emerges is a "discursive space" of competing power claims. The discursive horizon of Hegel's views of women and the family are defined on the one hand by the rejection of political patriarchy (which mixes the familial with the political, the private with the public), and on the other by disapproval of and antagonism toward efforts of early female emancipation.

This essay is divided into two parts: by using the traditional method of text analysis in the first part I explore *the logic of oppositions* according to which Hegel develops his views of gender relations and of female subordination. In particular I focus on the complex relationship between reason, nature, gender and history. Second, having outlined Hegel's views of women in his political philosophy, I situate his discourse within the context of historical views on women and the family at the turn of the eighteenth century. I read Hegel against the grain; proceeding from certain footnotes and marginalia in the texts, I move toward recovering the history of those which the dialectic leaves behind.

Women in G. W. F. Hegel's (1770–1831) Political Thought

In many respects Hegel's political philosophy heralds the end of the traditional doctrine of politics, and signals its transformation into social science. *Geist* which emerges from nature, transforms nature into a second world; this "second nature" comprises the human, historical world of tradition, institutions, laws, and practices (*objektiver Geist*), as well as the self-reflection of knowing and acting subjects upon objective spirit, which is embodied in works of art, religion, and philosophy (*absoluter Geist*). *Geist* is a transindividual principle that unfolds in history, and whose goal is to make externality into its "work." *Geist* externalizes itself in history by appropriating, changing, and shaping the given such as to make it correspond to itself, to make it embody its own subjectivity, that is, reason and freedom. The transformation of substance into subject is attained when freedom and rationality are embodied in the world such that "the realm of freedom" is actualized, and "the world of mind [is] brought forth out of itself like a second nature." The social world is *Substance*, that is, it has objective existence for all to see and to comprehend;[5] it is also *subject*, for what the social and ethical world is can only be known by understanding the subjectivity of the individuals who compose it.[6] With Hegel's concept of objective spirit, the object domain of modern social science, that is, individuality and society, make their appearance.

Does his concept of *Geist* permit Hegel to transcend the "naturalistic" basis of gender conceptions in the modern period, such as to place the relation between the sexes in the social, symbolic, historical, and cultural world? Hegel, on the one hand, views the development of subjectivity and individuality within the context of a human community; on the other hand, in assigning men and women to their traditional sex roles, he codifies gender-specific differences as aspects of a rational ontology that is said to reflect the deep structure of *Geist*. Women are viewed as representing the principles of particularity (*Besonderheit*), immediacy (*Unmittelbarkeit*), naturalness (*Natürlichkeit*), and substantiality (*Substanzialität*), while men stand for universality (*Allgemeinheit*), mediacy (*Vermittlung*), freedom (*Freiheit*), and subjectivity (*Subjektivität*). Hegel develops his rational ontology of gender within a logic of oppositions.

The thesis of the "natural inequality" of the sexes

On the basis of Hegel's observations on the family, women, and the rearing of children, scattered throughout the *Lectures on the Philosophy of History*, I conclude that he was well aware that differences among the sexes were culturally, symbolically and socially constituted. For example, in the section on Egypt, Hegel refers to Herodotus' observatations "that the women urinate standing up, while men sit, that the men wear one dress, and the women two; the women were engaged in outdoor occupations, while the men remained at home to weave. In one part of Egypt polygamy prevailed; in another, monogamy. His general judgment on the matter is that the Egyptians do the exact opposite of all other peoples."[7]

Hegel's own reflections on the significance of the family among the Chinese, the great respect that is shown to women in this culture, and his comment on the Chinese practice of concubinage again indicate an acute awareness that the role of women is not naturally but culturally and socially defined.[8]

These passages show a clear awareness of the cultural, historical, and social variations in family and sexual relations. Nevertheless, although Hegel rejects that differences between "men" and "women" are naturally defined, and instead sees them as part of the spirit of a people (*Volksgeist*), he leaves no doubt that he considers only one set of family relations and one particular division of labor between the sexes as rational and normatively right. This is the monogamic sexual practice of the European nuclear family, in which the woman is confined to the private sphere and the man to the public. To justify this arrangement, Hegel explicitly invokes the superiority of the male to the female while acknowledging their *functional complementarity* in the modern state.

The "superiority" of the male

The most revealing passages in this respect are paragraphs 165 and 166 of the *Philosophy of Right* and the additions to them. In the Lasson edition of the *Rechtsphilosophie*, Hegel writes that "The natural determinacies of both sexes acquire through its reasonableness *intellectual* as well as *ethical* significance."[9] This explicit reference to the "natural determinacies of the sexes" is given an ontological significance in the next paragraph:

Thus one sex is mind in its self-diremption into explicit self-subsistence and the knowledge and volition of free universality, i.e. the self-consciousness of conceptual thought and the volition of the objective final end. The other sex is mind maintaining itself in unity as knowledge and volition in the form of concrete individuality and feeling. In relation to externality, the former is powerful and active, the latter passive and subjective. It follows that man has his actual substantive life in the state, in learning, and so forth, as well as in labour and struggle with the external world and with himself so that it is only out of his diremption that he fights his way to self-subsistent unity with himself. In the family he has a tranquil intuition of this unity, and there he lives a subjective ethical life on the plane of feeling. Woman, on the other hand, has her substantive destiny in the family, and to be imbued with family piety is her ethical frame of mind.[10]

For Hegel, men's lives are concerned with the state, science, and work in the external world. Dividing himself (*sich entzweiend*) from the unity of the family, man objectifies the external world and conquers it through activity and freedom. The woman's "substantial determination," by contrast, is in the family, in the unity and piety (*Pietät*) characteristic of the private sphere. Hegel suggests that woman are not *individuals*, at least, not in the same measure and to the same extent as men are. They are incapable of the spiritual struggle and diremption (*Entzweiung*) which characterize the lives of men. In a passage from the *Phänomenologie* concerned with the tragedy of Antigone, he indicates that for the woman "it is not *this* man, not *this* child, but *a man* and *children in general*" that is significant.[11] The man, by contrast, individuates his desires, and "since he possesses as a citizen the self-conscious power of universality, he thereby acquires the right of desire and, at the same time, preserves his freedom in regard to it."[12]

Most significant is the fact that those respects in which Hegel considers men and women to be spiritually different are precisely those aspects that define women as "lesser" human beings. Like Plato and Aristotle, Hegel not only assigns particularity, intuitiveness, passivity to women, and universality, conceptual thought and "the powerful and the active" to men, but sees in men the characteristics that define the species as human. Let us remember that *Geist* constitutes second nature by emerging out of its substantial unity into *bifurcation* (*Entzweiung*), where it sets itself over and against the world. The process through which nature is humanized and history constituted is this activity of *Entzweiung*, followed by *externalization* (*Entäusserung*), namely the *objectification* (*Vergegenständlichung*) of human purposes and institutions in a world such that the world becomes a home for human self-expression. Women, since they cannot overcome unity and emerge out of the life of the family into the world of *universality*, are excluded from history-constituting activity. Their activities in the private realm, namely, reproduction, the rearing of children, and the satisfaction of the emotional and sexual needs of men, place them outside the world of *work*. This means that women have no history, and are condemned to repeat the cycles of life.

The family and political life

By including the family as the first stage of ethical life (*Sittlichkeit*), alongside "civil society" and "the state," Hegel reveals how crucial, in his view, this institution is to the constitution of the modern state. The family is significant in Hegel's political architectonic because it is the sphere in which the right of the modern individual to particularity (*Besonderheit*) and subjectivity (*Subjektivität*) is realized.[13] As Hegel often notes, the recognition of the "subjective moment" of the free individual is the chief strength of the modern state when compared to the ancient polis. In the family the right to particularity is exercised in love and in the choice of spouse, whereas the right to subjectivity is exercised in the concern for the welfare and moral well-being of other family members.

The various Additions to the section on the family, particularly in the Griesheim edition of the *Philosophy of Right*,[14] reveal that Hegel is concerned with this institution, not like Aristotle in order to discipline women, nor like Rousseau to prepare the true citizens of the future, but primarily from the standpoint of the freedom of the male subject in the modern state. Already in the *Philosophy of History*, Hegel had observed that the confusion of familial with political authority resulted in *patriarchalism*, and in China as well as in India this had as consequence the suppression of the freedom of the will through the legal regulation of family life and of relations within it. The decline of *political patriarchy* also means a strict separation between the private and the public, between the moral and intimate spheres, and the domain of public law. The legal system stands at the beginning and at the end of family; it circumscribes it but does not control its internal functioning or relations. It recognizes and administers, along with the church, the marriage contract as well as legally guaranteeing rights of inheritance when the family unit is dissolved. In this context, Hegel allows women certain significant legal rights.

He radically criticizes Kant for including women, children and domestic servants under the category of *jura realiter personalia* or *Personen-Sachen-Recht*.[15] Women are persons, that is, legal-juridical subjects along with men. They are free to choose their spouse;[16]

they can own property, although once married, the man represents the family "as the legal person against others."[17] Nevertheless, women are entitled to property inheritance in the case of death and even in the case of divorce.[18] Hegel is against all Roman and feudal elements of the law that would either revert family property back to the family clan (*die Sippe*), or that would place restrictions on its full inheritance and alienability.[19]

The legal issue besides property rights that most concerns Hegel is that of divorce. Divorce presents a particular problem because, as a phenomenon, it belongs under two categories at once. On the one hand, it is a legal matter just as the marriage contract is; on the other hand, it is an issue that belongs to the "ethical" sphere, and more specifically to the subjectivity of the individuals involved. Hegel admits that because the bodily-sensual as well as spiritual attraction and love of two particular individuals form the basis of the marriage contract, an alienation between them can take place that justifies divorce; but this is only to be determined by an impersonal third-party authority, for instance, a court.[20] Finally, Hegel justifies monogamy as the only form of marriage that is truly compatible with the *individuality* of personality, and the subjectivity of feeling. In an addition to this paragraph in the Griesheim lectures he notes that monogamy is the only marriage form truly compatible with the equality of men and women.[21]

Contrary to parroting the prejudices of his time, or ontologizing them, as Benjamin Barber suggests, with respect to the right of the free choice of spouse, women's property and divorce rights, Hegel is an Enlightenment thinker, who upholds the transformations in the modern world initiated by the French revolution and the spread of the revolutionary Code Civil. According to the Prussian *Das Allgemeine Landrecht* of 1794, the right of the free choice of spouse and in particular marriage among members of the various *Stände* – the feudal stratas of medieval society – was strictly forbidden. It was legally stipulated "that male persons from the nobility . . . could not enter into marriage . . . with female persons of peasant stock or the lesser bourgeoisie (*geringerem Bürgerstand*)."[22] If such marriages nonetheless occurred, they were declared "null" and the judges "were not empowered to accept their continuation."[23] To avoid social dilemmas, the lawgivers then distinguished between "the lesser" and "the higher bourgeoisie."

Hegel's position on this issue, by contrast, follows the revolutionary proclamations of the French Assembly which, codified as the "Code Civil" in 1804, were also adopted in those parts of Germany conquered by Napoleon.[24] Social strata differences are irrelevant to the choice of spouse and must not be legally regulated: the free will and consent of two adults (as well as of their parents), as long as they are legally entitled to marriage (that is, have not been married before or otherwise have falsified their civil status), is the only relevant point of view.

Yet Hegel inserts an interesting detail in considering this issue, which is wholly characteristic of his general attitude toward modernity. Distinguishing between the extremes of arranged marriages and the wholly free choice of spouse, he argues that: "The more ethical way to matrimony may be taken to be the former extreme or any way at all whereby the decision to marry comes first and the inclination to do so follows, so that in the actual wedding both decision and inclination coalesce."[25] Presumably this decision can also involve such relevant "ethical" considerations as the social background and appropriateness of the spouses involved. Consideration of social origin and wealth are now no longer legal matters to be regulated, as they were in feudal society, but personal and ethical criteria to be kept in view by modern individuals, aware of the significance, as the British Hegelian Bradley named it, of "my station and its duties."

While Hegel certainly was ahead of the Prussian legal practices of his time, and endorsed the general transformations brought about by the French Revolutionary Code Civil, he was, as always, reluctant to follow modernity to its ultimate conclusion and view the choice of spouse as a wholly individual matter of love and inclination between two adults. Hegel's views on love and sexuality, when placed within the larger context of changes taking place at this point in history, in fact reveal him to be a counter-Enlightenment thinker. Hegel surreptitiously criticizes and denigrates attempts at early women's emancipation and seeks to imprison women once more within the confines of the monogamous, nuclear family which they threatened to leave.

The Question of Free Love and Sexuality: The Thorn in Hegel's Side

Hegel's 1797–8 "Fragment on Love" reflects a more romantic conception of love and sexuality than the tame and domesticized view of marriage in the *Rechtsphilosophie*. Here love is given the dialectical structure of spirit; it is unity in unity and separateness; identity in identity and difference. In love, lovers are a "living" as opposed to a "dead" whole; the one aspect of dead matter that disrupts the unity of love is property. Property separates lovers by making them aware of their individuality as well as destroying their reciprocity. "True union or love proper exists only between living beings who are alike in power and thus in one another's eyes living beings from every point of view . . . This genuine love excludes all oppositions."[26]

Yet the discussion of the family in the *Philosophy of Right* is in general more conservative and criticizes the emphasis on free love as leading to libertinage and promiscuity. One of the objects of Hegel's greatest ire is Friedrich von Schlegel's *Lucinde*, which Hegel names "Die romantische Abwertung der Ehe" ("the romantic denigration of love").[27] To demand free sexuality as proof of freedom and "inwardness" is, in Hegel's eyes, sophistry, serving the exploitation of women. Hegel, in smug bourgeois fashion, observes:

> Friedrich v. Schlegel in his *Lucinde*, and a follower of his in the *Briefe eines Ungennanten*, have put forward the view that the wedding ceremony is superfluous and a formality which might be discarded. Their reason is that love is, so they say, the substance of marriage and that the celebration therefore detracts from its worth. Surrender to sensual impulse is here represented as necessary to prove the freedom and inwardness of love – an argument not unknown to seducers.

And he continues:

> It must be noticed in connexion with sex-relations that a girl in surrendering her body loses her honour. With a man, however, the case is otherwise, because he has a field for ethical activity outside the family. A girl is destined in essence for the marriage tie and for that only; it is therefore demanded of her that love shall take the form of marriage and that the different moments in love shall attain their true rational relation to each other.[28]

Taking my cue from this footnote in the text, I want to ask what this aside reveals and at the same time conceals about Hegel's true attitudes toward female emancipation in this period. The seemingly insignificant reference to Friedrich Schlegel's *Lucinde* is extremely significant in the context of the struggles for early women's emancipation at this time.

Remarking on the transformations brought about by the Enlightenment and the French revolution, Mary Hargrave has written:

> The close of the eighteenth and the beginning of the nineteenth centuries mark a period of Revolution for men and Evolution for women. The ideas of the French Revolution, that time of upheaval, of revaluing of values, of imperious assertion of the rights of the individual, swept over Europe like a quickening wind and everywhere there was talk of Liberty, Equality, Fraternity, realised (and perhaps only realisable) in that same order of precedence. . . .
>
> The minds of intellectual women were stirred, they became more conscious of themselves, more philosophic, more independent . . .

France produced a writer of the calibre of Madame de Stäel, England a
Mary Somerville, a Jane Austen; and Germany, although the strong-
hold of the domestic ideal, also had her brilliant intellectual women
who, outside their own country, have perhaps not become as widely
known as they deserve.[29]

In this work devoted to *Some German Women and their Salons*,
Mary Hargrave discusses women, both Jewish and Gentile, such as
Henriette Herz (1764–1847), Rahel Varnhagen (1771–1833), Bettina
von Arnim (1785–1859), and Caroline Schlegel (1763–1809). Of particular importance in this context is also Karoline von Günderode
(1780–1806), the most significant woman German poet of the
Romantic era, in love with Hegel's high-school friend, Hölderlin.
These women, through their lives and friendships, salons and
contacts, and in some cases through their letters, publications and
translations, were not only forerunners of the early women's
emancipation, but also represented a new model of gender relations,
aspiring to equality, free love and reciprocity.

Definitive for Hegel's own contact with these women and their
ideals, was the so-called Jenaer Kreis, the Jena circle, of the German
Romantics, Friedrich and August Wilhelm Schlegel, Novalis,
Schleiermacher, and Schelling. The journal *Athäneum* (1798–1800)
was the literary outlet of this circle, frequented by Goethe as well as
Hegel after his arrival in Jena in 1801. The "Jena circle" had grown
out of friendship and literary cooperation among men but counted
Caroline Schlegel among its most influential members. She had
extraordinary impact on the Schlegel brothers, and was the inspiration for many of Friedrich Schlegel's literary characters as well
as for his views on women, marriage and free love.[30] It is widely
believed that Caroline Schlegel was the model for the heroine in the
novel *Lucinde*.

Born as Caroline Albertina Michaelis, in Göttingen, as the
daughter of a professor of Old Testament, Caroline was brought up
in an intellectual household.[31] Following traditional patterns, in 1784
she married a young country doctor Georg Böhmer and moved from
Göttingen to Clausthal, a mining village in the Hartz mountains.
Although she suffered from the narrowness of her new surround-
ings and from the lack of intellectual stimulation, she remained here
until her husband died suddenly in 1788. Caroline, who was then
mother of three, lost two of her children after her husband's death.
With her daughter Auguste Böhmer, she returned to the parental
city. At Göttingen she met August Wilhelm Schlegel, six years her
junior, who fell in love with her. In 1792 she left Göttingen for
Mainz, the home now of her childhood friend Teresa Forster, born
Heym. In December 1792 the city fell to the French under General

Custine; the aristocrats fled and the republic was proclaimed. Teresa's husband, Forster, who was an ardent republican, was made president of the Jacobin Club. His wife, no longer in sympathy with his views, left him but Caroline stayed on and worked in revolutionary circles. In the spring of the following year, 1793, a German army mustered from Rheinisch principalities, retook Mainz. Caroline was arrested and with her little daughter Auguste was imprisoned in a fortress. After some months, her brother petitioned for her release, offering his services as an army surgeon in return, and August Wilhelm Schlegel exercised what influence he could to obtain her freedom.

Caroline was freed, but was banned from the Rheinisch provinces; even Göttingen, her home town, closed its doors to her. She was now pregnant, expecting the child of a French soldier, and August Wilhelm arranged for her to be put under the protection of his brother Friedrich, then a young student in Leipzig. A lodging outside the city had to be found for her; here a child was born, but did not live. In 1796, urged by her family and realizing the need for a protector, Caroline agreed to become August Schlegel's wife and settled with him in Jena. She never really loved Schlegel, and with the appearance of the young Schelling on the scene in 1798 a new love started in her life. Caroline's daughter, Auguste, died in July 1800. Schlegel settled in Berlin in 1802, and the increasing estrangement between them was resolved by a divorce in 1803. A few months later, she and Schelling were married by his father, a pastor, and they lived in Jena until her death in 1809.

Hegel lived in the same house with Caroline and Schelling from 1801 to 1803, and certainly the presence of this remarkable woman, an intellectual companion, a revolutionary, a mother, and a lover, provided Hegel with a flesh and blood example of what modernity, the Enlightenment and the French revolution could mean for women. And Hegel did not like what he saw. Upon her death, he writes to Frau Niethammer: "I kiss a thousand times over the beautiful hands of the best woman. God may and shall preserve her as befits her merit ten times longer than the woman of whose death we recently learned here [Caroline Schelling], and of whom a few here have enunciated the hypothesis that the Devil had fetched her."[32] A damning and unkind remark, if there ever was one!

Whether Hegel should have liked or approved of Caroline, who certainly exercised a caustic and sharp power of judgment over people, making and remaking some reputations in her circle of friends – Schiller's for example – is beside the point. The point is that Caroline's life and person provided an example, and a very close one at that, of the kinds of changes that were taking place in women's lives at the time, of the possibilities opening before them, and also of the transformation of gender relations. In staunchly defending women's place in the family, in arguing against women's education except by way of learning the necessary skills to run a household, Hegel was not just "falling prey to the prejudices of his time." "His time" was a revolutionary one, and in the circles closest to Hegel, that of his Romantic friends, he encountered brilliant, accomplished and nonconformist women who certainly intimated to him what true gender equality might mean in the future. Hegel saw the future, and he did not like it. His eventual critique of Romantic conceptions of free love is also a critique of the early Romantics' aspirations to gender equality or maybe some form of androgyny.

Schlegel's novel *Lucinde* was written as a eulogy to love as a kind of union to be enjoyed both spiritually and physically. In need of neither religious sanction – Lucinde is Jewish – nor formal ceremony, such true love was reciprocal and complete.[33] In the *Athäneum's* Fragment 34, Schlegel had defined conventional marriages as "concubinages" to which a "marriage à quatre" would be preferable.[34] *Lucinde* is a critical text, juxtaposing to the subordination of women and the duplicitous sexual conduct of the times a utopian ideal of true love as completion between two independent beings. Most commentators agree, however, that *Lucinde*, despite all noble intentions, is not a text of female emancipation: Lucinde's artistic pursuits, once they have demonstrated the equality of the lovers, cease to be relevant. The letters document Julius's development as a man, his *Lehrjahre*, his movement from sexual desire dissociated from respect and equality to his attainment of the ultimate companionship in a spiritually and erotically satisfying relationship. Women are idealized journey-mates, accompanying the men on this spiritual highway. "Seen on the one hand as the complementary opposites of men, embodying the qualities their counterparts lack, they are on the other, complete beings idealized to perfection."[35] Although in a section of the novel called "A dithyrambic fantasy on the loveliest situation in the world,"[36] there is a brief moment of reversal of roles in sexual activity which Julius sees as "a wonderful . . . allegory of the development of male and female to full and complete humanity,"[37] in general in *Lucinde*, the spiritual characteristics of the two genders are clearly distinguished.

In his earlier essays such as "Über die weiblichen Charaktere in den griechischen Dichtern" and "Über die Diotima" (1793–4), composed after meeting Caroline Schlegel Schelling, and being enormously influenced by her person, Friedrich Schlegel had developed the thesis – to be echoed later by Marx in the *1844 Manuscripts* – that Greek civilization decayed or flourished in proportion to the degree of equality it accorded to women. In particular, Schlegel emphasized that inequality between men and women, and the subordination of women, led to a bifurcation in the human personality, whereby men came to lack "innocence, grace and love," and women "independence." As opposed to the crudeness of male–female relations in Homer, Sophocles in Schlegel's eyes is the poet who conceives his male and female characters according to the same design and the same ideal. It is Antigone who combines the male and female personality into an androgynous ideal: she "desires only the true Good, and accomplishes it without strain," in contrast to her sister, Ismene, the more traditional feminine, who "suffers in silence."[38] Antigone transcends these stereotypes and represents a blending of male and female characteristics; she "is the Divine."

Read against the background of Schlegel's views, Hegel's generally celebrated discussion of Antigone in the *Phenomenology of Spirit* reveals a different message. In Hegel's version of Antigone, she and Creon respectively stand for "female" and "male" virtues, and forms of ethical reality. Antigone represents the "hearth," the gods of the family, of kinship and of the "nether world."[39] Creon stands for the law, for the city, human law and the dictates of politics that are of "this world." Their clash is a clash between equal powers; although through her acknowledgment of guilt, Antigone presents that moment in the dialectic of action and fate which Hegel considers necessary, it is eventually through the decline of the family and the "nether world" that Spirit will progress to the Roman realm of law and further to the public light of the Enlightenment. Spiritually, Antigone is a higher figure than Creon, although even the most sympathetic commentators have to admit that what Hegel has accomplished here is "an apologia for Creon."[40]

Ironically, Hegel's discussion of *Antigone* is more historically accurate in terms of the condition of Greek women, their confinement to the home, and the enormous clash between the newly emerging order of the polis and the laws of the extended family on which Greek society until the sixth and seventh centuries had rested than was Schlegel's.[41] But in his version of Antigone, Hegel was not simply being historically more accurate than Schlegel; he was robbing his romantic friends of an ideal, of a utopian vision. If Antigone's greatness derives precisely from the fact that she represents the ties of the "hearth and blood" over and against the polis, notwithstanding her grandeur, the dialectic will sweep Antigone in its onward historical march, precisely because the law of the city is public as opposed to private, rational as opposed to corporal, promulgated as opposed to intuited, human as opposed to divine. Hegel's narrative envisages no future synthesis of these pairs of opposites as did Schlegel's; whether on a world-historical scale or on the individual scale, the female principle must eventually be expelled from public life, for "Womankind – the everlasting irony [in the life] of the community – changes by intrigue the universal end of the government into a private end."[42] Spirit may fall into irony for a brief historical moment, but eventually the serious transparency of reason will discipline women and eliminate irony from public life. Already in Hegel's discussion of Antigone, that strain of restoration-ist thought, which will celebrate the revolution while condemning the revolutionaries for their actions, is present. Hegel's Antigone is one without a future; her tragedy is also the grave of utopian, revolutionary thinking about gender relations. Hegel, it turns out, is women's gravedigger, confining them to a grand but ultimately doomed phase of the dialectic, which "befalls mind in its infancy."

What about the dialectic then, that locomotive of history rushing on its onward march? There is no way to disentangle the march of the dialectic in Hegel's system from the bodies of the victims on which it treads. Historical necessity requires its victims, and women have always been among the numerous victims of history. What remains of the dialectic is what Hegel precisely thought he could dispense with: irony, tragedy and contingency. He was one of the first to observe the ironic dialectic of modernity: freedom that could become abstract legalism or selfish pursuit of economic satisfaction; wealth that could turn into its opposite and create extremes of poverty; moral choice that would end in a trivial project of self-aggrandizement; and an emancipated subjectivity that could find no fulfillment in its "other." Repeatedly, the Hegelian system expunges the irony of the dialectic: the subject posits its opposite and loses itself in its other, but is always restored to selfhood via the argument that the "other" is but an extension or an exteriorization of oneself. Spirit is infinitely generous, just like a woman; it gives of itself; but unlike women, it has the right to call what it has contributed "mine" and take it back into itself. The vision of Hegelian reconciliation has long ceased to convince: the otherness of the other is that moment of irony, reversal and inversion with which we must live. What women can do today is to restore irony to the dialectic, by deflating the pompous march of historical necessity – a locomotive derailed, as Walter Banjamin observed – and by giving back to the victims of the dialectic, like Caroline Schlegel Schelling, their otherness, and this means, in true dialectical fashion, their selfhood.

Notes

Some of the material in this essay formerly appeared as Seyla Benhabib and Linda Nicholson, "Politische Philosophie und die Frauenfrage," in Iring Fetscher and Herfried Münkler, eds, *Pipers Handbuch der politischen Ideen*, vol. 5 (Piper Verlag, Munich and Zurich, 1987), pp. 513–62. I would like to thank Linda Nicholson for her agreement to let me use some of this material here. This chapter was previously published in *Feminist Interpretations and Political Theory*, ed. Mary Lyndon Shanley and Carole Pateman (Polity, Cambridge, 1991).

1 Joan Kelly Gadol, "Some Methodological Implications of the Relations Between the Sexes," *Women. History and Theory* (University of Chicago Press, Chicago, 1984), pp. 1ff.

2 Cf. Genevieve Lloyd, *The Man of Reason: "Male" and "Female" in Western Philosophy* (University of Minnesota Press, Minneapolis, 1984); Patricia J. Mills, *Woman, Nature and Psyche* (Yale University Press, New Haven, 1987); Benjamin Barber, "Spirit's Phoenix and History's Owl," *Political Theory*, 16.1, 1988, pp. 5–29.

3 Cf. Heidi Ravven, "Has Hegel Anything to Say to Feminists?", *The Owl of Minerva*, 19.2, 1988, pp. 149–68.

4 Barber, "Spirit's Phoenix and History's Owl," p. 20. Emphasis in the text.

5 Hegel, *Hegel's Philosophy of Right*, trans. and ed. T. M. Knox (Oxford University Press, Oxford, 1973), para. 144, p. 105.

6 Ibid., para. 146, pp. 105–6.

7 G. W. F. Hegel, *Vorlesungen über die Philosophie der Weltgeschichte*, in *Hegels Sämtliche Werke*, ed. G. Lasson, vol. 8 (Leipzig, 1923), p. 471. Translated by J. Sibree as *The Philosophy of History* (New York: Dover, 1956), p. 205. Since Sibree's translation diverged from the original in this case, I have used my translation of this passage.

8 *Philosophy of History*, trans. Sibree, pp. 121–2.

9 I have revised the Knox translation of this passage in *Hegel's Philosophy of Right*, para. 165, p. 114, in accordance with Hegel, *Grundlinien der Philosophie des Rechts*, ed. Lasson, para. 165, p. 144. Emphasis in the text.

10 *Hegel's Philosophy of Right*, ed. Knox, para. 166, p. 114.

11 G. W. F. Hegel, *Phänomenologie des Geistes*, ed. J. Hoffmeister, Philosophische Bibliothek, vol. 114 (Hamburg, 1952), p. 326. Translated by A. V. Miller as *Hegel's Phenomenology of Spirit* (Oxford University Press, New York, 1977), p. 274. Emphasis in the text.

12 Ibid.

13 *Hegel's Philosophy of Right*, ed. Knox, paras. 152, 154, p. 109.

14 Cf. the excellent edition by K. H. Ilting, prepared from the lecture notes of K. G. v. Griesheim (1824–5), *Philosophie des Rechts* (Klet-Cotta, Stuttgart, 1974), vol. 6.

15 *Hegel's Philosophy of Right*, ed. Knox, Addition to para. 40, p. 39; cf. also Griesheim edition, para. 40 Z, pp. 180–1.

16 *Hegel's Philosophy of Right*, ed. Knox, para. 168, p. 115.

17 Ibid., para. 171, p. 116.

18 Ibid., para. 172, p. 117.

19 The one exception to this rule is the right of primogeniture, that is, that the oldest son among the landed nobility receives the family estate. It has long been observed that here Hegel indeed supported the historical interests of the landed Prussian gentry against the generally bourgeois ideology of free and unencumbered property and commodity trans-

actions, which he defended in the rest of his system. However, on this issue as well, Hegel is a modernist insofar as his defense of primogeniture among the members of the landed estate is justified not with reference to some family right but with reference to securing an independent income for the eldest son of the family, who is to function as a political representative of his class. Cf. *Hegel's Philosophy of Right*, ed. Knox, para. 306 and Addition, p. 293.

20 Ibid., para. 176, p. 118.

21 *Philosophie des Rechts*, Griesheim edition, para. 167 Z, p. 446.

22 Hans Ulrich Wehler, *Deutsche Gesellschaftsgeschichte* (C. H. Verlag, Darmstadt, 1987), vol. 1, p. 147.

23 Ibid.

24 Emil Friedberg, *Das Recht der Eheschliessung* (Bernhard Tauchnitz, Leipzig, 1865), pp. 593ff.

25 *Hegel's Philosophy of Right*, ed. Knox, para. 162, p. 111.

26 G. W. F. Hegel, "Love," in his *Early Theological Writings*, trans. T. M. Knox (University of Pennsylvania Press, Philadelphia, 1971, p. 304).

27 *Hegel's Philosophy of Right*, ed. Knox, para. 164 Addition, p. 263; cf. Griesheim edition, p. 436.

28 *Hegel's Philosophy of Right*, ed. Knox, para. 164, p. 263.

29 Mary Hargrave, *Some German Women and their Salons* (New York: Brentano. n.d.), p. viii.

30 Cf. ibid., pp. 259ff; Kurt Lüthi, *Feminismus und Romantik* (Harmann Böhlaus Nachf., Vienna, 1985), pp. 56ff.

31 Cf. ibid., pp. 251ff.

32 G. W. F. Hegel, *The Letters*, trans. Clark Butler and Christiane Seiler (Indiana University Press, Bloomington, 1984), p. 205.

33 Friedrich Schlegel, *Friedrich Schlegel's Lucinde and the Fragments*, trans. and introd. Peter Frichow (University of Minnesota Press, Minneapolis, 1971); cf. Sara Friedrichsmeyer, *The Androgyne in Early German Romanticism*, Stanford German Studies, vol. 18 (Peter Lang, New York, 1983), pp. 151ff.

34 Schlegel, *Lucinde and the Fragments*. p. 165.

35 Friedrichsmeyer, *Androgyne*, p. 160; cf. also, Lüthi, *Feminismus und Romantik*, pp. 95ff.

36 Schlegel, *Lucinde and the Fragments*, pp. 46ff.

37 Ibid., p. 49.

38 Cited in Friedrichsmeyer, *Androgyne*, p. 120.

39 Hegel, *Phenomenology of Spirit*, p. 276.

40 George Steiner, *Antigones* (Oxford University Press, New York, 1984), p. 41.

41 Hegel's reading of Antigone is more inspired by Aeschylus, who in his *Oresteia* exposed the clash between the early and the new orders as a clash between the female power of blood and the male power of the sword and the law. The decision to speak Orestes free of the guilt of matricide is signaled by an astonishingly powerful statement of the clash between the maternal power of birth and the paternal power of the law. Athena speaks on behalf of Orestes: "It is my task to render final judgement: / this vote which I possess / I will give on Orestes' side

/ For no mother had a part in *my* birth; / I am entirely male, with all my heart, / except in marriage; I am entirely my father's. / I will never give precedence in honor / to a woman who killed her man, the guardian of her house. / So if the votes are but equal, Orestes wins." Aeschylus, *The Oresteia*, trans. David Grene and Wendy O'Flaherty (University of Chicago Press, Chicago, 1989), pp. 161–2.

42 Hegel, *Phenomenology of Spirit*, p. 288.

Index